Design for Today

Schools Council Design and Craft Education Project
This Project was set up in 1968 at the University of Keele and
continued there for five years with the help of a Schools Council
grant of £73,710. Its main aims were to survey the range of design
and craft activities in secondary schools, to identify educational
objectives in design and craft teaching, and to examine methods of
validating the effectiveness of design and craft curricula in attaining
those educational objectives.

Project team
Director: Professor S. John Eggleston
Senior Research Fellows: A. R. Pemberton, D. Taberner
Field Officer (from 1971): Louis Brough
Writer/Editor (from 1971): Russell J. Hall

Design for Today

Schools Council Design and Craft Education Project

Edward Arnold

First published 1974
by Edward Arnold (Publishers) Ltd
25 Hill Street, London W1X 8LL

ISBN: 0 7131 1805 9

Set in 10 on 12pt Times Roman and printed in Great Britain by BAS Printers Limited, Wallop, Hampshire.

Contents

List of Case Studies

List of Filmstrip Notes and Commentaries

Preface

This volume and its associated publications represents part of the outcome of the Schools Council development project in Design and Craft Education. The project commenced in 1966 when the Schools Council generously financed a feasibility study to explore the possibilities of development that might spring from the existing school curricula in woodwork, metalwork and related activities with particular reference to the needs of the older age groups in the secondary schools. The Schools Council decision was in response to the enthusiastic initiatives of a large group of teachers in schools, colleges and universities who, with heads, advisers and administrators had met together to formulate proposals on a number of occasions at Leicester throughout 1965.

The feasibility study outlined a range of promising developments that were already taking seed in the schools and, in response to the report of this study (published as Schools Council Working Paper No. 26 *Education Through the Use of Materials*) the Council made a series of further grants to enable a major development study to take place at the University of Keele. Overall the project continued for six years with a total grant amounting to some £70,000.

Working with me at Keele for all or some of the time have been Louis Brough, Russell Hall, Allan Pemberton, Denis Taberner and our secretary Mrs Gillian Hope. But the efforts of our team at Keel have been hugely augmented by the work of the teachers in the schools and of their students. Most crucial has been the work of those in the trial schools in England and Wales and, later, in Northern Ireland and the British schools in Germany where the exhaustive initial work was undertaken, much of it initiated by the work of a number of teacher co-ordinators who were relieved of some of their normal teaching duties for varying periods by their local education authorities in order to participate in the Project. These were: Mr D. C. Crook, Mr R. W. Draycon, Mr G. Hughes, Mr D. Hunt, Mr T. Maguire, Mr G. Martin, Mr B. S. Nicholson, Mr J. D. Parker, Mr Paulden, Mr D. V. Pyatt, Mr J. Richards, Mr J. Ridge, Mr P. L. Small, Mr E. Swan, Mr A. Wagstaff and Mr R. Waterhouse.

But in addition to the work in the trial schools many other teachers in the design subjects in other schools in various parts of Britain and the rest of the world gradually came to be involved in the general exchange of ideas that sustained and enhanced the development. A notable part of the project was also played by the specialist advisers and inspectors of the local education authorities in whose schools we were working. But over and above the contribution of the design specialists there was also the more general contribution of other teachers in the schools, the head teachers and local authority officers and the members of the various examination boards, most notably those of the North Western Secondary Schools Examinations Board who joined us in introducing entirely new examinations in design education. These contributions were at all times abundant and generous and their importance is reflected throughout the publications as is the outstanding assistance that was received from members of the Inspectorate, from the officers of the Schools Council, from a wide range of industrial and commercial organizations and from our publishers. Much of this support reached the team through the representative advisory committee which, under the chairmanship of Professor G. H. Bantock, effectively guided the project throughout its existence.

The varied publications of the project are only a part of its outcome. There are many others including the development of new strategies of examination in the design subjects, the in-service training of design teachers and the by now self-perpetuating development of ideas in the schools. These are at least of equal importance. Indeed, we hope that the publications are seen not as an end but as a means to such continuing development throughout the whole field of design education.

JOHN EGGLESTON

Acknowledgments

Acknowledgment is due to the following who agreed to the reproduction of their specially-prepared material in the Case Studies in this book:

T. Pettit   Aireville Secondary School, Skipton, Yorks
M. Wharton   Kesteven Education Authority, Sleaford, Lincs
E. James   Blue School, Wells, Somerset
O. Bailey   Heronswood School, Welwyn Garden City, Herts
R. Duffield   Beckfoot Grammar School, Bingley, Yorks
E. ab Iorweth   Aberconwy School, Conway, Caernarvon
Mrs M. Grice   Hartcliffe Comprehensive School, Bristol
J. Heath   Bowland County School, Grindleton, Yorks
E. Ballam   Endon Secondary School, Endon, Stoke-on-Trent, Staffs
R. M. Scott   Clondermont Secondary School, Londonderry, N. Ireland
M. Ettridge   St Augustine's Roman Catholic School, Trowbridge, Wilts
J. D. Walker   Forest-of-Needwood High School, Rolleston-on-Dove, Staffs
T. Maguire   St Augustine's Secondary School, Belfast, N. Ireland
J. Comer   St Paul's Secondary School, Bessbrook, Newry, Co. Down
A. Thomas   Llangefni County Secondary School, Llangefni, Anglesey
W. G. Diamond   Paddington Comprehensive School, Mount Vernon, Liverpool
R. Jones   Ysgel Dyffryn Conwy, Llanrwst, Denbigh
A. Wagstaff   Hatfield High School, Ash Hill, Doncaster, Yorks
A. Finch   Longslade Upper School, Birstall, Leics
R. Draycon   Inner London Education Authority
W. G. Skinner   Principal, Melton Mowbray College of Further Education, Melton Mowbray, Leics
W. P. C. Mills   Headmaster, Brierley St Secondary Boy's School, Crewe, Staffs
J. Parker   Parkside High School, Leeds, Yorks
R. Pace   Stainbeck High School, Leeds, Yorks
Miss M. Ratcliffe   New Hayes Comprehensive School, Liverpool
E. Swann   Crewe Grammar School for Boys, Crewe, Cheshire

The Publisher's thanks are also due to the following for permission to use copyright material:

Jack Thomas and Cheshire County Council for an article from *Education in Cheshire* which is quoted on pp. 266–7; the Central Office of Information, Weetabix Ltd, Cuticura Laboratories Ltd and Times Newspapers Ltd for advertisements which appear on p. 46; Weekly Post Newspapers Ltd, Slough Observer Ltd, Westminster Press Ltd for newspaper reports which are reproduced on p. 116; Ladybird Ltd, United Rum Merchants Ltd, Encyclopaedia International Ltd, Buchanan Booth's Agencies Ltd, Co-operative Wholesale Society Ltd, The Save the Children Fund and Rowntree Mackintosh Ltd for advertisements which are reproduced on pp. 101–103 and in the Design and Craft filmstrip *Value for Money*; Henry Grant for photographs 3.9, 3.10, 4.6, 5.16, 5.17, 5.22, 5.23, 7.1, 7.2, 9.22; John Lawson Reay for photographs 4.10, 5.15.

Introduction

The preparation of young people to meet the problems, responsibilities and demands of adult life has always, very properly, been a major aspect of school work. Educating a child for his future is a process that starts on his first day at school and continues until he leaves. The educational validity of such work may be broadly accepted; indeed, in today's rapidly changing social and economic conditions the need for such work becomes increasingly urgent.

Craft teachers have long been aware of the need for research into the practice and objectives of craft education. Changes in society are reflected in the rapidly changing approaches and methods in our schools. Advances in technology, for example, have resulted in the introduction of new materials, new tools and new techniques.

The publication of Schools Council Working Paper 26 *Education Through the Use of Materials*[1] led to the setting up, in 1968, of the Schools Council Research and Development Project in Design and Craft Education, under the directorship of Professor S. J. Eggleston, at the University of Keele Since that date the Project team have been helped by teachers and their students (in the materials subjects—art, craft, home economics—and the humanities and sciences as well) in a wide range of trial schools throughout Britain.

At the heart of the Project's work has been the development of problem-solving approaches suitable for use in secondary schools. These approaches and their development and implementation at various levels throughout the school are the subject of *Materials and Design: A Fresh Approach*,[2] a book written for teachers in service and teachers in training. Students are encouraged to identify design problems, investigate them, produce and realize solutions and finally to evaluate the end-products.

Design for Today builds upon the design approaches examined in *Materials and Design: A Fresh Approach* and looks at some of the ways in

1

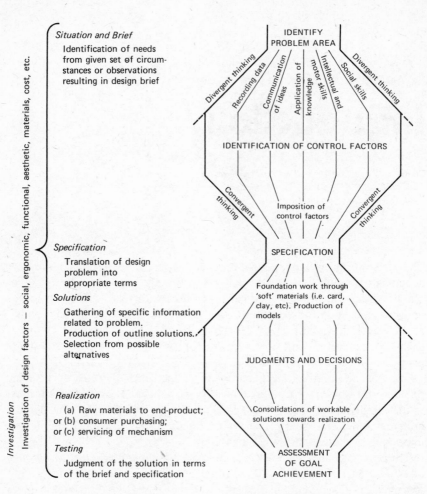

A design process for secondary schools.

which they may be applied in activities relevant to the needs and interests of students of a wide range of abilities.

If we examine these needs and interests it is clear that they may be divided into four main categories: those related to the home, the community, leisure activities and work. Although there are many instances of overlap and interrelation we have found it convenient to divide this book into four similar areas:

—Materials and Domestic Life;
—Materials and Community Development;
—Materials and Leisure;
—Materials and Work.

The suggestions outlined in this book seek to promote a co-ordinated approach in which work already taking place may be further developed through a close association with other subject areas. In addition, the aim is to help teachers to locate aspects of practical design work not yet included in their curriculum.

Five filmstrips have been prepared to introduce specific topics that may be used as a basis for design work. Commentaries and frame reproductions appear in Chapters 3 and 6. The filmstrip titles are: *Houses and Homes*[3], *Value for Money*[4] (design and consumer discrimination), *Helping Out*[5] (design and community action), *Design and the Environment*[6], and *Playthings*[7] (the design of play equipment).

You Are a Designer[8] introduces students to the problem-solving approach, first in a general, descriptive way and then by listing and detailing the factors that may need to be considered at various stages during a design process and suggesting a range of key questions that a student may need to ask. Thus it will be useful both as an introduction to designing and as a 'memory jogger' whenever a design process is being put into action.

Also aimed at students is *Connections and Constructions*[9], a resource book designed to assist the development of appropriate fabrication techniques when designing and making products in a wide range of hard and soft materials.

A series of filmstrips has been produced to introduce certain principles essential to much design and craft work. Fourteen subjects—including shape, form, colour, texture, ergonomics, and materials and tools—are covered in nine filmstrips. Commentaries and frame reproductions of this series appear in *Looking at Design*[10].

The background to new developments in the materials subjects and the role they have to play in education in a changing society are examined in *Education Through Design and Craft*[11]. This book pays particular attention to aims and objectives and factors of examination and assessment.

It was felt that certain specialized areas of work required more detailed attention than was possible in the above publications. For this reason three supplementary teachers' books have been produced—*Design and Karting*[12], *The Creative Use of Concrete*[13] and *Designing with Plastics*[14]. In each case the emphasis is, of course, on a design-based approach. Introductory filmstrips *Kart-Ways*[15] and *Designing with Concrete*[16] support two of these publications.

In addition, the National Council for Educational Technology has, in association with the Design and Craft Education Project, produced a film, *Design With a Purpose*, which looks at the work of a group of fifteen-year-old students involved in designing and making play equipment for infant school children as part of an experimental Mode III CSE course. The film may be used by teachers' groups as a focus for discussion and development, and for students it offers an introduction to the requirements, and flexibility, of a design process. *Design With a Purpose* is distributed by the EFVA and is available from the National Audio Visual Aids Library, Paxton Place, Gipsy Road, London, SE27 9SR.

Section 1
Materials and Domestic Life

1
Design in the Home

The scope for work under the theme of 'Materials and Domestic Life' is enormous. Many schools have organized entire courses of this nature for their senior students bringing in aspects of finance, consumer discrimination, local government, as well as the more obvious activities related to family care, home maintenance and decoration.

The breadth of the subject opens up many possibilities for integration or co-ordination with other subjects. It is probable that most teachers on a school staff, through their own subject disciplines, personal interests and experience, could make a useful contribution. In this respect, as in others, no two schools will have identical resources. This section outlines some of the factors that may influence the contribution made by the materials subjects, allowing as much breadth as possible for individual contributions and development according to a school's particular resources and needs.

Figure 1.1 illustrates the range of activities that may be appropriate in this area of work. The arrows indicate those to which the materials subjects may make a substantial contribution in terms of practical, workshop-based, activities. Additional contributions may be made by other subject areas in a study of the social services, option mortgage and rent rebate schemes, finance, the local and national tax structure, banking, marketing and mass communication, changes resulting from development within the European Economic Community, and so on.

Figures 1.2, 1.3, 1.4, and 1.5 specify in a little more detail what a consideration of 'The Home', 'Other People', 'Finance' and 'Environment' might mean in terms of practical design work, some parts of which are directly applicable to workshop activities. For some of the wider aspects material is available in the form of booklets, simulation exercises, posters and slides from Shelter (see bibliography) which is intended to be used in a linked-subject situation and which tries to acquaint students with some of the legal, financial and environmental problems with which they might be faced later in life.

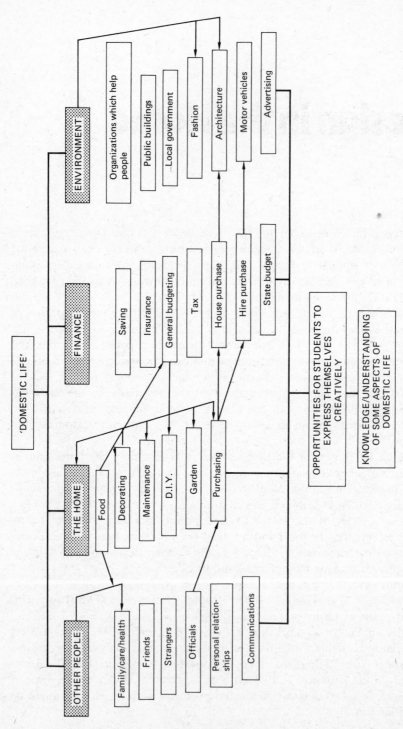

1.1 Range of possible activities in 'Materials and Domestic Life' schemes of work.

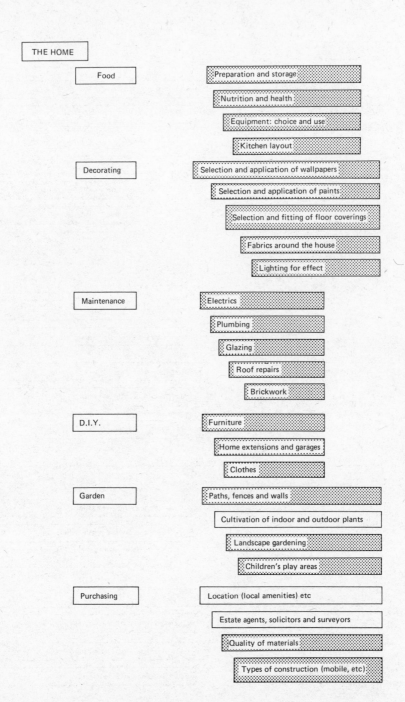

THE HOME

Food
- Preparation and storage
- Nutrition and health
- Equipment: choice and use
- Kitchen layout

Decorating
- Selection and application of wallpapers
- Selection and application of paints
- Selection and fitting of floor coverings
- Fabrics around the house
- Lighting for effect

Maintenance
- Electrics
- Plumbing
- Glazing
- Roof repairs
- Brickwork

D.I.Y.
- Furniture
- Home extensions and garages
- Clothes

Garden
- Paths, fences and walls
- Cultivation of indoor and outdoor plants
- Landscape gardening
- Children's play areas

Purchasing
- Location (local amenities) etc
- Estate agents, solicitors and surveyors
- Quality of materials
- Types of construction (mobile, etc)

1.2 Approaches to 'The Home' theme. (Shaded areas indicate possible topics to which the materials subjects may contribute. Unshaded areas indicate other possible topics. This is not intended to be a complete list.)

OTHER PEOPLE

Family/Care/Health

The working mother

Who does what

Family planning

Size of house

Communal amenities in house

"Private" spaces in house

Collective choice of furnishings and dec-oration

Friends

Choice of friends

Activities with friends, holidays, etc

Strangers

Visitors from abroad, etc

Personal introduction and what to talk about

Writing to strangers

Officials

Local Council Officials (building regulations)

Police (motor vehicle regulations)

Personnel in welfare organizations

Trades Unions

Personal Relationships

Sex Education

Relationships within and outside the family

Communications

Mobility of people — how do we move about?

Radio, television and the telephone

1.3 Approaches to 'Other People' theme. (Shaded areas indicate possible topics to which the materials subjects may contribute. Unshaded areas indicate other possible topics. This is not intended to be a complete list.)

10

```
FINANCE

    Saving              Banks

                            Post Office

                                Building Society

                                Investments

    Insurance           National Insurance

                            Pensions

                                Personal insurance

                                Property insurance

    General Budgeting   Income and Expenditure

                            Food

                                Clothes

                                Entertainment

                                House Improvement

                                Motor Vehicles

    Tax                 Direct

                            Indirect

                                Methods of Coding

    House Purchase      Mortgages

                            Rates

                                Land values

                                Cost of materials and sub-
                                contracting

    Hire Purchase       Major household items — furniture etc

                            Motor vehicles

    State Budget        Social Services

                            Subsidized Industries

                                Exports and imports
```

1.4 Approaches to 'Finance' theme. (Shaded areas indicate possible topics to which the materials subjects may contribute. Unshaded areas indicate other possible topics. This is not intended to be a complete list.)

ENVIRONMENT

Organizations which help other people	Consumer protection
	Citizens Advice
	Welfare Organizations
Public Buildings	Libraries
	Baths
	Civic Centres
Local Government	Election of Councillors
	Officers of Local Government
	Services — Health etc
Fashion	Clothes
	Make-up and hair styles
	Health/Cleanliness/Food
Architecture	Patterns of settlement
	Contemporary problems — slums etc.
	Modern methods of building
	Survey of possible future trends
Motor Vehicles	Social implication of motor vehicles
	Transport problems
	Range of vehicles available
	Possible developments
Advertising	Reasons and methods
	Discrimination

1.5 Approaches to 'Environment' theme. (Shaded areas indicate possible topics to which the materials subjects may contribute. Unshaded areas indicate other possible topics. This is not intended to be a complete list.)

'Design in the Home' is such a large area of work—ranging from the simple problems associated with the fabric of the building to large-scale social problems—that far greater impact is likely to be achieved if the staff concerned are prepared to plan a co-ordinated programme for any particular study topic. It may be helpful to start by examining the total framework and analysing the various aspects of work against the availability of suitable staff, accommodation and facilities. From such a starting point it may become clear that a degree of team teaching is essential, because individual teachers may not be able to contribute their talents with the maximum effectiveness while working in isolation.

Few schools will be fortunate enough to have staff qualified in some of the specialist areas such as insurance, banking and building, but most large commercial organizations offer an advisory service to the public and are eager to supply schools with publications, and in many cases films, wall charts and other visual aids. Indeed, many organizations gladly accept invitations to send speakers to schools.

An enormous amount of help is available at both local and national level and it is suggested that an important aspect of the work lies in the exploration and utilization, by both students and teachers, of these professional resources.

The fabric of the home

It has been said that a house is a machine for living in. Although such a definition may put a distorted emphasis on the process of home-making the far-reaching effects of technology on domestic life cannot be denied.

A brief survey of technology in the home may therefore be a useful basis for a discussion of the ways in which design is important in home and garden.

Developments in the building industry

Let us first consider the exterior fabric of the home. For centuries the main building materials have been bricks or local stone. These have had to be laid on site by skilled craftsmen. The process is 'labour intensive' and therefore expensive and time-consuming.

In recent years experiments with other materials have indicated ways in which the building process may be shortened, undertaken by less-skilled craftsmen and produced more cheaply. The pre-casting of concrete for the manufacture of standard units on a batch production basis is an example of this. Recent developments in plastics have also contributed, notably in roofing materials, guttering and piping.

The growth of 'do-it-yourself'

A parallel to the introduction of new processes in the building industry is the development of the 'do-it-yourself' movement which has grown considerably in recent years. Contributory factors in this growth include the introduction of products such as self-adhesive tiles and non-drip paints which the unskilled householder can apply with the minimum of trouble, the development of a wide range of 'amateur' tools such as paint rollers, and the marketing of furniture and other items in kit form for home assembly.

The introduction of new materials and processes has been accompanied, and their use promoted, by the widespread availability of information in the do-it-yourself field. A visit to any newsagent will reveal a large number of popular do-it-yourself magazines; almost every shopping area has a do-it-yourself shop. These are frequently supported by television programmes concerned with various aspects of home maintenance or improvement.

Other factors contributing to the growth of the do-it-yourself industry are the increasing costs of skilled labour and changing attitudes towards house ownership. The undeniable economic advantages of property ownership now induce many people to stretch themselves to their financial limits in order to own property, a desire encouraged by the building industry and the building societies.

But high labour costs lead them to undertake as much work as possible themselves. The renovation of an old house or the development of a new one may contain elements of financial necessity, personal challenge and leisure pursuit.

Renovation as a service to the community

Examples of renovation work are not uncommon. Some schools take the opportunity to undertake such work as a form of service to the community. The following comments were made by a lady who received help from local secondary school students:

Some time ago my husband and I, both over sixty, faced a severe domestic crisis. Our financial reserves were drained and we were compelled to sell our house to avoid bankruptcy. The only accommodation we could find was an old cottage that had stood empty for a year. It was not in a fit state to be occupied; the floor was rotten with dry-rot, the walls were soaked with damp, window frames were falling apart and the whole of the interior needed redecorating.

As a result of our financial and domestic problems my husband suffered a nervous breakdown and was not physically able to undertake the work. At the height of our difficulties we were approached by a local schoolmaster with a proposal. He suggested that his students—both boys and girls—be allowed to undertake repairs and redecoration. With some trepidation we agreed. The children set to work with a will and within six weeks, working one day each week, they had transformed the derelict cottage into a home. The work continues and my husband and I continue to be amazed at the transformation that is taking place.

To the school children this work may seem to be only a different sort of lesson; I don't know. But to my husband and me their work helped us out of a desperate situation and brought us back to a point where we can begin to meet life with pleasure and confidence. Many of them come to see us after school and although they don't know it their friendship, their cheerfulness and enthusiasm have been great sources of encouragement to my husband and me. We feel that we are part of a family again.

One advantage of this approach is that students are able to become aware of social problems and to form relationships with people in the community.

Building projects

An increasingly popular do-it-yourself activity is the development of property by adding extra working or living space. The work may involve concreting, bricklaying, roofing, plumbing, electrical installation and joinery. The range of ready-made components to aid such activities is increasing almost day by day, though the accompanying skills required for their proper fitting are not always available. A background knowledge of the practical demands of building assignments is desirable and may be provided by real involvement at secondary school level.

'Case Study: Building a Garage' describes such a project which arose out of the difficulties encountered in motor vehicle work because of lack of space. In the design and construction of a garage the students were able to experience a wide variety of building processes.

Case Study

Building a Garage

The work entailed the design and construction of a multi-purpose building incorporating a garage. A point of interest is that the school, although having a catchment area of approximately 140 square miles accommodates only 150 students.

Our students come from tiny schools, many from widely scattered homesteads. A good number of leavers go to work which can have no foreman and they must, therefore, rely on their own ability to make decisions and to see them through. Because of such factors we endeavour to provide our students with experiences that will enable them to work on their own initiative and to develop an honesty of purpose as reliable citizens.

What we attempted

When we were asked to participate in an experimental 'Design for Living' project it was felt that the work should meet a local need and fit the circumstances of this small rural school. Out of this grew the idea of constructing a concrete raft 13·4 × 4·25 m and at one end building a brick garage for use by parents and the local community. On the remaining 6·09 m of raft a room was to be built for senior girls to practise aspects of house maintenance.

With the exception of the housecraft room, which is to await the approval or otherwise of a new headmaster, all the work was completed in two years using two groups of students and working only in the period May to July. A quite professional standard was achieved by boys of 13 to 15 years, on a total budget of £80. We managed, with the aid of demolition timber, to end up just £5 over our original allocation. The garage is in extensive use now and, as commercial garage repair and maintenance charges rise, will be even more so.

16

1.6 The completed garage.

Organization

In a small school it is difficult to organize elaborate schemes of integration with teams of teachers. In our case all the materials subjects are taught in one room by one teacher! In the event, it was clear that co-operation would be of a minimal nature, but when asked for it was freely given. The nature of the work permitted it to be split up into convenient sections, boys to participate or withdraw as their individual work demanded. Visitors often query whether all the work was done by boys and the answer is—'Yes, easily!' For example, they dug a $3 \times 1 \cdot 37 \times 1 \cdot 22$ m hole in hard shale in their dinner break as a 'bit of fun'.

As always, the hardest part was planning and drawing. Boys who did best at this were not always confident on practical work, while boys who showed qualities of leadership were often a pleasant surprise to us.

It was inevitable that some aspects of the work tied in with maths and English, such as ordering materials by letter and phone, and surveying and calculating quantities and costs.

Outline of the work schedule

Briefly, the order of procedure was as follows:

Stage 1:
    Discussion of factors influencing design.
    Design by drawing.

17

Surveying and preparing block plan of site.

Estimating quantities.

Preparation of scale drawings.

Submission of plans for approval of Board of Governors and County Architects.

Excavation of site.

Preparation of concrete formwork.

Concreting (the school had free use of the Council's mixer).

Stripping and tidying site (all formwork was re-used as scantlings and garage doors).

Stage 2:

Manufacture of window joinery.

Building of brickwork and windows to eaves.

Placing roof timbers (covered with corrugated asbestos sheet and four sheets of clear 'Apex').

Pointing and painting.

Exterior plumbing.

It is not proposed to give detailed accounts of the work involved at every step. However, the following observations may be of interest.

Stage 1:

—Help and advice was readily available from the Local County Planning Office.

—The site was easily drained into a lower lane gutter by pipe and clinker trench.

—76 mm quarry bottoms formed the main hardcore and 12 mm to dust was used for the concrete aggregate (it is necessary to stipulate the correct proportion of 'dust', or sand must be added).

—2·44 × 1·22 m sheets of 9 mm building quality colombian pine ply were used for the pit formwork.

—Two 4·57 mm wide steps were cast *in situ* at the top of each end of the pit—the remaining steps were a movable timber unit.

Stage 2:

Some of the organizational aspects of this second period of work are summarized on the following table:

Activity	Students	Allocation of time
Designing/ Planning	12 boys (3H) 14 boys (3W)	Mainly during technical drawing lessons
Practical work	10 boys (3H) 10 boys (3W)	Mainly during craft lessons in period Easter-Summer Extra time at end of term

18

Familiarizing the students

The students taking part at this stage were already familiar with the work of the preceding students in building the raft but had not studied the details that had been decided upon. The general scope and purpose of the project were outlined to them and former drawings explained. It was emphasized that these designs for the building were not complete and that several modifications still had to be made. They were asked, therefore, to consider the general planning approach afresh and to make a list of all factors they could think of which should be taken into account when designing such a building.

The procedure we followed to help the students understand the total implications of the design was confined to clearly defined stages:
1 The preparation of a suitably scaled outline drawing of the raft.
2 The addition of the brickwork, taking into consideration factors decided upon by the students, e.g., length and width of a vehicle with doors open and space needed to work all around a vehicle with garage doors closed.
3 The drawing of brickwork, paying due regard to bonding and stability.
4 Consideration of lighting and window sizes and drawing of elevations to show positions of windows.
5 Consideration of materials available for the roof covering, eaves and gutters (this influenced the design of the centre truss and purlins).
6 Consolidation of ideas for doors and gables (using material stripped from the concrete formwork of the raft).
7 Detailing methods of fixing windows and doors.

Bricklaying

Following this, all the boys had a good appreciation of the task and a fair idea of how work would proceed. In deciding on the allocation of work it was agreed that all should have some share in laying bricks. Supervision of bricklaying had to be clear and precise before each period of outside work was commenced. In addition, frequent visits had to be made by the teacher to check that standards were being upheld; work that was allowed to lean or go out of line was ruthlessly taken down and rebuilt before the mortar had time to set. It was surprising how quickly boys 'caught on' and a competitive spirit developed in working plumb, level and clean. Various ideas were suggested as aids but they were found to be time-consuming and the boys were generally happier with traditional methods.

Despite such care there is some evidence, if one applies a craftsman's standard, that the brickwork was done by the students. If a school is

B

contemplating work of this nature the following points may be helpful :

—Work must start on a clean, tidy site and it must be left clean and tidy.

—Mortar must be of even consistency from mix to mix to keep courses level and free from twist—this is particularly important as sill and eaves are approached.

—Students working from inside are more likely to build out of plumb than those working from outside.

—The allowance for vertical joints must be known and stick gauges supplied in the early stages.

—Corners must be built up three or four courses ahead of main wall (put best students on corners !).

—Pillars can mysteriously go out of plumb overnight !

—Adequate time allowance must be made for pointing up work neatly and leaving site tidy.

—Make allowance for the weather—in dry conditions bricks and preceding work need wetting ; when working between showers mortar tends to get thin and courses tight with a sloppy finish to wall faces.

—Scaffold planks must be wide ; if slash-sawn boards are used they should be doubled in thickness.

—Larch pads must not be forgotten where fixing is to take place— cutting out hard compo is no work for small boys.

—Window frame ties are fixed as the jambs go up so have a supply handy or they tend to be forgotten.

—Each boy should have a plumb level to hand.

—Boys love to handle mortar ; insist on barrier cream or Vaseline.

After the brickwork was finished and windows fixed in, it was decided that concrete lintels were too heavy and cumbersome so cuprinolled timber was substituted. The prefabricated truss was placed in position and bricked in. Beam and gable over-doors fixed, purlins nailed on and built into the gable ready for the roof-covering. This was corrugated asbestos with four sheets of clear 'Apex' for overhead light. Plastic guttering, downspout, couple-brackets, stop-ends, heads, etc, are supplied in proprietary brands and the boys were surprised when they found out just how many different items were needed.

Conclusions

The building itself will be a valuable addition to the school, and of great benefit to the boys who made it. All the boys enjoyed the experience and it was undoubtedly worthwhile. The contributions made by each boy can be readily discussed by the teacher but it is extremely difficult to assess everything in an objective way. How do you mark a cheerful willingness to help others ? Or a boy who worries when things go wrong? It is possible to be objective about more tangible matters like the skills attained by the students, the way in which they worked as a team and the way in which the students themselves assessed the benefits of the experience. All along the line this project suggested that as a motivator and a continual source of meaningful work we should go on putting up buildings. But there must be an end somewhere so one needs to examine the lasting way in which the building may involve our students.

We feel that buildings like ours can provide valuable scope for decoration, plumbing, lighting, soft and hard furnishings. Interior fittings can be altered at will and girls could be drawn into the scheme to a greater extent. Teacher training programmes could well be adjusted to include the implications in the design of these structures together with methods of planning work schedules for youngsters. At the same time, emphasis should be placed on how such work may help link the school and its students to the outside community. We think we have managed to illustrate that craftwork, as well as having intrinsic interest, can be real, can be related to the world outside and moreover can have some element of the problems 'why and how' built in.

This is not achieved easily and may best be sought in the planning stages, which means less time spent in supervision of the practical work and more in design. When boys see the teacher so concerned I feel it is 'bread cast upon the waters'.

In all the ferment of ideas in craft teaching one aspect that may be overlooked is that of time. How much is justified in reaching a certain end and how does it fit into examinations? Again this leads to speculation on how much an assessor will be able to appreciate what is clear to the teacher concerned. Will he be able, amongst all the divergent trends in craft, to cope with the total field of design concepts from the artistic to the technological? Clearly the stresses that will be thrown upon the craft teacher will demand men of high calibre and energy— even for classes of ten or a dozen.

Even allowing for such problems, project work should be a permanent feature of a senior programme, but with certain reservations. It must not be allowed to dominate the craftroom or timetable merely for the sake of being on a project but be seen as one valid aspect of the general work. It must meet a genuine need, preferably outside the school. It should contain the seeds of its own continuity.

These projects, and the design process generally, are epitomized by the lad with an IQ of 90 who eagerly wants to make a step for his father's caravan in mild steel and hasn't a clue. 'Bring a sheet of drawing paper, Henry, sit next to me, and let's think about it.'

How could it ever be otherwise?

Case Study

Building a Fifth-Form Centre

With the increasing number of senior students and the recommendations of the Newsom Report in mind quite a number of schools have given some thought to the provision of some kind of 'centre' or special accommodation for senior students. Not all schools may be able to build their own fifth-form centre, although the experience of one school indicates that such a project could have value.

We realized that it is essential to cater for the needs of the non-academic senior student, and that we must offer something that the formal approach of earlier school life has not been able to supply. To this end, it was felt that an activities centre for senior students would be a necessity. However, as the LEA has such heavy commitments on major building programmes, it was appreciated that we should have to wait an indeterminable time for this much-needed asset.

1.7 The completed 'phase one' building.

So we decided to tackle the job ourselves. After some six months of discussion between the various school departments it was possible to set down proposals on paper, in which the senior students, too, had their say. As a result the building was designed and the plans produced by the technical drawing department. These were approved by the local planning officer and the education authority agreed to supply the materials. The costing was done at the school.

When work first began, four groups of boys, about twelve in each, were moulded into a form 4P (for project) and they put in the equivalent of about three-and-a-half hours weekly on the site, returning to their woodwork and metalwork rooms when the weather was bad. This class is directed by a bricklayer demonstrator employed on a part-time basis, together with members of the craft departments when available.

1.8 Interior view of the building.

1.9 Preparations for 'phase two'—a motor engineering workshop and common room.

The building programme

The programme was planned to be carried out in two phases, phase 1 being 18 m long by 7·5 m wide, containing a light craft room, a school shop, an administration office, entrance hall and toilets. Phase 2 will comprise a common room and a motor engineering workshop, this to be 21 m by 12 m, the completed centre being L-shaped.

The first phase has a felt-covered flat roof. Floors are solid, surfaced with thermoplastic tiles. The outer leaf of the cavity walls is constructed of rustic brick to match the existing school buildings. The inner leaf and internal are of light-weight load-bearing concrete blocks, chosen because of their insulation and nailing or fixing properties. The ceiling is insulation board covered with asbestos tiles.

The only difference in the construction of the two stages of the work is in the types of roof used. The second phase will have a 6·75 m pitched roof of RDA trusses spanning 12 m. These will carry purlins and common rafters. The final covering will consist of battens on felt and interlocking tiles.

Heating is by electrical power which was installed by the local authority to enable part of the building to be put into immediate use.

Advice was sought and most readily given by the Architects' Department, also by a variety of outside experts, including the fire departments and manufacturers and suppliers of materials and equipment.

Solving problems

There were, of course, difficulties that were not anticipated. One which caused us much concern in the early stages was the constant flooding of the trenches for the foundations. As we did not have the use of mechanical pumps to keep them dry, the problem was overcome by laying land drains around the entire workings, a move which succeeded admirably.

Plastering also presented difficulties. It was found that boys could tackle small areas with confidence. Large walls were therefore divided into panels by means of battens, and an element of competition was introduced between teams of plasterers with a view to the best finished surface.

At a later date, a 7·5 m steel girder had to be lifted into position to support the roof. A mobile crane was hired and the task achieved in about ten minutes, and, incidentally, at a very low cost.

It must be mentioned that the solving of these types of problems gave immense satisfaction to the boys concerned.

Careful time-tabling and planning ahead eliminated many hold-ups that could have occurred. In the early stages it was essential to have a room available, preferably a craft room, for work indoors during inclement weather. Roof trusses, door frames, lintels and all manner of fittings were made during these periods, but as work progressed beyond the roofings stage it was possible to plan indoor and outdoor operations to run simultaneously.

At this point it is appropriate to record that never has this scheme been solely a building project. We have always regarded it as an educational one, with vast scope for subject integration, and although primarily for those not fully occupied in examination studies, we have not overlooked its possibilities with regard to CSE Mode 3.

After construction

The spirit of this project will continue when the actual construction is completed. The centre will be the headquarters for all manner of work which can be regarded as contributing to the function of the community which a boy or girl will be joining in adult life, with due regard for both the vocational and the cultural. Groups will be engaged in such pursuits as modelling, wood carving, photography, cabinet making and sculpture, in as many media as possible, and will include welding, casting and similar industrial techniques. It will also include automobile and motor cycle maintenance. In addition an emphasis will be put on the do-it-yourself' approach with an eye to future home making and the increasing use of power tools now readily available to the home handyman.

Students will exercise some choice in their programme of work, which may often be related to occupational interests, and in connection with this every effort will be made to establish a liaison with local industry. It cannot be too heavily emphasized that senior students will be encouraged to undertake tasks that are traditionally regarded as those of the teaching staff, and every effort will be made to raise the status of these young people. What they have already achieved is there to be seen.

Work will be undertaken on behalf of the rest of the school, e.g., small building construction for the rural science department, stage props for school dramatic productions and general maintenance of school equipment.

We hope in this way to overcome the formal school atmosphere as far as possible and to ensure that the curriculum will be such that the students will see a relevance to adult life.

* * * * *

Interior design

If a house is a machine for living in then for the majority of people, perhaps, it is a machine that functions poorly. In many cases it only functions at all because its occupiers are prepared to compromise between what they would like to do and what the accommodation forces them to do.

The ideal solution to this problem is the individually designed house, but for the average person this is no more than a dream. Nevertheless, some useful changes can be effected within the shell of a building. It is not uncommon, for example, for householders to remove partition walls to form one large room from two smaller ones and provide greater access and freedom of movement. (This operation is greatly facilitated by the increasing tendency to build with non-load-bearing interior walls.) Because of these and other possibilities it is, therefore, realistic to talk to young people at school about the interior design of living accommodation and the possibilities of internal structural alteration.

The utilization of space

A consideration of the functions of rooms is a useful starting point for the study of interior design in the home. Any such investigation will usually begin with the people who use a particular room and the activities they are likely to pursue there.

The kitchen, for example, may be considered as a workshop or production unit in which the mother, and other members of the family, will be involved in processes such as food preparation, laundry work and similar activities. This room may contain a range of mechanical and electrical equipment such as a cooker and a refrigerator. The washing machine usually has to be

26

accommodated there too. In addition, there will be a need to solve problems associated with storage of food, utensils and other things to which easy and safe access is necessary.

Further considerations include those of hygiene, suitability of wall and floor surfaces, and the provision for the safe and effective disposal of waste.

It is clear that interior design cannot be isolated from the physical activity of the room's occupants. Allied to these considerations are the additional needs of, for example, a mother who may have to supervise active and inquisitive toddlers while performing a multitude of other tasks. Thus, interior design will involve problems related to ergonomics, accommodation, circumstances of use and selection of materials, and therefore presents a wide range of work relevant to the interest of young adults.

The teenager and the home

Other rooms present similar problems to those encountered in kitchen design. In many modern homes the sitting and dining areas are incorporated into one room. Within this room people of different ages and interests may attempt to pursue different activities at the same time. Sometimes these activities may be in conflict as, for example, when one person is watching the television while another is doing homework, possibly sharing a table with someone who is having a meal. Under conditions of this sort conflict can arise simply because a single space cannot successfully accommodate such a range of activities.

The teenager is particularly vulnerable in such circumstances. How, for example, can friends be entertained with any degree of privacy when only one living room is available? This raises the question of the broader use of other rooms. Need bedrooms function only as bedrooms? How feasible is the idea of turning a teenager's bedroom into a bed-sitter? What sort of equipment would be required? Could the teenager undertake the work without outside help?

Many secondary school students are faced with problems of this nature in their own homes and the study of such problems therefore has an unquestionably realistic basis. Students may be encouraged to solve some of their own problems through the preparation of drawings, three-dimensional models and colour schemes which might form the basis of actual conversion work at home—perhaps undertaken in a way that provides an attractive form of home/school/student collaboration.

The use of caravans

The increasing popularity of the caravan, both as a holiday home and as a more permanent residence, offers scope for the involvement of secondary school students in worthwhile interior design activities. Even a straight-

27

forward study of the amenities in a caravan can be illuminating when considering the confined space into which everything has to be fitted. But a deeper understanding of how this may be achieved and actual experience of working to such constraints may be useful and may best be offered by involving students in a practical assignment.

Caravan shells are easily obtained; if finances do not permit the purchase of a new unit there should be little difficulty in obtaining an older, but sound, caravan at a fraction of the original price. Removal of the interior fittings can quickly create an empty space that will provide an excellent starting point for a variety of design briefs. One such project is described in 'Case Study: Caravan Layouts'.

Design and decor

Whether one is considering a caravan, kitchen or bed-sitter, decoration is an important aspect of interior design. The majority of students will see the relevance of education in the selection and use of fabrics, paint and wallpaper. Such work may involve aesthetic factors, practical experience and consumer discrimination.

Closely allied to decoration is the question of lighting. Schools have involved their students in a variety of experiences related to 'lighting for effect'. When dealing with mains electricity, however, there is always a need for basic knowledge to be harnessed to a desire to create some special effect with electric lighting. Clearly this is of the utmost importance where the rewiring of a room may be necessary. The way in which one school kept a balance between 'expressive' and 'knowledge' requirements is described in 'Case Study: A Home Maintenance Course'.

There is also scope for 'home' schemes to be undertaken in the context of community development projects, thus widening the range of possible outcomes and involvement of students.

The following comments were made by fourth-year students after a project in which they planned and carried out extensive redecoration in the homes of a number of old people:

I did not like the idea at first because being in an exam form I did not think it would be very beneficial to us, but I did enjoy and benefit from it. It's something I'll never forget! Two girls, a boy and myself were given the living room to redecorate. We took it in turns to paste the paper and also to put it up so each one gained some papering experience. I learnt how to speak to old people and how to work with my fellow decorators. Although the old lady had a brighter, cleaner home the project of making her happy and a member of the community was not over and my friends and I have returned several times to see her.

I learnt an awful lot, how to put up wallpaper, colour schemes, what paints to use and where to put them and how to go about doing them, but I learnt even more by doing a written project on the work. I found out how the job was done properly by going into shops and asking for different kinds of leaflets and pamphlets.

My opinions of the project at first were that it wouldn't work, it was a good idea but it wouldn't work. My opinions of the project at the end were (1) a good job done, (2) the project was taken up by time well spent, (3) a job done with a good thought in mind, i.e., an old lady who could not even afford a pot of paint had her whole bungalow redecorated for no expense either for her or for us.

My friend and I had to make a set of cupboards so we had to go out and buy some wood. We came up with complications about buying the wood but after about four weeks we started.

The group I was in set about the work by first of all dividing up into several smaller groups so that two people were decorating the kitchen, two people decorated the hall and three or four people started decorating the dining room. The first thing we had to do was wash down the walls and skirtings and ceiling of the rooms we were decorating. The last room we decorated was the bedroom the old lady slept in. She had not wanted it redecorated but changed her mind later. One or two boys dug up the weeds in the small patch of land at the back of the garden, so that it looked a little more presentable. I learnt a little bit of what lonely lives some people live. The person whose house I was in seemed to have no one who really seemed to care about her or to see she had enough coal and food in the home. Her only friend seemed to be an old gentleman who lived a few doors away from her. I would like to do something similar to this project again but also I think it would be a good idea if we could go out on 'meals on wheels' service, etc, or to help in a hospital or an infant school.

This service could be improved by having our own transport to get there and back. So we can get there earlier and we don't have to leave so early.

I wish this project went further afield to nursery homes, hospitals, schools, etc.

I was very pleased with the result, the work was not first class but the next thing to it. I think we should do the decorating in one whole week, instead of leaving the house in a mess, until the next time we came. It would relieve the owners. To have a whole week of decorating would mean the work could be done quicker.

My opinion at first of the project was that it was a waste of time as we had our exams coming up. From this project I learnt more about old people in general and their attitude to young people. I also learnt how to decorate a home and how to set about it. At the end of the term I was very pleased with what we had done as we had made one old person happy. It helped a lot of us to work together well and to get to know each other's ideas. It was a good basis to start on, so as in the future we will be able to build it up into something helpful to the community.

In any interior design problem—whether bedsitter or caravan, involving reconstruction or redecoration—our students may come to realize that design is ultimately concerned with people and their quality of life rather than with things.

Design has the power to influence personal relationships by providing an environment in which they can develop harmoniously. The home is not merely a machine for living in, but a designed environment which affects people's actions and responses.

Case Study

Caravan Layouts

In the following project, undertaken as part of a technical drawing course, the brief was made as wide as possible to allow the students maximum freedom of interpretation. Nevertheless, in order to spur the group beyond the idea of a mobile holiday base, the brief did offer some suggestions for possible uses. It said:

The school has been offered a caravan shell, 5 m long, 2 m wide and 2 m high (internal dimensions).

The design and fitting of the interior has been left to the school, dependent on its eventual use. Various claims have been made, for instance, the geography/biology departments envisage it as a mobile centre for field studies, while the careers and art departments see it as a mobile library and exhibition centre. And there are many other ways in which the shell could be used.

You are asked to consider how you would use the vehicle and then suggest a layout which would enable the caravan to be used for that purpose.

NB. If used as a field studies centre the main living accommodation would be under canvas.

Some of the end results were encouraging. Because the students knew the assignment was part of their technical drawing course the final solutions tended to be well presented, accurate and well drawn.

Our design process

But the end result is only part of the picture; we tried to assess the process by which the students had arrived at their solutions. This is something we are attempting to introduce into many aspects of our work. We find that the quality of drawing does not suffer when problem-

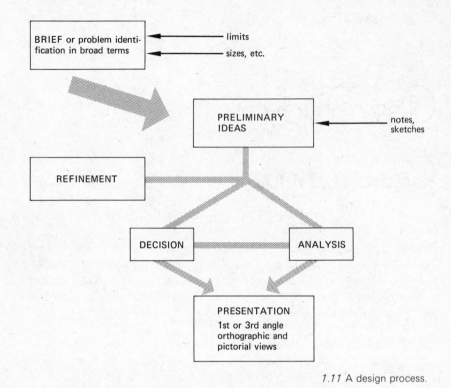

BRIEF or problem identi-
fication in broad terms ◄——————— limits
◄——————— sizes, etc.

PRELIMINARY
IDEAS ◄——————— notes,
sketches

REFINEMENT

DECISION ═══════ ANALYSIS

PRESENTATION
1st or 3rd angle
orthographic and
pictorial views

1.11 A design process.

solving approaches are applied. Before starting our assessment we tried
to get a clear impression of what the design process involves. Although
this may be a very flexible process, for our purposes we introduced the
steps illustrated in the diagram.

Although it was realized that the group was not going beyond the
'proposal' stage, relevant problems were earnestly considered and
realistic solutions suggested. Technical drawing offers scope for the
development of the 'designer approach' to practical problems and opens
up possibilities of engaging students in work where the actual construction of the end-product would not be possible. Surveys of road
networks, transportation in general, communications and town planning
involving the provision of shopping, housing and other amenities all
come readily to mind.

*1.12–1.15 Students' drawings. 1.12 was produced during an early investigation and idea-
generating stage. Some solutions are shown in 1.13, 1.14 and 1.15.*

BLUE SCHOOL CARAVAN DESIGN. 1

① PROBLEM IDENTIFICATION: Required, caravan interior design for caravan to be used by the school as a field study centre. This mobile base could be used on: geography and geology trips to make studies of landforms, rocks, town and country planning, land-use, farming etc.; and science trips to make studies of plants, trees and animal life in the country.

One of the main uses of the mobile study centre would be on single day trips to make on-the-spot investigations of various things.

A well furnished, functional interior is required with plenty of cupboard space for the storage of scientific equipment. Equipment in the caravan should fold away neatly leaving a light, roomy and airy interior. Large windows are required for good lighting. A roof vent or windows with built-in ventilators would provide excellent ventilation. Ample locker space, and cubby holes would encourage tidiness.

CONSIDERATIONS:
- WEIGHT
- DISTRIBUTION OF WEIGHT
- COST
- MATERIALS AVAILABLE
- STORAGE SPACE
- WORKING SPACE
- MOVING SPACE
- RANGE OF EQUIPMENT TO BE INCLUDED
- OVERALL SIZE OF CARAVAN.
- CAN OUTSIDE SURFACES BE USED?
- WINDOWS/DOORS

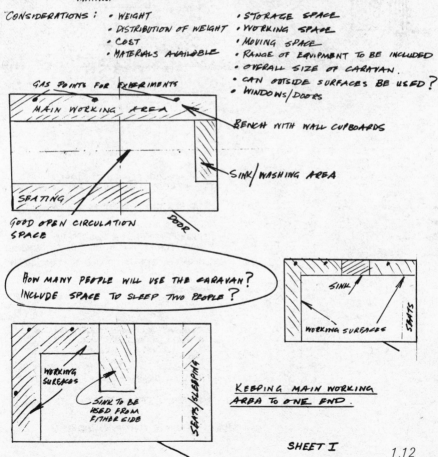

GAS POINTS FOR EXPERIMENTS

MAIN WORKING AREA

BENCH WITH WALL CUPBOARDS

SINK/WASHING AREA

SEATING

GOOD OPEN CIRCULATION SPACE

DOOR

HOW MANY PEOPLE WILL USE THE CARAVAN? INCLUDE SPACE TO SLEEP TWO PEOPLE?

SINK

WORKING SURFACES

SEATS

WORKING SURFACES

SINK TO BE USED FROM EITHER SIDE

SEATS/SLEEPING

KEEPING MAIN WORKING AREA TO ONE END.

SHEET I

1.12

WELLS BLUE SCHOOL FIELD STUDY CARAVAN

LOCATION PLAN OF INDIVIDUAL UNITS   1cm = 1ft.

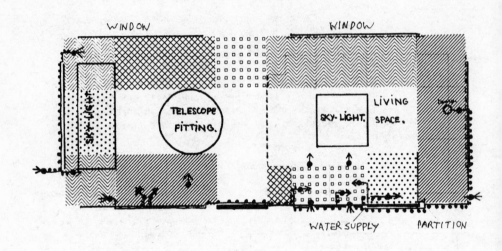

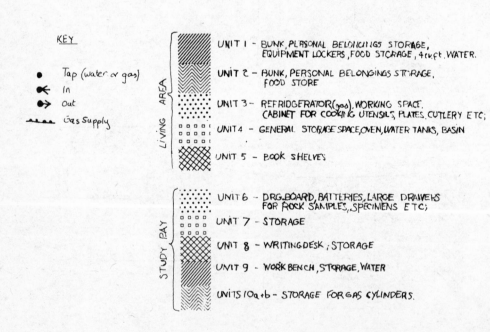

KEY

- Tap (water or gas)
- In
- Out
- Gas Supply

LIVING AREA

UNIT 1 – BUNK, PERSONAL BELONGINGS STORAGE, EQUIPMENT LOCKERS, FOOD STORAGE, 4 cu.ft. WATER.

UNIT 2 – BUNK, PERSONAL BELONGINGS STORAGE, FOOD STORE

UNIT 3 – REFRIDGERATOR (gas), WORKING SPACE. CABINET FOR COOKING UTENSILS, PLATES, CUTLERY ETC;

UNIT 4 – GENERAL STORAGE SPACE, OVEN, WATER TANKS, BASIN

UNIT 5 – BOOK SHELVES

STUDY BAY

UNIT 6 – DRG. BOARD, BATTERIES, LARGE DRAWERS FOR ROCK SAMPLES, SPECIMENS ETC;

UNIT 7 – STORAGE

UNIT 8 – WRITING DESK; STORAGE

UNIT 9 – WORK BENCH, STORAGE, WATER

UNITS 10a + b – STORAGE FOR GAS CYLINDERS.

GAS SUPPLY

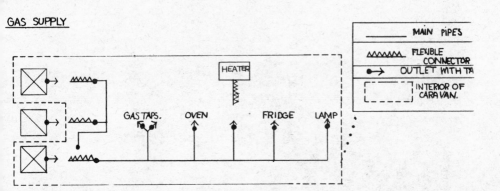

	MAIN PIPES
∿∿∿∿	FLEXIBLE CONNECTOR
•→	OUTLET WITH TAP
⌐ ¬	INTERIOR OF CARAVAN.

GAS TAPS.   OVEN   HEATER   FRIDGE   LAMP

WATER SUPPLY

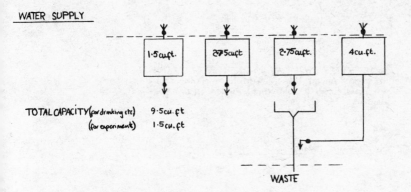

1·5 cu.ft.   2·75 cu.ft.   2·75 cu.ft.   4 cu.ft.

TOTAL CAPACITY (for drinking etc)   9·5 cu. ft
(for experiment)   1·5 cu. ft

WASTE

ELECTRICITY SUPPLY

This supply has a restricted use of only lighting the study bay
with small 6W fluorescent tubes. The three batteries are recharged
either by wind-powered dynamos or water wheel dynamos.

Re-charge sockets.

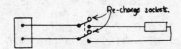

3 circuits are built similar to this, one for each tube.

**N.B. ALL GAS AND WATER PIPES
CAN BE FITTED BETWEEN THE
INNER AND OUTER WALLS OF
THE CARAVAN.**

1.13

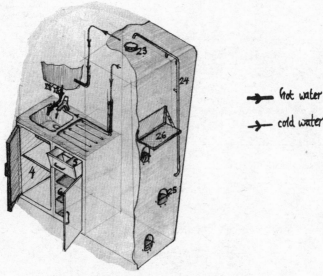

→ hot water

⇀ cold water

ABOVE SCRAP VIEW SHOWS REAR NEARSIDE OF CARAVAN. Step holes are provided up the side for access to top of cold water storage tank from outside. A plate folds out from the side to enable a person to stand within easy reach of the filler cap.

⬭ Indicates seating

┈┐
   ┊ Indicates line of curtain partition
   ┊ when required

Caravan interior design for Mobile Study Centre or Headquarters proposed for use by the School, Wells. Cold water is stored in a tank. Gas is supplied by a cylinder fixed outside caravan on towing gear. Accomodation for sleeping two people can be made if necessary. Refrigerator, cooker, toilet, plates, saucepans, etc., storage space for personal belongings are provided for use if needed. Storage space for technical books, chemicals, equipment, maps, samples etc., is provided in connection with the caravan's intended use primarily as a scientific study centre. The caravan would be useful on biological expeditions for taking samples, making observations and making on-the-spot analyses during prolonged stays at study bases. Used on geographical trips, observations of weather, land forms etc., could be made using the caravan on prolonged trips. The caravan could have numerous other uses, these two above uses are only two obvious ones.

36

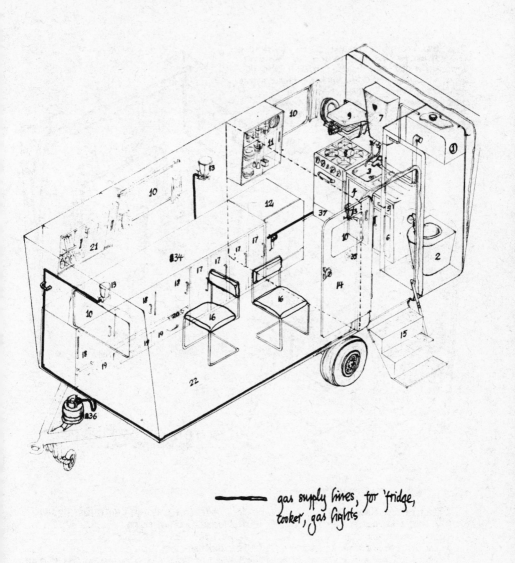

gas supply lines, for 'fridge, cooker, gas lights

SCALE: 1" = 1'   ISOMETRIC PROJ.ⁿ
NO ISOMETRIC SCALE USED

1.14

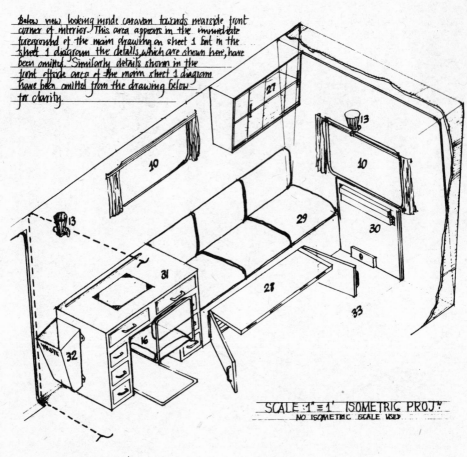

Below view looking inside caravan towards nearside front corner of interior. This area appears in the immediate foreground of the main drawing on sheet 1 but in the sheet 1 diagram the details, which are shown here, have been omitted. Similarly details shown in the front offside area of the main sheet 1 diagram have been omitted from the drawing below for clarity.

SCALE 1" = 1' ISOMETRIC PROJ.ⁿ
NO ISOMETRIC SCALE USED

Key to main diagrams, sheets 1 & 2

1. Fillable, cold water storage tank.
2. Chemical toilet, removable inner bucket. Situated in private compartment.
3. Steel sink unit and draining board.
4. Cupboard for storing mops, brushes, dusters, gas cylinder etc.
5. Drawer for cutlery.
6. Cupboard for storing tinned food or food which doesn't need a refrigerator.
7. Hot water supply/heater, taking water from cold water tank.
8. Cooker.
9. Grill + plate warmer.
10. Window.

11. Cupboard for storing cups, saucers, plates, etc, dishes.
12. Refrigerator with working top.
13. Gas light.
14. Lockable outer door.
15. Retractable steps, stowed up in caravan when not in use.
16. Seats.
17. Lockers for personal equipment.
18. Lockers/cupboards for scientific equipment and instruments.
19. Drawers for clothes.
20. Slot for housing bed in stowed position (see sketch, sheet 2).
21. Cupboard for books, chemicals etc.
22. Outline, on floor, of tiltings shown in diagram, sheet 2.
23. Filler cap for cold water storage tank.
24. Hand rail, external.
25. Step holes.

Sketch showing bed in position for use on unstowing from housing shown at **20** on main diagram, sheet 1.

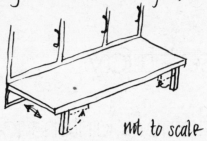

not to scale

Sketch showing table in position for use on unstowing from storage position shown at **30** on diagram, sheet 2.

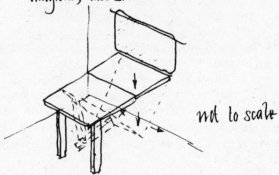

not to scale

26. Foot plate, retractable, for access to cold water tank filler cap.
27. Cupboard space.
28. Trays in cupboard for maps, documents, samples etc.
29. Seat, convertible into bed.
30. Collapsible table, shown in stowed position, (see sketch, sheet 2).
31. Desk with drawers, working top etc.
32. Waste bin
33. Outline, on floor, of fittings shown in main diagram, sheet 1.
34. Working top.
35. Coat hook.
36. Gas supply cylinder.
37. Storage space under cooker.

1.15

Case Study

A Home Maintenance Course

Some schools have attempted to rationalize their approach to the many aspects of home maintenance and improvement by developing a single scheme of work which introduces most, if not all, of these aspects.

The course began to take shape when we realized that there was a need for practical involvement in an area of materials and domestic life where the work was suitable for both examination and non-examination students. The fact that a main emphasis lay in home electrics, home decoration and plumbing enabled us to get the project off the ground.

As the seeds of the project were being sown, it was necessary to consider what the students might gain from it. The main conclusions were that it should:

1 aid the decision of a future career;
2 encourage students to be of subsequent service to the community, especially to those less fortunate than themselves;
3 enable students to maintain their future homes at minimum cost;
4 provide the opportunity to gain first-hand experience and knowledge of a range of scientific principles;
5 provide a chance to practice diagnostic forms of problem solving.

Setting up

Our first problem was to obtain a suitable room. It must have smooth walls for decorating, a water and electricity supply, and an area in which we could fasten pipes and fittings. We decided that, above all, this must be a separate room or area so that classes not involved in the project would not interfere with work in hand. This was not easy to find. Our school has prefabricated aluminium walls; flat ones are difficult to come by.

Nevertheless, we managed to secure a disused changing room which had the potential we needed. A suitable wall surface was provided by erecting sheets of chipboard. The room was divided into three booths to enable different areas of work to be experienced separately by different students at the same time. A wash-basin in an adjoining lavatory provided our water supply and a neighbouring store with a main fuse-box was the answer to our electrical needs. To complete the scene, mock ceiling joists were fitted into the booth in which the electrical work was to be undertaken and an old mock fireplace was resurrected from the stage property room to give a greater feeling of realism.

The time taken to design, construct and erect these fixtures was good experience for the students, although the desire to get on with the real thing caused some frustration. But it was not long before the booths were completed and we were able to bring in the various tools and materials we would need to start the project.

Before starting constructional work it was necessary to consider a range of safety factors—especially on the electrical side where it becomes necessary to use reduced voltage. I also had in mind several possible wiring circuits and pipe runs, so we had to ensure that the booths were flexible enough to meet all demands. Stop-cocks to isolate the water supply were inserted at various points.

As a result of this kind of planning, we were able to list the various fittings and materials we would require. Once the initial stock has been obtained it can, with care, be used over and over again. We ordered a small wash-basin, WC cistern, small galvanized tanks, copper pipe, electric cable, switches, paste and paper, brushes, and so on. It is, of course, necessary to add further items on occasions as the work develops. In addition, a few items have to be replaced annually.

Getting started

As the various pieces of equipment were unpacked, the students offered suggestions concerning how and where they should be placed. The general enthusiasm shown at this stage continued throughout the project. During the constructional phase of the work a basis of know-how and experience of certain techniques was established as students studied the fittings available, decided which one most suited the job in hand and then carried out the necessary practical work.

The students did not always work from detailed drawings so when, for example, circuits were checked the result was sometimes a blown fuse. This quickly brought the error home and did not need to be accompanied by a reprimand from the teacher. Likewise, students were quick to comment critically if their paper-hanging colleagues did not make the pattern match properly. Again, disappointment resulted in further thinking and investigation when the water did not flow; a discovery about one-way stop-cocks was soon made. The evident joy and relief when the water finally flowed served to reinforce the lesson that had been learnt.

The co-operation of other departments throughout the project added considerably to the value of the whole experience. Lessons given by the art mistress helped the students to gain a firmer grasp on the principles of interior decoration. Detailed discussions in the science department, aided by battery-powered models, set the pattern for much of the electrical work. Additional useful information was obtained from magazines and text-books, and valuable outside assistance was provided by parents who had professional experience in the kinds of work we were undertaking. One big advantage of such sources is the up-to-date information they are able to provide. Further help was given by the local electricity board who supplied us with some useful leaflets and sent one of their staff to talk to the students.

1.16 Work on light fittings in one of the booths.

Future developments

So this was the way in which we established our working area. Now we are intent on developing the facilities and using what we already have to help subsequent groups of students become aware of the proper and safe way of maintaining and installing a range of household equipment. We are considering building-in a series of basic faults, such as sticking ball-valves and leaking tap washers. Another possible development is the study of central heating.

Already, students are suggesting that they could help each other paper their rooms at home. Many have asked to stay after school to complete a circuit in the booths. To have such feedback is encouraging and this, coupled with the positive influence the course has had over the careers of a number of boys, supports my belief that more of this work should be considered in future school timetables.

*   *   *   *   *

Further developments

The points so far discussed are those that are directly concerned with the technical aspects of the home and the human factors related to its use. But in addition to these there are other equally important aspects inherent in the relationship between materials and domestic life.

Diagnostic design in the home

Attempts to improve the home environment frequently make considerable use of modern technology. Electronic and mechanical aids to living are to be found in every home, not only as major tools in the kitchen but also in the recreational aspects of home life. Most teenagers have access to a record player and a radio, and a major target upon attaining the age to hold a driving licence is a vehicle of some sort. When such equipment fails repairs may be costly and this is, again, a frequent inducement to do-it-yourself solutions.

The process of repair follows a particular pattern of design which is, initially, diagnostic. It involves locating the area of the fault, then tracing the fault itself. Subsequently, the mechanism may be dismantled to extract the faulty part and replace it. Little of this can be done without a clear understanding of the mechanism, its principles of operation and the functions of its parts. In terms of school work it demands intellectual skills that may be different from those applied in the process of turning raw materials into an end-product. Some diagnostic design was involved in the work described in 'Case Study: A Home Maintenance Course'.

Links with the world of work

In the context of equipment repair and maintenance the demands of domestic life are to some extent a microcosm of the demands of industry in that many industrial processes are now automated to a point where the actual production is done by automatic machinery while the main human contribution lies in the diagnosis and repair of faults. In addition, the repair and maintenance of television sets, motor vehicles and domestic and office equipment represents an ever-widening area of employment.

It will be seen, therefore, that training in diagnostic skills through courses of motor vehicle maintenance, karting and work with domestic equipment is justified both directly and, perhaps more importantly, indirectly in terms of the intellectual skills involved—skills which will have application both in domestic life and in future employment.

2
Consumer Discrimination

Let the buyer beware?

The importance of consumer discrimination in domestic life is clear. Indeed, the evaluation and selection of manufactured items—from soap powders to cars—is an inescapable part of life in today's society. But most people have little knowledge of the actual production of what they buy and are therefore unable to make first-hand judgments of quality. So where do ideas of value for money originate? On what basis do we discriminate between two comparable products?

Ideally, judgment is based on the type and quality of materials, construction, performance, appearance and price. To some extent students are able to gain a body of knowledge and experience related to these factors from the work normally undertaken in the materials-based subjects. Nevertheless, there is considerable scope for the development of more structured activities in this field in which the various elements are pulled together to enable the student to make a more informed and independent judgment.

In practice, discrimination may frequently be based merely on two grounds—price and prejudice. And in the encouragement—or even, on occasions, the generation—of prejudice, the pressure of advertising, is of central importance.

The influence of advertising

The essence of advertising is persuasion. To use reasoned argument in order to persuade people to buy a particular product seems a valid form of propaganda and, indeed, could be expected to assist the process of discrimination.

But the advertiser's concern cannot be solely to assist discrimination. His appeal is therefore rarely directed towards reason alone but also towards the more emotional responses that may be triggered by associating a product

45

If the firm's office party is the only time ou're on an equal footing with the men, perhaps you're working for the wrong people.

People talk a lot about 'equality of opportunity'. In spite of all the chat, most firms haven't changed much. It's still the men who snap up the executive positions, while the girls are expected to be satisfied with the duller, routine jobs. Even today, you won't find many women in the management dining room.

An old-fashioned view. The RAF thinks this is a hopelessly old-fashioned outlook. To us, it's your ability that matters, not whether you're a man or a woman. You get the same chances of promotion and you share the same privileges - even as the most junior woman officer you're a full member of the Officers' Mess. It makes for a friendlier world to live and work in on an equal footing with your male colleagues.

A special sort of person. Of course, we offer more, we ask more. If you're merely looking for a job you can do mindlessly from 9 to 5, then the RAF is hardly the place to look. But if you want an opportunity that will stretch your abilities, and reward you for doing so, then you're the kind of person we'd like to talk to. Come and see us at your nearest RAF Career Information Office (address in phone book) or post the coupon.

RAF officer
EXECUTIVE

"Shopping used to really depress me until I discovered Ayds."

Mary before Ayds: Her 8lb, 5ft, 3in, Size 16.
Mary after Ayds: As 7lb, 5ft, 3in, Size 10.

Start the Ayds plan tomorrow and by this time next month you could be pounds lighter.

Vanilla
Flavour

Ayds.
Vitamin and Mineral

One month's Slimming Plan in every box.
Ayds Division of Carter-Wallace Ltd., Maidenhead, Berks.

Granny knew best

Granny knew that you only get out of life what you put into it - and that went for food especially.

That's why Granny would have approved of Weetabix. Because it's made with natural whole wheat, and nobody knew better than granny that pure wheat, whole wheat, is just packed with nourishment.

Weetabix gives you 3 vitamins of the B group, iron and don't forget the bran which is so good for your digestion! Granny would certainly have approved of that.

All you add is milk and sugar - and a hearty appetite. As Granny would say "Now you've had a good start to the day"

What could be more natural?

Weetabix

2·1 Persuasion—different techniques for different 'markets'. These advertisers appeal to the desire for a slim and attractive figure (Ayds), for a return to old values (Weetabix) and for equality (WRAF). Understatement and wit, too, have a place in the ad-man's armoury (The Times).

with the private hopes, fears, prejudices, and anxieties that beset the average human being.

And if these appeals can be disguised within a reasoned argument, so much the better.

It seems likely that young people now at school will be subjected to this type of persuasion in an increasingly sophisticated form throughout their lives. It is therefore just as important to teach students to discriminate between rival advertising claims as it is to teach them to discriminate between products. And in view of the fact that advertising employs almost all forms of visual and aural communication it is unlikely that consumer discrimination can be taught effectively within a curriculum in which art, design and English are considered as separate and unrelated areas of knowledge. The case for co-ordination here is overwhelming.

The place of marketing

Although a basic understanding of advertising is important in consumer discrimination it is sometimes forgotten that this is only one of a number of marketing techniques used by a manufacturer to increase the sales of his product.

Other areas of study include built-in obsolescence (of which fashion is one aspect), packaging, point-of-sale display, free gifts, cut prices and distribution methods.

It is clear that there are many opportunities for fruitful links with other subjects here. The strong emphasis on visual communication gives added weight to the argument for some form of collaboration with the art department in this area of study. The kinds of work that may be carried out in this respect are illustrated and described by Anthony Horrocks in Chapter 4 of *Attitudes in Design Education*.[17] (Chapter 6, by Peter Goldman of the Consumers' Association, is also relevant.) Similar opportunities exist for links with the social studies area of the curriculum. Built-in obsolescence, for example, offers a wide area for the discussion of such points as:

—disposal problems, pollution;
—psychological obsolescence, fashion;
—the need (or otherwise) for continuing employment for the majority of people;
—conservation and recycling of supplies of raw materials.

Perhaps the most valuable contribution that the workshops can make to the study of the place of marketing in consumer discrimination is in the organization of simulated exercises. The potential of this area of work is discussed later in this chapter.

Consumer testing

Where schools have undertaken consumer discrimination work this has most often been in the form of *Which?*-style tests of products such as soap powders, cosmetics, various types of floor-covering and electric light bulbs. In addition to the more obvious values of this type of work there is scope for students to become involved in the design of valid comparative tests and testing equipment. The possibilities are illustrated in 'Case Study: Product Testing' and 'Case Study: Developing a Critical Awareness'.

Organizing a marketing project

Simulated exercises involving product design are discussed in Chapter 9 of this book. In these the emphasis is usually on organizational design and production planning, and the constructional requirements of a product which is to be produced in quantity. Nevertheless, there is no reason why aspects related to marketing should not be given more prominence; after all, these play an extremely important role in industrial design.

Although many of the factors discussed in Chapter 9 will apply equally to a simulated 'marketing project' there are a number of points worthy of special consideration in this different context. These points are examined in the following pages.

Aims and objectives

The aims and objectives of a simulated marketing operation will be similar in many respects to those of a project in which the emphasis is on production (see figure 9.1, Chapter 9). Product design will almost certainly continue to play an important part, as will factors related to communication with 'clients', working as a member of a team, and specifying and assessing roles in the production process.

An important additional aim, however, is to enable the student to have a better understanding of how manufacturers attempt to influence consumer choice, and so be better able to exercise rational judgment when buying products and services.

It is clear that the difference between the kind of work described below and that discussed in Chapter 9 is largely one of emphasis. And, particularly when working with average or less able students, it is important that this difference be reflected in the complexity of the work undertaken. The amount of data collection and analysis, marketing planning, preparation of display and packaging material, and so on, could be considerable, and if this is to be combined with a lengthy and complex product design and manufacturing process then the result is likely to be a very long, drawn-out project demanding a degree of stamina and co-ordinating ability quite beyond most students. Ways of overcoming this problem are discussed later in this chapter.

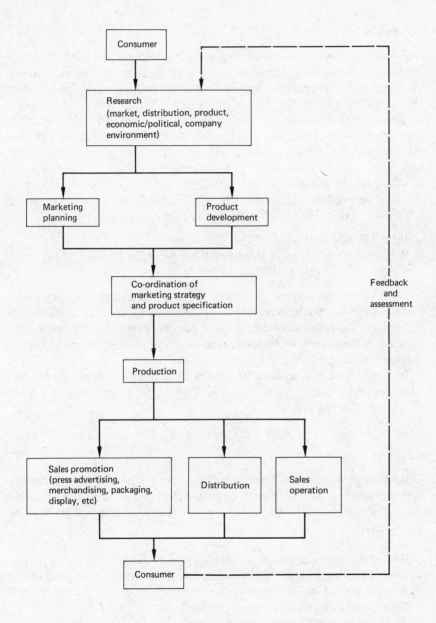

2.2 There is a clear similarity between the 'marketing process' illustrated here and the design process diagram (page 2). Both start with a situation (the consumer), progress through investigation (research), specification and production to assessment and feedback.

The marketing process, like the design process, may be fairly complex and will almost certainly incorporate several design processes—the design of packaging, display material, distribution systems, and so on.

Starting points

The starting point for a marketing project could be the need to design products to be sold at a school fête or garden party or at some other fund-raising event. It is possible that the first step could be a factory visit, but this would have to be very carefully organized if the students are to come away with any real idea of how marketing—not an easily demonstrable area of work—fits into the whole picture. An additional potential difficulty is that manufacturers are understandably less willing to expose their marketing operation to public gaze than they are their production lines.

Whatever the motivation, the initial aim will be to select one or more items to be produced and sold. This will involve market research during which the students will need to answer such questions as:

—Who will buy the product?
—What are the needs or problems of these potential customers? (In other words, what will they be likely to buy?)

These questions may be dealt with in group discussion or they could form a basis for preliminary fieldwork, perhaps using questionnaires. In either event the result should be a list of possible products for manufacture which will then need to be evaluated in terms of the potential market, production facilities, and so on.

In one school the students started with a brainstorming session (see *Materials and Design: A Fresh Approach*[2], Chapter 5) and produced a list of 80 items for discussion.

Choosing a product

Once a range of possible items for production has been drawn up further investigation will be necessary in order to select one of these and to enable product design work to start. Among the questions that will have to be answered are:

—What competitive products are likely to be available?
—What advantages should our product have over competitive products?
—What is the size of the market?
—What production facilities are available?
—What price range should we aim for?
—What more do we need to know about potential customers (age, sex, etc)?
—How much can be spent on raw materials, packaging, advertising materials, etc?

Many of these questions may be dealt with at a relatively superficial level at this stage. For example, the cost of raw materials and packaging can only be estimated very roughly until the design work is much more advanced. Nevertheless, such factors will affect the choice of product and will need to be taken into account, even if it is only at the level of deciding that a fairly small product will be needed if materials stocks are not to be exhausted.

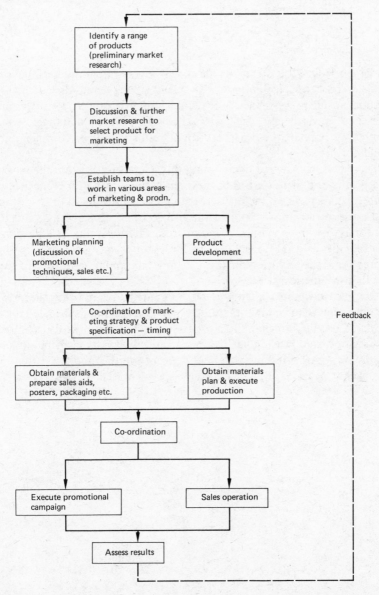

2.3 An approach to organizing a marketing project.

c

Some teachers feel that it is undesirable for their students to examine similar products during their investigation work: it is argued that this will reinforce their preconceptions (see *Materials and Design: A Fresh Approach*, Chapter 6). In a marketing project, however, this examination is essential if the work is to be comparable with commercial reality; many promotional campaigns, for example, are built around the favourable comparison of a product with its competitors.

Production problems?

If the work is to be of real value it will involve quantity production. As modern marketing techniques are a result of the economics of mass production in our present society it would be unrealistic to consider them in isolation. Nevertheless, as suggested above, there is a danger here that combining both of these aspects could result in a very complex and unwieldy project.

There are two ways of overcoming this. One is to separate the marketing and production aspects so that they can be tackled by different groups, or different classes. The difficulty here is that a certain amount of co-ordination and cross-fertilization is vital if the project is to be a success, and this in itself may become so complicated as to negate the value of separating the two activities. A joint factory visit by both groups may go some way towards overcoming this by demonstrating how marketing and production fit together in practice.

Alternatively, the students could be guided towards the selection of a product which can be manufactured fairly simply without the need for many hours of production planning. A product which requires little more than an assembly and packaging line may be ideal. It may even be possible to simply buy products for resale and concentrate the students' attention on the packaging and sales promotion aspects of the marketing operation.

Case Study

Product Testing

The project described here was undertaken by a class of fourteen- to fifteen-year-old girls as part of their home economics course. Their work is also illustrated in the filmstrip Value for Money.[4]

Advertising techniques

Work began with a talk on advertising. The girls then looked at a number of advertisements and discussed the ways in which advertisers try to persuade the consumer to buy their products.

Several techniques were identified. Some advertisements suggested that by using a particular product consumers could improve their status in some way. For example, purchasers of a certain brand of carpet would have a beautiful home; users of a particular aftershave lotion would become more sexually attractive; the only way to be a perfect mother is to dust baby's bottom with a certain brand of baby powder, feed him a certain brand of tinned food and wash the family's clothes with a certain washing powder.

Another technique could be seen in advertisements in which products were compared in superficial and unscientific ways with no technical information of real value being given. A good example was a certain company's petrol mileage test in which a brand of petrol was compared with the same brand without a 'mileage ingredient'.

A similar 'comparison' technique was noted in a washing powder advertisement. The copy claimed that:

Impossible stains—blood, sweat and chocolate pudding—washing in ordinary powder don't come out. Soaked in . . . (an enzyme detergent) —they do!

The girls noticed that different processes—washing and soaking— were being compared as well as different powders. This raised a number of questions:

—Was the test making a fair comparison?

—What would happen if the stains were **soaked** in ordinary powders?

—What would happen if the stains were hand washed in the biological detergent?

From subsequent discussion it was clear that although the girls knew the names of popular brands they had no knowledge of comparative performances or relative prices of washing powders. They were, however, able to quote slogans and catch-phrases from television advertisements.

Planning tests

An examination of washing powder advertisements suggested that they were designed to persuade rather than to offer hard information that would help the purchaser to make a valid comparison. Indeed, the only way to obtain real knowledge of comparative performance seemed to be to set up some kind of testing process.

It was obviously essential to wash fabrics. Several girls volunteered to bring in actual garments worn by toddlers, but this approach proved unsatisfactory because the clothes varied in texture and in the range of stains they carried. Some form of standardization was necessary, both of fabric and the stains that were to be tested.

Choice of fabric presented no problem. A large sheet of cheap white cotton was purchased from a local market. It was washed to ensure that it carried no stains or residue from the manufacturing process. Then it was cut into twenty-four rectangles approximately 600 × 450 mm ready for specimen stains to be added.

The range of stains was discussed at length. A selection that any housewife and mother might meet in her weekly wash was finally listed:

1 tea with milk and sugar;
2 blood (ox blood was used for the tests);
3 car oil;
4 damson juice in syrup;
5 beetroot in vinegar;
6 shoe polish;
7 foundation face cream;
8 cream-based lipstick;
9 pearlized lipstick.

The stains were applied evenly in a standard pattern to each piece of fabric and allowed to soak in and dry for twenty-fours.

Tests and results

Five biological and seven non-biological powders were tested. As far as possible all the powders were purchased from one large supermarket in order to establish a consistent price basis.

The soak test was carried out first. Powder and water were mixed according to instructions on each packet. The instructions proved remarkably similar across the whole range of powders, both in terms of the water temperature and quantity of powder specified. One ounce of powder to one gallon of water at 40°C satisfied the requirements in every case. This would seem to indicate that no powder is significantly more powerful than others and economy cannot therefore be achieved by using less per wash.

After a five-and-a-half hour soak each sample was held up to the window for inspection. Judgments about stain removal were made on a three-point scale:

C—clear of any stain;
S—slight stain visible;
H—heavy stain visible.

The judgments were recorded and the sample was then hand-washed for five minutes in an attempt to remove remaining stains. The judgment of stain removal was repeated. Figure 2.4 shows the results obtained.

2.4 Table of results—soak and wash test.

SOAK and WASH

	TEA	BLOOD	OIL	FRUIT JUICE	SHOE POLISH	BEET. VIN.	LIPSTICK (cream)	MAKE UP	LIPSTICK (pearl)
BIOLOGICAL									
ARIEL	c/c	s/s	H/H	c/c	H/s	c/c	H/s	H/c	H/H
RADIANT	c/c	s/s	H/H	c/c	H/s	c/c	H/s	H/c	H/H
OMO	c/c	s/s	H/H	c/c	H/s	c/c	H/s	H/s	H/s
FINE FARE	c/c	s/s	H/H	c/c	H/s	c/c	H/H	H/s	S/s
TESCO	c/c	s/s	H/H	c/c	H/s	c/c	H/c	H/s	H/s
NON BIOLOGICAL									
PERSIL	s/c	s/s	H/H	c/c	H/s	c/c	H/s	H/s	H/s
DAZ - Blue	c/c	s/s	H/H	c/c	H/s	c/s	H/H	H/s	H/s
TESCO SUPER	c/c	s/s	H/H	c/c	H/H	c/c	H/H	H/s	H/s
FINE FARE - Blue	s/s	s/c	H/H	c/c	H/s	c/c	H/s	H/s	H/s
SURF - White	c/c	s/s	H/H	c/c	H/s	c/c	H/H	H/s	H/s
TIDE - Blue	c/c	s/c	H/H	c/c	H/s	c/c	H/s	H/S	H/s
TIDE - White	c/c	s/s	H/H	c/c	H/H	S/s	H/s	H/s	H/H

The second test involved hand washing. A fresh mixture of each powder was prepared and a new sample was hand washed for three periods, each of five minutes. At the end of each period judgments were made of the degree of stain removal. The results are shown in figure 2.5.

2.5 Table of results—wash test.

A table of comparative costs was also compiled (figure 2.6). Several packets were found to carry boldly printed price reductions such as '3p off Recommended Price'. The girls were surprised to discover that no packet carried a recommended price and it was therefore impossible to say from what original price the '3p off' had been deducted. Some suggestions for recommended prices were obtained from *Shaw's Guide* but, of course, few housewives carry such a guide when shopping.

It was found, too, that although all the packets were a standard size the guaranteed weight of powder varied from 25 to 29 oz. The price per packet could not therefore be compared. Only by working out the cost per ounce could a fair comparison be made. It then became possible to assess the accuracy of advertisements which suggested that one particular brand offered more powder than others for the same money.

When the cost factors shown in figure 2.6 were compared with the performance levels recorded in the other two tables, the girls concluded that some of the cheapest powders appeared to offer best value for money. They were surprised to discover that advertisements were unreliable and seldom offered hard facts that would help the consumer.

	Retail Price	Actual Price	Weight	Special Offer	Cost per oz.
BIOLOGICAL					
ARIEL	23	20p	28ozs	2½p off	.7p
RADIANT	22½	19p	27ozs	3p off	.7p
OMO	20½	17p	26ozs	2½p off	.65p
FINE FARE		16p	28ozs	none	.57p
TESCO		16½p	28ozs	none	.59p
NON BIOLOGICAL					
PERSIL	22	22p	29ozs	none	.76p
DAZ . Blue	19½	16p	26ozs	2½p off	.61p
TESCO SUPER		14p	25ozs	none	.56p
FINE FARE . Blue		13p	25ozs	none	.52p
SURF . White	15½	15½p	26ozs	none	.51p
TIDE . Blue	15½	15½p	26ozs	none	.51p
TIDE . White	15½	15½p	26ozs	none	.51p

NOTE:-
RETAIL PRICE FROM SHAWS GUIDE

Indeed, some vital information such as the recommended price appeared deliberately to be withheld. In other cases, to obtain a 'free offer' it was found that the customer was committed to further purchases.

Value of the project

Consumer discrimination is clearly a valuable element of design education, particularly in the context of home economics. There can be little doubt that the girls involved in this project became alert to some of the pressures exerted on consumers by sophisticated marketing techniques. Their first-hand experience of finding out for themselves appeared to make a marked impression on them. Their teacher felt that they were beginning to view the business of purchasing in a far more critical way.

Case Study

Developing a Critical Awareness

The following report has been extracted from an article describing the part played by the science department in a 'practical projects' course for third-year students. Although the course involved also woodwork, metalwork, plastics, technical drawing, home economics and needlework there was no attempt at co-ordination and no restriction was placed on an individual teacher's choice of work or method of approach. Consumer testing found its place in the course as a result of the experience of the science teacher.

Birth of the project

About two years ago I set an examination question to all the forms throughout the school, ranging from first to fifth years, which I then taught. The students were asked to look at two television advertisements to see if the claims that they made were valid. If they felt they were not valid they were asked to explain how they would have conducted the experiments illustrated in the advertisements.

One advertisement compared two soap powders. A garment was washed for three minutes in one powder and a similarly soiled garment soaked overnight in the other. The second advertisement showed two cars driving around a circular track. One car stopped after a short time ; the other, whose petrol, the manufacturer claimed, contained a 'mileage ingredient', travelled a greater distance.

I was somewhat shocked by the response to this question. Many students maintained that 'it must be right if it's on the telly'. Others thought that if they identified one result as being invalid, the other ought to be valid. Across the range of forms a wide variety of answers was produced, most of which seemed highly unsatisfactory. It appeared, therefore, that our teaching had failed in a rather fundamental area— that of developing a critical awareness !

Washing and wearing

In order to encourage the development of this awareness a course of work was devised in which the students were asked to design experiments to test and compare a range of materials. Two of these assignments were :

—An investigation of the 'wearing ability of a number of materials such as wool, silk, Terylene, acetate fibres, cotton, nylon and linen. (Tests were also undertaken on apparent thicknesses and textures.)
—Comparison of the effectiveness of various washing powders. (This was followed by a chemical analysis of the powders to determine the content of bleach, soap, washing soda, etc.)

The most open-ended of all the standard problems is that concerned with the comparison of the effectiveness of washing powders. Most groups start with a number of different materials and a number of different powders. They standardize the amount of water used, the length of washing time, the temperature of the water, the amount of powder, the type and amount of staining on each material, and so on. Not every group, perhaps, will have identified every factor. The temperature of the water, for example, has been forgotten on several occasions. In the main we feel that this approach is logical and meets the needs of the assignment.

The students also usually take a critical approach to the application of stains to the fabrics. A wide range of stains is considered but standardizing on quality and density calls for great care.

In practical work, two powders are used on a single material—white cotton. The washing is usually carried out in a small machine we built ourselves, although some groups elect to use the larger commercial model in the home economics room.

3
Work with Motor Vehicles

The influence of the motor vehicle on our lives is undeniable. It offers many benefits—mobility, convenience, speed—but the price society pays for these benefits is high. A thousand miles of motorway span the country. Towns built before this century are torn apart to provide easier passage or parking for motor vehicles. In congested areas the levels of noise and atmospheric pollution are high. When the demands of the vehicle and the pedestrian conflict the results are sometimes inconvenient, sometimes fatal: eleven thousand children under fifteen, for example, are killed or severely injured every year. If increasing car production over recent years is maintained the number of cars on the road now—12 million—is likely to double by 1980.

In the circumstances, then, it is not surprising that an increasing number of schools are seeing the need for an introduction to the safe and responsible use of the motor vehicle. Courses developed in recent years tend to be of two rather distinct types—pre-driver training and driver training. Pre-driver training has been defined as

. . . classroom tuition aimed at the inculcation of responsible and considerate attitudes to other road users, and covering such matters as licensing and insurance, car safety, the Highway Code, road signs, and traffic law. In addition some elementary driving instruction is normally given in a car using . . . (a) suitable off-street manoeuvring area. The aim is not, however, to turn out a driver, but rather someone who is prepared for the responsibility of learning to drive, and who possesses the knowledge he will later need as a background to driving skills. Driver training, on the other hand, has its emphasis on 'in-car' tuition, extends to driving on the public highway and generally aims at producing competent and safe drivers. It follows that it is appropriate only for pupils who are 17 years old, or nearly that age.[18]

This account of motor vehicle work is concerned solely with pre-driver training, which, it is argued, may be justified as more than an adjunct to the concern for road safety. It is seen in some schools as one of the optional extensions of general design activities in the lower part of the school. In addition, there is much educational potential in the whole range of social and environmental aspects of the subject. (See figure 3.1.)

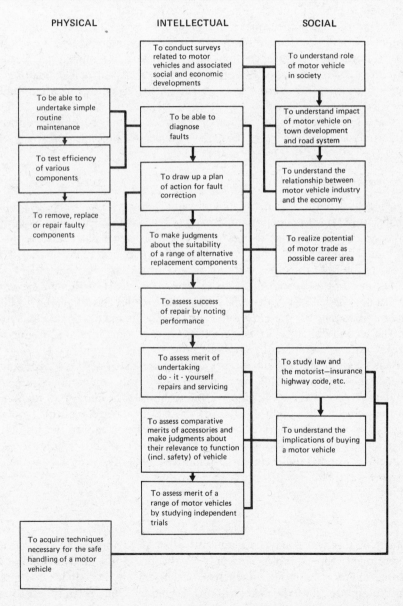

3.1 Aims and objectives of motor vehicle work.

The attraction of motor vehicle work

Work with motor vehicles has many obvious attractions for students. Their interest in cars and motor cycles is an important motivating factor. The relevance of theory as an essential preparation for more advanced practical work is seen and understood, particularly if introduced in short sessions as required to amplify and extend practical experience.

The work—both theoretical and practical—is self-evidently 'real', not contrived, and so attracts many who need, as an important additional motivation, the reassurance that their activities are related to real-life situations. Most students welcome the opportunity to tackle 'man-sized' problems instead of those which are obviously scaled down or simplified for school use.

For some students the attraction of this work extends beyond the utilitarian or recreational and lies in the career prospects it presents at many levels.

The teaching pattern

The teaching pattern frequently employed in motor vehicle work is a fairly unstructured one in which the opportunity to explain a feature of assembly or operation is taken as it presents itself. This approach will, of course, continue, but at least two common problems associated with the work indicate the need for other methods to accompany it.

The first of these problems is the number of students. Although the work is usually carried out with some fraction of a full class—half is typical— the number can still present a somewhat difficult organizational challenge.

The second difficulty arises from the fact that some jobs are suitable for group work while others can only be done by an individual.

One solution may be to use work-cards. Such cards need not necessarily specify the steps needed to carry out a particular job, but should require the student to record the tools he used, the techniques he employed, the name of the part, and its condition. If work-cards, or job-sheets, of this type are used from the early stages when bench work is being carried out on parts, then a body of recorded observations and methods will be available to each student for individual reference. Examples of work-cards are given on pages 87 and 88.

Links with other subjects

Much of this work may overlap with other departments. In the science department, for example, the study of the principles of two- and four- stroke engines, batteries, magnetism, electrical circuits, dynamos, fuses, and so on, are an established part of the syllabus. Quite often it needs only a slight degree of co-operation to bring the practical engineering aspects of one department into alignment with the theoretical aspects of another. The opportunity also exists to introduce carefully planned integrated courses.

Another strong link exists with the art department in the study of body-work styling. In one school styling exercises are carried out in the art room and the results assessed by the motor vehicle group for production problems and mechanical suitability. For several years the Vauxhall Motor Company undertook a schools' competition which exploited this aspect of motor vehicle work.

Limits

Even though the following section contains references to problems associated with motor vehicle work it is important at this point to stress some of the salient dangers associated with this topic, since these may limit the extent to which a school may feel able to undertake motor vehicle work.

On educational grounds it seems valueless to have several engines that do not work. Having said that, there is the inherent danger of ensuring a supply of engines that do run, or will run when necessary repairs have been undertaken, that in turn leaves students with a dangerously inadequate knowledge and skill. Here the competence of those responsible for organizing a course must be considered. The rate at which fundamental change is taking place in motor vehicle design often means that even the most enthusiastic amateur is unaware of some of the implications. Changes in suspension systems and the replacement of dynamos with alternators and forthcoming electronic circuitry are points in question. To help ensure that safe and up to date methods of working are maintained it may often be helpful to seek the guidance of the motor trade or departments in technical colleges where courses on motor vehicle technology are undertaken.

The question of safety, though mentioned elsewhere, must also be stressed. The movement, lifting and jacking up of a motor car can be hazardous and unless proper facilities and equipment are supplied and understood some aspects of the work must be omitted. A teacher must ensure that he is aware of his obligations in this respect; he would be wise to obtain parental agreement for each student engaged in motor vehicle work. Insurance cover must also be examined and the views of the local authority sought. The HMSO pamphlet *Driver Training for Young People*[18] will be useful here.

Starting off

The focus of attention for students in this area of work is, naturally enough, the motor vehicle itself, whether their interest is first excited by a scooter, motor cycle, car or kart. The underlying motivation is much less likely to

3.2 Starting off—driving experience can provide valuable motivation

be, as it is for more mature individuals, the desire to travel from one place to another; more often it lies in the desire to control a moving machine.

Harnessing initial interest

One of the ways in which teachers attempt to harness this interest is by giving students, at the outset, the opportunity to experience these sensations by providing them with karts which, subject to certain safeguards, they may drive around the school playground, on tennis courts or, more rarely, on a track. It soon becomes apparent, even to those who may at first exhibit a reckless disregard for safety, that the control of a machine at speed entails a high degree of responsibility, both for the sake of the machine and other drivers. This is particularly the case when others from the same group have spent a great deal of time and care putting the machine in perfect working order to begin with. Thus, right from the start, the twin aspects of a motor vehicle course are demonstrated: the first concerned with the machine, the second with its responsible and controlled use.

The experience of driving, as noted by many teachers, has considerable value as a 'carrot' to motivate those who might otherwise not be ready to make the fullest use of a motor vehicle course.

Facilities

Possession of the correct facilities is essential, not only to ensure the safety of students working on or beneath vehicles, but also to aid the organization of a structured course. Some schools are fortunate in having workshops with access and ramps leading to double sliding doors, hoists, roof tracks, hydraulic lifts and, above all, sufficient space allocated for the storage, maintenance and driving of motor vehicles. Inspection pits are not recommended and it is stressed that adequate provision must be made for the disposal of exhaust fumes. In addition, the storage of petrol, even in small quantities, needs special care and should be approved by an officer of the fire service. The advice of the local authority should also be sought and appropriate British Standards consulted.

When such facilities are not available many teachers regard the erection of a garage as the first step towards specialized provision. The way in which one school tackled this undertaking is described in 'Case Study: Building a Garage'. A motor vehicle course may therefore begin at several removes from the machine itself.

Engines and other parts will be needed for practical work or as demonstration models. (Small engines should be used for testing.) These are often obtained from garages or breaker's yards, as MOT write-offs or by accepting vehicles and parts given as presents. Gifts of this sort have sometimes proved an embarrassment because of the amount of work needed to put the vehicle in working order. Care must be taken to avoid littering school premises with unwanted parts. Some motor manufacturers are happy to supply parts or assembled training engines at cheap rates.

In addition to these more obvious requirements, many tools and items of testing equipment can be made within the school, either as part of a course or during work which precedes it. The range of useful tools which can be made is large and includes screwdrivers, axle-stands, brake adjusting spanners, plug spanners, adjustable spanners, brake bleeding equipment, ramps, sprocket pullers, tyre levers and screwjacks.

But again it must be stressed that load bearing tools such as axle-stands, ramps and screwjacks must be tested carefully to ensure safety.

Organization

Work on motor vehicles may be conveniently divided into tasks which are critical and those which are less so. Early practical work carried out by students with relatively little knowledge would obviously be of the latter kind. One might think of very simple tasks to begin with: washing or polishing bodywork, for example, wheel changing or carrying out a pre-journey check. Later, normal servicing operations could be included: greasing and the cleaning, adjustment or replacing of items like spark-plugs, contact points, and so on. More complex jobs can then be under-taken, such as tappet adjustments, and the examination and lubrication or repair of body parts like window winding mechanisms, bonnet catches and door handles.

Initial problems

It is at the point where young and relatively inexperienced students are given tasks of a critical nature—that is, concerned with the mechanical operation or performance of a working vehicle—that the greatest demands are made on the teacher in terms of organization. The difficulty, quickly realized by any teacher unwise enough to let this happen, is that the careless or incorrect assembly of parts may result in the damage or non-operation of a previously working vehicle, with the result that his own limited and expensive time may have to be devoted to locating and remedying the fault—a time-consuming and frustrating business.

The solution is, of course, to prevent this situation occurring. The maintenance and repair of working vehicles should be carried out only by students sufficiently experienced to do so. For less experienced students, still at the stage of acquiring basic knowledge, work on individual components on the bench may be the most suitable approach. An additional advantage of bench work is that it can be carried out in well-lit conditions without the problems of difficult access and poor visibility which inevitably accompany some operations on a vehicle. At the same time, this method presents the opportunity to instil good habits of work—careful dismantling and re-assembly of parts, laying out of the pieces in a methodical sequence, and so on.

The 'spare-parts' technique

Even in these conditions, however, inexperienced students should not work on the school's only alternator or carburettor. Mistakes will inevitably be made and parts fitted incorrectly or even lost. For this reason some schools adopt what might be called a 'spare-parts' technique whereby several pieces of equipment—starter motors, fuel pumps, back axles, carburettors, alter-nators, and so on—are kept in stock. If parts from an item are broken or lost they can be supplied from another. When necessary the units are dis-carded and replaced. Experience indicates that units used on this basis may have a school life of about two years before replacement.

A similar system is often employed with the less critical tasks associated with bodywork repairs. Initially, damaged body panels are taken from scrapped vehicles. The intention is not, at this stage, to restore the part to a professional standard but to restore its shape and particularly its strength. All the normal finishing operations are applied—from paint-brush to spray gun.

Planning a course

Early problems with inexperienced students may also be eased through careful planning of the first year of a motor vehicle course. Quite often, the first term contains a large element of theoretical work. In the second this knowledge is reinforced by practical work, and in the third most of the learning is done through practical tasks.

Once a body of practical knowledge has been gained, the transfer of activity to operational vehicles should certainly be made. Work on any machine is, of course, critical and should be undertaken with care; this is particularly so with school vehicles which are used to give students driving experience and must therefore be in perfect mechanical condition, with MOT if applicable. A teacher cannot take the risk of permitting work on operational vehicles to be undertaken by students who are not thoroughly competent and responsible.

Practical work

The element of developmental design associated with the redesign of components or constructions is rarely large in motor vehicle work, except in kart construction where it has an important part to play. In the majority of motor vehicle courses developmental design work finds expression largely through diagnostic activities, that is, the tracing and correction of faults in the various systems of the machine.

Diagnostic design

Diagnostic design and problem solving makes rather different demands on the student than do forms of design associated with working through an idea from raw materials to end-product. What is required in diagnostic work is the ability to conceptualize what is, or may be, happening inside a series of functioning components. But however great is a student's ability to do this, it is unlikely that he will be able to develop sufficient knowledge or skill without the practical experience of taking actual components to pieces and re-assembling them in working order.

Diagnostic forms of design, therefore, are usually found as the culmination of a practical course. As with other aspects of motor vehicle work, the ability to diagnose and trace faults should be tackled as part of a structured development. Bench rigs—of the ignition system, for example—might be investigated and the components—coil, distributor, battery, etc—laid out

The components are mounted on a metal frame. By switching the ignition on and turning the distributor drive by hand the plugs will spark. Faults can be introduced or worn parts can be substituted for diagnostic tests.

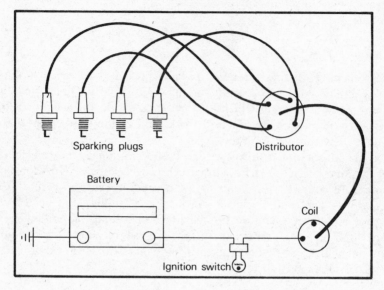

3.3 Ignition system bench rig.

on a board as in figure 3.3. The rigs enable the teacher to introduce a fault, perhaps by setting the contact points incorrectly.

An alternative to a rig displayed on a board is an actual stripped-down chassis. The one illustrated in figure 3.4 is in full working order. The advantage here is that the component parts of a system are shown in their actual position and relationship which helps a student to orientate himself when faced with a real problem.

From the tracing of faults in one system it is a logical extension to trace a fault which may lie within any one of a number of systems. A starting fault, for example, may lie within the electrical system, the fuel system or it may be mechanical in origin. The main thing is that the student should approach a diagnostic investigation in a methodical manner and systematically exclude one possibility after another. Indeed, it has been the experience of many teachers (and car-owners) that a random approach often results in a longer time being needed to trace the fault, or even the complete failure to trace it at all. Occasionally a school is fortunate enough to have a test rig of professional standard and in this situation the teacher is able to introduce a fault into any part of a system by operating the appropriate switch.

It is possible to apply a systematic approach to fault analysis; this applies to fault finding beyond the motor vehicle situation and therefore students

3.4 Stripped-down chassis.

3.5 Test rig.

may usefully be encouraged to understand the principles of the approach, so that it will be of use to them when attempting to repair any faulty piece of mechanical equipment.

Further developments of this work take diagnostic problems from the relatively simple environment of the bench or working rig to normal operational machines where the problems are more critical and both the tracing and the correction of a fault are complicated by limited access to the components.

Situation   Before any repair work can be undertaken it is necessary to collect information about the apparent fault.

Analysis   Once all reasonable evidence has been collected it is possible to decide what may or may not be related to the fault.

Isolate   This may involve the systematic testing of a sequence of components that operate in relation to each other until the exact fault is located.

Rectify   At this stage it is necessary to decide why the fault occurred —the replacement or repair of a component may not be sufficient.

Test   This ensures that the fault has been correctly repaired and that the equipment operates satisfactorily.

Ergonomics

Ergonomic aspects of design are important not only to the comfort, but also to the safety of the driver and passengers. Some practical work— related partly to motor vehicles, but more particularly to karts—may be carried out on slotted angle-iron test rigs. Among the factors to be considered are comfort, visibility from the driving seat, view of the instrument panel, and the ability to reach all the essential controls with the minimum of body movement.

One way of establishing an understanding of some of these aspects that has proved practical for use in schools is by examining the main driving controls. Students are asked to design three sets of controls: one each for a lorry, a family saloon and a sports car. Initially, they list the possible controls under three headings: those required by law, those considered desirable and those considered luxuries.

Under the first heading are included a speedometer, brake, horn, lights switch, windscreen wiper switch and washer. Those which might be considered desirable include an oil pressure gauge, brake failure warning, seat belt warning and an ammeter. The luxuries list includes such items as a radio, record player, stereo tape system and rev. counter. The significance of some of these varies, of course, according to the vehicle; an item considered luxurious in one vehicle—an oil pressure gauge, for example, in a family saloon—might be considered desirable in another—in a sports car for example.

At the second stage the students accord a number of points to each item— one to ten. Those which rate high numbers are placed closest to the driver while lower numbers are placed further away. Next, they consider the actual layout of the dashboard and the design of the instruments. Final conclusions are expressed in the form of a plan drawing indicating the location of the items in relation to the driving position. This is amplified by a drawing of the driver's view of the instrument panel.

Performance

Many schools have competition karts which are maintained and repaired by students. Since a kart is a relatively safe vehicle and the conditions under which it performs are not normally dangerous, greater concentration is possible on aspects of performance, particularly speed. Work on karts is therefore ideally suited to the study of the problems of tuning and the redesign of components to improve performance. This area of work is discussed in more detail in *Design and Karting*[12].

General design problems

There is considerable scope for the tackling of general design problems within a motor vehicle course. A typical example is a project carried out by a group of fourth-year boys which involved the conversion of an old van to facilitate group driving instruction. Through discussion they formulated a specification with three main factors:

1 the van should be able to accommodate up to eight students (eight being a half class);
2 there should be easy access from the driving seat into the body of the van;
3 those in the rear of the van should be able to see and hear what the driver was doing.

From this point work continued on an individual basis, each student translating his ideas into notes and sketches. These ideas were then brought together and group discussion established a final choice.

The students decided to alter the construction of the body in order to ensure easy access and good visibility. Since this resulted in a severe reduction in the strength of the remaining parts chassis modifications had to be made to reintroduce adequate strength. Accommodation was provided by making and fitting two bench seats and finally a colour scheme was chosen and the bodywork re-sprayed.

Another school extended the scope of its motor vehicle course by involving students in the design and construction of a driving simulator. This involved problems of ergonomics when considering the position of the seat and controls. Electronic circuitry was incorporated into the apparatus so that a number of faults could be simulated. To ease the students' difficulties of acquiring correct sequences of starting the engine and driving off a tape recording was connected to the simulator.

Roadcraft

For many students, particularly those who do not wish to continue to examination level, motor vehicle work may not be pursued for its own sake. It may be viewed principally as a means to attain mobility by buying and maintaining their own vehicle. For this reason many teachers see the logical culmination of a motor vehicle course as *driving instruction* in which the vehicle, now known and understood, is used for the purpose for which it is intended.

The advantages of this extension are considerable. Far from being merely a gimmick to attract those who might otherwise respond reluctantly to formal training, the benefits seen are those of providing not only experience of basic skills—starting, signalling, positioning, gear changing, stopping— but also an entire background to the responsible use of the motor vehicle and its effect on society. Work of this sort is of clear importance. In some schools this is recognized by promoting roadcraft not just as the culmination of a practical course but as a second, parallel strand to the practical work.

Driving instruction must, of course, be carefully prepared.* This preparation often takes the form of a number of talks and simulated road situations. A course in roadcraft commonly looks at six aspects which affect the handling of vehicles: the health of the driver, the road, the vehicle itself, traffic circulation, safety, the Highway Code. (See *Driver Training for Young People*[18].)

The health of the driver

Driver health is often taken for granted, but it is most necessary that students should recognize medical conditions that impair judgment. In

---

*Whether or not school driving instruction produces better drivers ('better' being measured in terms of number of accidents) is the subject of present research. The assumption cannot be made that school driving instruction leads to an improvement in these terms.

terms of school work eyesight tests are of obvious importance. Simple ones can be arranged by using standard eye test cards; colour blindness can be tested in the same way.

Similarly, long and short sight may be easily tested over a range of, say, ten feet to five hundred yards. Tunnel vision is another phenomenon about which students can be made aware. This is important because peripheral vision has no relationship to long or short sight.

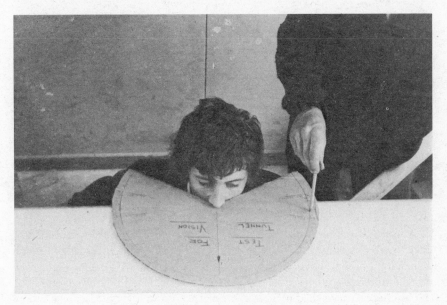

3.6 A simple technique for testing peripheral vision.

The speed of a driver's reaction is another factor of importance. Reaction tests provide the sort of competitive element that students enjoy. There are two related aspects of physical reaction: the first concerned with the time taken to respond to a stimulus and the second with the ability to react correctly when faced with a situation in which more than one response could be made.

It is not suggested, of course, that these tests are objectively accurate. Their purpose is simply to make the student aware of the importance of such factors.

A simple reaction tester is illustrated in figure 3.7. A graduated rod is dropped and the student must catch it before it hits the floor. His speed of reaction is shown by the distance travelled by the rod before being caught. This is a simple, limited test because the student is anticipating what will happen and is, so to speak, primed.

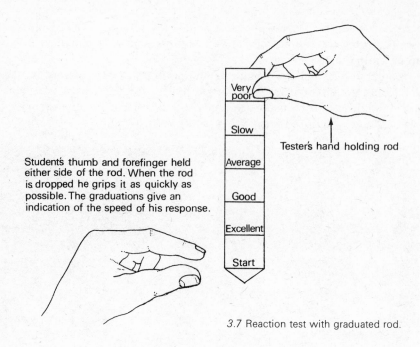

Student's thumb and forefinger held either side of the rod. When the rod is dropped he grips it as quickly as possible. The graduations give an indication of the speed of his response.

Tester's hand holding rod

Very poor
Slow
Average
Good
Excellent
Start

3.7 Reaction test with graduated rod.

A more searching test is that illustrated in figure 3.8. Here, the student is faced with three lights and must act in a prescribed manner depending on which light flashes. An extension of this is the normal MOT driving reaction test in which a student must stop a car as quickly and safely as possible. Graduated whitewashed markings on the playground enable the result to be measured.

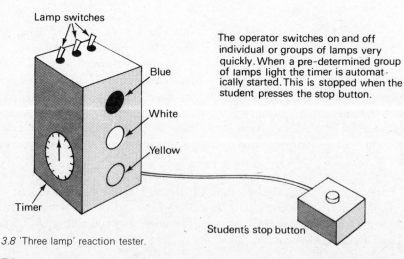

Lamp switches

The operator switches on and off individual or groups of lamps very quickly. When a pre-determined group of lamps light the timer is automatically started. This is stopped when the student presses the stop button.

Blue
White
Yellow
Timer

Student's stop button

3.8 'Three lamp' reaction tester.

The third aspect of health which is of concern is the effects of fatigue, alcohol or drugs on the ability to react quickly and decisively. The debilitating effects of fatigue and alcohol on speed of reaction and general performance are well known, but the inclusion of drugs will serve to remind students that even mild drugs like aspirin or hay fever tablets combined with mild alcohol can produce a dramatic lowering of performance.

The importance of these aspects of health and reaction speed are certainly not lost on those who are planning future road systems. Their suggestions include the removal of the control of the vehicle from the driver altogether!

The road

The road itself, obviously an important factor, is the subject of further work. The intention here is to take into account a number of different types of road surface, the materials of which they are made and the frictional qualities each has. In addition, there is opportunity to study the effects of fallen leaves, water, ice and snow on road surface qualities.

The vehicle

The mechanical safety of the motor vehicle is a major aspect of engineering work. In terms of roadcraft, however, it is important to consider other factors which relate to the performance of the vehicle in motion. Considerations like those of momentum, stability and force of impact are intended to give students some idea of how drivers and vehicles act when in motion. Understanding of these factors enables them to appreciate the importance of making a correct decision in a continuously changing situation, and also to anticipate what is likely to happen to a vehicle as a result of its speed, position on the road, curvature of the road surface, and so on.

Traffic circulation

Studies of driver health, the road and the vehicle are aspects of the total traffic situation. Studies of traffic engineering and its effects on traffic circulation act as a focus, therefore, for knowledge gained in these other areas.

Work in this area is concerned particularly with traffic flow in towns and cities. Those which are newly built can take the requirements of the motor vehicle into account. In some places—Birmingham, for example—large-scale alterations are made within existing developed areas. Other towns, built to facilitate the traffic flow of other ages, are often able to effect only small-scale changes; and even these frequently arise as a result of the existence of some potential hazard.

Problems of traffic circulation can be framed in local terms. For example, the traffic layout of an old town without special provision for traffic flow can be contrasted with a modern town incorporating pedestrian walkways, cycle tracks, underpasses, flyovers, etc. Or, where planners have attempted to improve traffic circulation via small-scale changes in an old town, layouts of the traffic flow before and after the amendments can be compared and the students encouraged to discuss the effects of changes and suggest alternatives.

Another simple but effective basis for study is a model of the town layout. This has the advantage that it is familiar to students. With the aid of model cars, common road situations can be staged, safe methods of negotiating particular areas can be worked out, parts of the town planned for traffic flow are easily distinguished from those which have been adapted, routes can be timed to ascertain which have the fastest traffic flow, and so on.

3.9 Students studying traffic flow.

Safety

Local town models—or maps if an extended area is to be covered—can also be used to assist the analysis of road accidents. One school has developed this work to a fairly high level. The local road safety officer provides

76

the school with a monthly accident report. This gives information regarding the types of vehicles involved, the time of day, weather conditions, road surface conditions, speed limit within the area, and so on. The position is pin-pointed on the map or model and, through discussion, an attempt is made to decide why the accident occurred, which driver was to blame or whether a number of drivers contributed, and how it might have been avoided.

Work of this sort cannot fail to establish that, in addition to vehicle or traffic-direction failure, a major cause of accidents is the behaviour of drivers—giving ambiguous signals, or none at all, acting or reacting with aggression, and so on. Such discussion has considerable value as a warning to students and a reminder to them of the kinds of behaviour they should avoid when placed in a practical driving situation.

The Highway Code

Accident analysis also serves to remind students of the purpose and importance of the Highway Code and the need to familiarize oneself with the current requirements. This importance is not only related to an understanding of road markings, signals and procedures, but also to the need to standardize what might otherwise be a wide variety of interpretations of certain instructions.

When studying the Highway Code it is natural to consider also the seriousness of the abuse of traffic laws through an understanding of the endorsement system and of various Road Traffic Acts.

Driving instruction

The maintenance and roadcraft aspects of a motor vehicle course are often regarded by students as preliminaries to the actual experience of driving. This can present the teacher with a difficult organizational problem, but this can be overcome through careful planning and the presentation of an appropriate blend of theory and practice.

Organization

Once the class has been introduced to the controls in the normal way, driving usually begins in a four-wheeled vehicle rather than on a motor cycle or scooter. This may at first seem paradoxical but the reason is simply that having a wheel at each corner of the vehicle enables the student to concentrate on what he is doing without worrying about balance. In addition, the presence of a qualified driving instructor* in the passenger seat helps to

---

*In some schools the teacher acts as the driving instructor. Where this is the case he or she is required by the Road Traffic (Driving Instruction) Act of 1967 to be registered with the Ministry of Transport.

ensure trouble-free early runs. Some schools have even gone to the length of fitting their vehicles with dual controls.

One organizational difficulty is that few vehicles of manageable size can hold more than three students at one time. And if the teacher is acting as instructor, what is the remainder of the group doing? One solution to this situation lies in having different activities underway at the same time—perhaps using work-cards for those engaged on mechanical work. Alternatively, driving instruction is often provided outside school hours.

The driving area

First experience normally follows what common sense dictates and takes place in some large, unobstructed area on private land; the school playground often proves ideal, although the teacher must ensure that the surface is strong enough. Manoeuvring is therefore reduced to a minimum with starting, stopping and gear changing providing adequate challenges at this stage.

Later, when the basic operations have been mastered, road lanes may be marked out and junctions indicated with bollards. Simulated traffic lights are easily made and can be controlled by students. Those driving—at an advanced stage there may be a number of assorted vehicles on the grid at any one time—are given a particular route to follow and must, of course, give way or signal their intentions as the situation demands.

3.10 Driving instruction in progress.

School driving tests and further instruction

Sometimes, as a conclusion to simulated experiences of this kind, a school conducts its own driving test. This often merits a certain prestige within the school since those who hold it may manoeuvre vehicles in and out of the garage, for example.

Later, of course, when students reach the age when they may hold a provisional driving licence, lessons may be arranged on the highway. The RAC organize a Junior Driving Scheme in which a local driving instructor, using the driving school's vehicle, provides instruction for three students at a time—those not driving observing and listening to the instructor's comments. This course is not concerned just with driving practice, but also with its theory and with aspects of roadcraft. There is also a companion scheme, known as the RAC/ACW scheme, which is concerned with the driving of two-wheeled vehicles.

Further extensions

It can be seen from the pattern that is beginning to emerge that motor vehicle work is capable of continued expansion. It has its basis in an area of work largely concerned with materials and tools, and this leads quite naturally into driving instruction and the various considerations of road-craft. The scope of the subject expands once again when, developing from roadcraft, the social aspects of motor vehicles are involved together with factors of selection and discrimination.

Changing attitudes

It is by no means uncommon for teachers to encounter antipathy and prejudice from their students when mentioning bodies and authorities whose job it is to support and control the motorist. Nowhere are these attitudes more marked than in connection with the police whom many youngsters regard as 'the fuzz—out to get me!'.

A certain softening of this attitude is sometimes discernible when, through their own experiences, they properly understand the importance of safety, both in terms of the vehicle's roadworthiness and their own personal behaviour. This can be reinforced by inviting the police to send a representative to the school to speak on road behaviour from the official point of view. It is something of a surprise to some students to discover that policemen, like teachers, are human beings too!

It is not unknown for this change in attitude to turn to actual respect when students are given the chance to see the police in training and observe the highly professional level to which they must aspire on behalf of others. This may lead not only to a greater understanding of the need for discipline on the roads and the observation of speed limits, but also a recognition that the police are there to help and support, not obstruct, the motorist.

A wider view

Many organizations connected with motoring are, like the police, prepared to send guest speakers to a school. Examples include the local road safety organizer, the AA or RAC, and representatives of the British Insurance Association. RoSPA have a lecturing team who will visit a school or arrange visits, including lectures, demonstrations and tests, for school parties to their headquarters in London. Garage proprietors and motor vehicle manufacturers, too, are able to give much assistance to those who may be considering some kind of career associated with motor vehicles.

Within the school many teachers attempt to foster a wider view by arranging inter-school quizzes, road safety competitions or photographic competitions (racing vehicles in action, for example). Some realization of the historical development of motor transport can be given by quite simple means such as a collection of assembled model kits.

Consumer discrimination

Another matter in which students often display a great deal of prejudice—or, at least, wishful thinking—is in their choice of a motor vehicle. If questioned at the beginning of a course as to their choice of vehicle they tend, not surprisingly, to favour the exotic and the dramatic. E-type Jaguars or Honda Ford motor cycles feature strongly in their selections.

The cold light of analysis of initial costs and maintenance and running expenses, however, quickly reveals to students that such vehicles are likely to be beyond their financial resources. The discussion is then open for the examination of more prosaic vehicles: mopeds, scooters, motor cycles, three-wheeled cars, older reconditioned vehicles, good second-hand ones and new ones in the lower price range.

For each category the initial cost may be noted together with the amount required to keep the vehicle in good working order, petrol consumption, tax and insurance, depreciation and resale value. In addition, of course, the intended use must be taken into account. A motor cycle, for example, is perhaps not the best vehicle on which to transport a girl friend to a social occasion. Or an old sports car may not be very suitable if one cannot afford spare parts, is not sufficiently competent to keep it properly tuned and maintained, or has a job where punctuality is important.

Interestingly, it is not unknown for considerations of this sort to effect a complete reversal of previous attitudes: whereas, for example, at the beginning of a course three-wheeled vehicles are often deprecated, being so far removed from an E-type or a Honda Ford, they are later often regarded as the most effective compromise between cost and weather protection.

Choosing between vehicles in this way is far more than a mere exercise; towards the end of a motor vehicle course many youngsters are preparing a vehicle of their own for use on the roads when they leave school, or may actually have it in use. For those who must purchase and maintain a vehicle with little help from parents the costs involved will probably be the highest yet faced by the young adult. The projection forward to a time when these expenses must be met from a wage packet is therefore a realistic aspect of consumer discrimination.

An obvious and often-used extension of this type of work is a study of new developments in vehicle design. These are usually studied with reference to driver and passenger innovations as well as mechanical innovation. Visits to motor shows are a frequent feature of this work.

Competitive sports

From the earliest days, student interest is usually primarily related to the speed and manoeuvrability of the vehicle—whether two-, three- or four-wheeled. This interest in competitive sports is an enduring one, and for some students it is the main focus of their attention. A young student in one school, for example, of low academic ability, saved his pocket money and earnings from a part-time job to travel to Le Mans for the twenty-four hour race. The entire expedition was planned and executed without help.

Competitive sports provide the link between motor vehicle work as described here and school karting activities. Frequently, the two are organized side-by-side so that karting provides an outlet for the students' interest. In fact, some extend their interest to karts which lie outside school specifications and seek to compete on the periphery of professional racing activities driving international class 250 cc karts.

3.11 Competitive karting.

Many students take a keen interest in motor cycle sports. Schoolboy scramble clubs are established in a number of places. The skill required of the student in demanding tests, sometimes deliberately performed at slow speed over difficult terrain, is considerable. Other students may take to trial riding and some have been known to act regularly as marshalls at RAC meetings.

It has already been mentioned that many organizations concerned with motor sports are prepared to send a guest speaker to a school, but the greatest enthusiasm is often reserved for the speaker who is also a competition driver. It goes without saying that anyone connected with an officially organized motor sport will give considerable emphasis to safety and the importance of responsible and controlled conduct. One spin-off from this emphasis should be the realization by the student that certain stylish vehicles—'chopped' motor cycles, for example—may be less attractive than a properly built competition vehicle.

Motor sports interest within school can act as a valuable stimulus in motor vehicle work. They should, however, remain 'the gilt on the gingerbread' and must not obscure the serious objectives of preparing a student for adult responsibilities on the highway.

Examination aspects

Much work in a motor vehicle course is often of an empirical nature; points are made and aspects illustrated as they occur during practical work. For some students it will be a non-examination pursuit and for these the explanation of, say, a cam as something designed to open a valve at a particular time is probably adequate. At the furthest extreme one might speak of sine and din/sine cams, high-lift cams and wide overlap cams. Indeed, most areas of motor vehicle work, like camshaft design, are capable of much detailed extension.

Between these two extremes a number of examination syllabuses are beginning to emerge. Most are concerned with a body of knowledge related to the mechanism itself, examined in a written paper, an extended essay and a practical test.

The essay, in particular, holds great potential for the expression of individual ideas and interests. It has been the experience of some schools that when a proper attitude to researching an idea is shown—as opposed to the mere copying of information from a book—the essay has revealed technical information, from manufacturers, of very recent origin, occasionally preceding its release to the general public.

Case Study

A Motor Vehicle Course

The school described here is a five-form entry co-educational all-ability school. Students range from those with difficulties where literacy is concerned to those attempting 'A' levels in several subjects in preparation for university entry. Motor vehicle courses have been in operation for several years.

The headmaster's comments

Some years ago, the headmaster realized that a course of study focused on vehicle work would have a special appeal for boys. He summed up his aims in this way:

A few years ago I was privileged to spend a year in the USA. One of the things about some Senior High Schools which I visited which impressed me greatly was the sense of purpose given to older students by realistic courses of vocational education, including highly developed courses in automobile engineering of a very sophisticated nature. These courses were allied to general education and it was most noticeable that they gave a stimulus and incentive to students which was not apparent in earlier parts of the school course. On my return I was determined to try to introduce something of this nature into our own curriculum.

It began with the appointment of an enthusiast as a teacher of metalwork and automobile studies, and grew until we were able to build our own garage, bought from school funds, and collect together a variety of old vehicles, some in running condition. Driving instruction (by a qualified instructor) followed naturally. This year a syllabus for CSE has been accepted.

The remarkable success of the project is due almost entirely to the teacher in charge whose enthusiasm has been caught by the boys (and one girl) taking the course. Boys whose main object in life was to escape as soon as possible from the drudgery of school have found a purpose and enthusiasm in this work which has transformed them as individuals. In one or two cases the transformation has been nothing short of miraculous, and boys from lower streams who would undoubtedly have left at fifteen are staying on in fifth-year courses to take CSE in a variety of subjects. They will work on cars as long as the teacher is prepared to stay after school, and discipline presents no problems at all on this course.

My chief regret is that our facilities are primitive compared with those in American schools, but facilities are a minor part of the course; imagination, inventiveness and enthusiasm play a much greater part in education than facilities.

Organizing the course

The vehicle course is organized to occupy four periods weekly (in two doubles) for both fourth and fifth year boys and leads to a CSE examination, now approved by the East Anglian Regional Board. In addition to a wide range of practical work and theory the course includes sections on the highway code, driver licencing, insurance, the effects of fatigue, alcohol and drugs, the importance of health, eyesight and mental approach, reaction times and stopping distances. Special conditions such as ice, tyre bursts, wind, floods and fords, skids and fog, first aid and accident assistance, are also considered. The balance between the theory and practical work is flexible. thus permitting maximum benefit from outdoor work when the weather is suitable. Preliminary driving instruction, although not included in the CSE syllabus, is provided on the school playground. More advanced instruction is arranged in conjunction with the RAC and several boys and girls have already left school having obtained their driving licence.

3.12 The garage—built by students.

3.13 Some of the vehicles used on the course.

3.14 Engine maintenance—checking the plugs.

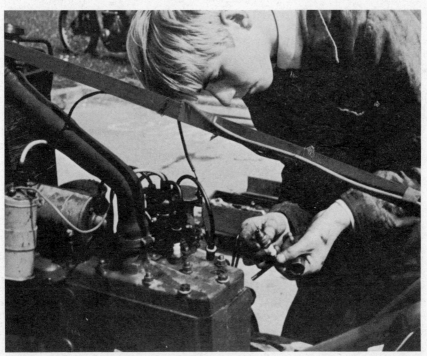

As always, a good deal of local initiative and expert 'scrounging' has been involved in getting together the necessary equipment. An engine is available on a stand for demonstration and experiment, together with a wide variety of other components that can be dismantled and rebuilt. A Ford Popular has been stripped of its body and maintained in running order together with a more conventional Standard 8.

At every stage the boys are encouraged to drive the vehicles upon which they have worked as a 'pay-off' for their effort. The driving sessions, however, are far from the teenage tear-up that might be feared on a large playground using bollards to set out a route.

A small classroom is used for much of the theory work and a wide variety of visual aids of both diagrammatic and question-and-answer form have been devised.

The ability of the boys, and in particular their mature and responsible attitude to vehicles and their use, is impressive, indeed both staff and parents have reported a significant change in attitude in many of the boys involved.

It would be misleading to present this as a quick and easy answer to our problems with less able boys. The work succeeds because of the dedication and hard work of the teacher involved, together with the fact that he is an autocross and rally driver, and that this no doubt affects his standing with the boys. As a result we cannot avoid the impression that vehicle work at Heronswood is very different from the omnipresent old car being torn to pieces in a school playground.

Appendix to Chapter Three

SPECIMEN JOB SHEET A

JOB Brake bleeding   DATE

VEHICLE

WORK TO BE DONE

      1 Check system for leaks and repair if required.

      2 Bleed the system.

      3 Check brake efficiency.

LIST TOOLS REQUIRED IN THE ORDER THEY ARE USED

LIST ANY OTHER EQUIPMENT OR MATERIALS REQUIRED

WHAT WERE THE FAULTS IF ANY
(Give details of part and condition)

DESCRIBE BRIEFLY THE STEPS NECESSARY TO CARRY OUT
THE JOB

Job checked by . . . .

SPECIMEN JOB SHEET B

JOB Cleaning and waxing a vehicle   DATE

VEHICLE

WORK TO BE DONE

     1 Wash bodywork.

     2 Wax bodywork.

     3 Clean upholstery and trim.

     4 Clean and check luggage compartment.

LIST TOOLS REQUIRED IN THE ORDER THEY ARE USED

LIST ANY OTHER EQUIPMENT OR MATERIALS REQUIRED

DO ANY ITEMS REQUIRE ATTENTION?
(Give details of part and condition)

DESCRIBE BRIEFLY THE STEPS NECESSARY TO CARRY OUT
THE JOB

Job checked by . . . .

Filmstrip

Houses and Homes*

Teachers' notes

A study of housing may be approached in a variety of ways. Its history may be considered not only in terms of the history of building structure but also in a sociological context in relation to population movement brought about by the development of industry. House design may be studied from the point of view of the social relationships of the people who occupy it. Although these approaches may involve aspects of history, geography, and so on, it is not uncommon to find them integrated under the banner of the social studies area of the curriculum.

But the study of housing would be incomplete without some account being taken of the scientific and practical aspects. Electrical circuits, plumbing and ventilation systems offer wide opportunity for the science teacher. Costing, financing and house purchase are provinces to which the mathematics department may contribute. Aspects related to house layout may be dealt with by the home economics department. In art a study of such things as colour schemes, wall decorations, and so on, is of importance.

The workshops can make a valuable contribution to studies related to house structure. A frequent first step is the collection and testing of a range of building materials. For example, porosity tests may be carried out on blue bricks, common bricks and a variety of facing bricks to demonstrate the importance of damp courses and cavity walling. Other suitable materials for examination include roofing tiles and slates, corrugated asbestos and plastic sheeting, and roofing felt.

Design work should not be restricted to technical drawing lessons; there is much scope for model making in the workshops.

These activities may be supported by visits to building sites. It is important that such visits are not arranged merely to fill in a spare day

*Design and Craft Education Filmstrip No. 10

towards the end of the summer term but *should be carefully prepared as a field exercise to find answers to problems that have arisen in the course of earlier studies.* Students should prepare lists of questions and points to look for so that their visit becomes a research exercise rather than a pointless wandering from one half-completed building to another.

It is suggested that a small exhibition of building materials be prepared so that students may handle the materials when asking questions after viewing the filmstrip.

Commentary

Houses like this are being built in large numbers all over the country. It is probably an ambition of many people, especially young newly-married couples, to live in a modern house with two or three bedrooms, a garage and a garden.

But there aren't enough modern houses to meet everyone's needs. And even if there were, many people couldn't afford to pay for them.

Most people still live in older houses like these. Because of their age they don't always have as many amenities as their owners would like. So they often add things like bathrooms and central heating. Many enterprising people tackle such jobs themselves using the wide range of materials now available—plastic piping and easy-to-install plumbing units, do-it-yourself central heating, and so on.

Very old houses may become so dilapidated that they have to be pulled down. Rehousing people presents serious problems for local authorities. In large cities there is not enough ground space for every family to live in a house of their own. One solution has been to build large blocks of flats.

A home—whether a house or a flat—does not always exactly meet the needs of the family living in it. For example, a teenager training for a job may have to study at home, and this is not easy if other members of the family want to watch television in the same room. So the teenager may have to use a bedroom as a study.

The bedroom also has to have storage space for clothes. Does this type of storage unit make the best use of the limited space available?

A student in college faces these problems but also has to find room for books and other things. Washing facilities may also have to be provided.

And this may be the only room in which to entertain friends, so the bed must also serve as a settee.

There are many people who have to live in one room, especially young people who have moved from their parents' home to another town in the course of their work or studies. Such a room is sometimes called a 'bed-sitter'. It needs to be designed carefully if it is to be an efficient and comfortable living unit.

This housewife is inspecting the kitchen of a new house before deciding what changes will need to be made if she buys the house.

Although husbands and other members of the family may take an interest in cooking, the kitchen is still usually the housewife's province. This is her workshop.

More accidents occur in the kitchen than any other room in the house. Some of these result, at least in part, from bad design. So it is important that the room be well designed—if possible to suit the physical size of the person who will use it most. For example, are the cupboards at the right height, or does the user have to stand in an awkward or unsafe position to reach them? Are they the right size for the things that have to be stored?

Are working surfaces and sinks at the correct height? The height of the sink is particularly important because saucepans of hot food or boiling water are handled at this point.

The relative positions of working surfaces and equipment are also important. In a kitchen a great deal of effort can be saved if things are arranged so that cooking, washing up, and so on, can be done easily and with a minimum of walking.

The use of models—or even full-size mock-ups—may be very helpful when planning a layout and deciding how to use a room to its best advantage.

Imagine yourself in a new home faced with a number of empty rooms. How would you decide what each one was going to be used for? How would you make best use of the space available? What provision would you make for small children? What furniture and equipment would you need? Which units could be built-in and which would need to be portable? What floor covering would be necessary? How much would it cost? Could you afford it? Would you get better (and cheaper) results if you designed and made some of your own fittings rather than buying everything? How would you decorate the rooms?

We could take these questions further and consider the design of the house itself. How many rooms are necessary? How large do they need to be? Can a kitchen, for example, be *too* large, resulting in unnecessary walking?

The problem is that no two families have exactly the same needs, but architects and builders produce large numbers of houses made to the same pattern. So people need to make changes to suit their own families. This model has been made to help someone decide what can be done to improve the layout of his own house.

The problem of house design doesn't end with building structure. There is also the design of the garden to consider. New houses usually have empty gardens as well as empty rooms.

Again, the needs of the people who will use the garden must be the starting point for design. Will small children use it as a play area? Will elderly people use it as a quiet place in which to relax? Will dad use some part of it to park the car? And where will mother hang out the washing?

If dad wants to grow flowers and his young son wants to play football in the same area their needs will conflict. How would you solve such a problem?

Other aspects of home design may be found in the renovation of old property, often undertaken by young people on behalf of the elderly or disabled, or by young couples who choose to start married life in a low-priced house of their own.

If you decided to renovate an old house what would you look for when you inspected it? This old house was renovated by senior students in a secondary school on behalf of an elderly couple in poor health. Let's compare it with a new property to see what problems they faced.

Inside the front door the floor was rotten and unsafe. This was caused by a fungus growth commonly known as 'dry rot'. The cavity under the floor had become sealed, thus creating an area of damp, still air. Fungus spores were then able to settle on the underside of the floor and establish a growth which eventually ate the timber away.

Air-bricks are always built into a wall below the level of wooden floors to allow air to circulate and keep it dry. In this case the small front garden had been covered with concrete to a level above the air-brick. Only this small vertical channel leading down to the air-brick was left. The channel became clogged with leaves, thus sealing off the passage of air to the space beneath the floor.

This picture shows the air-bricks in a new house. Note also that the timber joists have been treated with chemicals to preserve them from fungus attack.

The blue bricks are provided to stop moisture rising up the wall from the damp ground. This is called a 'damp course'. Other materials, such as special felt, may be used as a damp course. In old houses it is important to make sure that the walls contain some form of efficient damp-proof course.

The walls of our old house do not have an efficient damp course. This is one cause of the damage you see here, underneath the front window. You can see that the floor has been replaced with a special flooring type of chipboard. Before it was fitted the walls had to be treated chemically to kill the dry-rot fungus.

The wall was replastered and decorated, but within a fortnight the damp came through again. Although it is impossible to compensate fully for the lack of a proper damp course, some improvement was found after the walls had been stripped and sealed chemically to hold back the damp.

In new houses the outer walls are really two walls in one. A gap of about 5 cm is left between them to prevent damp from the outer wall spreading to the inner wall. The two walls are held together with metal tie rods. In the old house the walls are solid—as there is no cavity, moisture from the outside can soak right through.

Susceptibility to damp also depends on the quality of the bricks used. The surface of facing bricks—those on the left—is more water resistant than the surface of cheaper common bricks.

In this wall the common bricks will be protected by a decorative timber panel that fits into the recess. In addition, joints between window frames and brickwork have to be sealed. This picture shows several of these features —damp course, air-brick, facing bricks and sealed woodwork.

In comparison, the old house shows many defects—no effective air channel, perished brickwork that allows rain to soak in, and rotten window frames.

But the worst defect is in the cement rendering that has been applied under the window in an attempt to stop the damp. Notice how it has cracked and come away from the wall creating a pocket in which water collects. The problem has been made worse instead of better.

A common cause of damage to building structures is a faulty guttering and down-pipe system. In older buildings guttering and down-pipes were made of cast iron which rusted away and developed leaks. Asbestos cement was also used, but this is brittle and liable to crack. Both these materials need painting regularly to preserve them. The plastic guttering and piping shown here does not need painting.

A popular method of decorating some outside surfaces is by covering them with timber cladding. Timber used in this way is particularly liable to rot from the back and must be given strong preservative treatment before it is fitted.

Inside the house many things, such as water pipes and electric wiring, are deliberately hidden. In a new house all electric wiring is protected by a metal sheath like this.

After the plasterer has been to work all the wiring is covered and only switches and power points remain visible. If you were fitting a wall bracket or shelf and accidentally drove a screw through a hidden wire you could quite possibly kill yourself. In older houses the danger is greater since wiring may not be encased in a metal sheath. In addition, old wiring may be perished and need replacing to avoid the risk of fire.

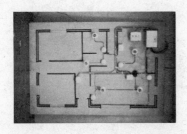

A great deal can be discovered about the various systems used in houses by constructing models, like this electricity circuit. But remember that any model involving electric circuits must be battery powered. Under no circumstances should mains power be used.

Do-it-yourself equipment is now available in many forms that bring renovation work within the capabilities of ordinary people. Plastic piping, for example, can be fitted without the need for soldered joints.

Modern tiling adhesives make it possible to apply a wide range of decorative and hard-wearing surfaces to kitchens and bathrooms.

The house you see here is the old house with which the students started. They have renovated it inside and out and turned it from a slum property into a cosy home for a retired couple. It involved hard, though enjoyable, work, but most of all it involved design and the solving of problems.

The kind of home we live in may depend on many things—what is available, how much we can afford, how carefully we think about our own particular needs, how much we are prepared to take decisions for ourselves. To what extent our house really becomes a home depends largely on how much of ourselves we are prepared to put into it.

Filmstrip

Value for Money*

Teachers' notes

The need for consumer discrimination in our daily lives is clear. The efforts of what has been called the persuasion industry—through newspapers, magazines, television, posters, direct mail, packaging, and so on—can hardly be avoided.

This filmstrip sets out to illustrate some of the techniques of the advertiser and show how objective comparisons of products can be made. The analysis of advertising techniques is by no means an exhaustive one; the teacher can extend the range of examples by offering additional samples for discussion and asking students to collect further material from newspapers and magazines. The Penguin Education publication *Break for Commercials*[20] in the 'Connexions' series is a useful source of additional examples.

There is a close similarity between product testing in consumer discrimination and the work carried out during the evaluation stage of a design process. In addition, as the students' book *You Are a Designer*[8] illustrates, the process of investigation, and so on, which, ideally, precedes the decision to purchase may be compared with a design process. Both start out with the discovery of a need or problem, go on to look at matters of function, aesthetics, and so on, and continue through realization (buying instead of making, in this case) and evaluation.

The practical work illustrated in the second half of this filmstrip is described in more detail in 'Case Study: Product Testing' in chapter 2 of this book.

*Design and Craft Education Filmstrip No. 11

Commentary

In some ways the quality of our lives depends on money. We work to obtain it. We need it to buy the things we want. But if we spend without getting value for money then we work for nothing.

The job of advertising is to persuade people to buy things. It is directed at everyone—even small children. The message of an advertisement may be in picture form, it may be in words, it may be a combination of the two. It may even be just a simple sound that comes to have a special meaning. The ice cream man's chimes persuade people—especially young children—that it would be nice to eat an ice cream, even though they were not thinking of ice cream until they heard the sound.

As children grow into young adults they usually become keenly aware of the need to present an attractive appearance to members of the opposite sex. This powerful drive is often used by advertisers to sell almost everything from swimsuits to cigars.

Young people spend a lot of time 'trying out' relationships with members of the opposite sex until a permanent partner is chosen. The social activities of entertaining and being entertained are very important to them. This advertisement encourages us to identify with the young couple. It suggests that the product they are drinking is associated with the young and attractive—and most people want to be young and attractive. Most people would also like to be rich—perhaps that is the reason for the setting of the illustration . . . panelled walls, ornate gold picture frame, butler hovering in the background (the butler also seems to represent those people who—for some un-explained reason—are too old to drink light rum).

Very many advertisements play on the desire most of us have to be accepted by those we respect—by being attract-ive, fashionable, smoking the right cigarette, driving the right car. But they don't always limit themselves to what might be considered the more superficial impulses and emotions.

Parents wish their children to do well at school and make a good career for themselves in the future. This advertise-ment suggests that by buying a set of encyclopaedias they will be helping to make this dream come true. The headline aims to flatter the reader into taking notice of the advertisement's message.

If you look closely at this picture you can see two more popular advertising techniques being used. First, the pub-lisher has used a well-known television personality to recommend his product. And, secondly, he encourages us to write for more information by offering a free record and a free booklet. Even the postage is free !

Here is another example of the use of personality to sell a product. Perhaps by drinking this brand of whisky we'll feel just a little bit like a dinner-jacketed TV-star ?

This is sometimes called the 'threepence off' technique. Every supermarket tries to make us buy more by showing us how much money we can save by doing so. This kind of advertising can, of course, be very useful—as every housewife knows. If we have the time and the facilities to 'shop around' we can buy where the bargains are.

Another popular way of advertising is to offer a free gift. Sometimes you have to collect packet tops, at other times coupons are given with every purchase. What these systems do is commit the purchaser to buying the same brand time after time. Advertisers call this 'brand loyalty'. It is clearly important in the sale of consumables like cigarettes, drink, petrol, and so on.

Not all advertising has a purely commercial basis. Advertisements like this help to provide the money that is needed to fight famine, poverty and disease.

At first sight this advertisement doesn't seem to have much in common with the last one. Their aims are very different. Yet every advertisement has one thing in common: in it the advertiser is trying to show *his* product in the best possible light. It may have draw-backs. Another product might serve our purpose better.

Knowing something about the techniques that an advertiser uses can help us to compare products—can help us avoid spending money on products that don't really suit us, or that we can't really afford. But to get good value for money we may also need to make *objective* comparisons between products—comparisons that don't rely on the claims of advertisers.

How can we make such comparisons? How can we find out if the claims made in advertisements are reliable? A class of fifteen-year-old girls made a study of washing powders to find out which offered the best value for money.

The local supermarket offered a wide range of washing powders. Most of them are advertised regularly on commercial television. Each one claims to be the best in some special way; perhaps it 'washes whiter' or 'gives more for your money' or contains some magic formula that 'will soak clothes clean the easy way'. Housewives are often shown using a particular powder and then refusing to exchange it for other powders.

How can we choose between the rival claims? Especially when there are so many price variations and special offers.

Here are some examples of special offers. Each claims that a deduction is being made from the 'recommended price'. The trouble is that the recommended price is not printed on the packet so the shopper does not know the price from which the deduction is being made.

Twelve powders were tested in this project. It is worth noting how the brand name often suggests cleanliness. For example 'daz' is obviously short for dazzle, 'tide' and 'surf' remind us of the sea washing against the beach, 'radiant' suggests that clothes will radiate cleanliness and brightness.

The ability of the powders to remove a wide range of everyday stains was tested. The stains included oil, tea with milk and sugar, damson juice in syrup, beetroot in vinegar, ox blood, two types of lipstick, shoe polish and foundation face cream.

Cotton fabric was used for the experiment. Twenty-four samples were prepared, first the dry stains were put on each separate fabric and the wet stains were then soaked through a number of the samples together.

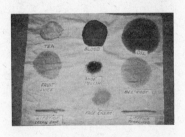

Each sample finally looked like this. The stains were allowed to dry in for twenty-four hours.

The maker's instructions were obtained from each packet. The instructions proved to be the same on every packet. One ounce of powder to one gallon of water at 40° C met the requirements for each brand. This seemed to indicate that no powder offered greater economy because it was more powerful; therefore advertisements making this claim appeared to be false.

The mixture for each powder was prepared before morning school. The bowls were carefully labelled.

A sample was put into each bowl and left to soak.

Six hours later each sample was lifted out and held up to the window. In its wet state stains that remained were clearly visible. Each was judged on a three-point scale; if the stain had disappeared it was marked 'clear', if a shadow of the stain remained it was marked 'shadow' and if a heavy stain remained it was marked 'heavy'. Remaining stains were then hand washed in the same liquid for five minutes and the same judgments were made again.

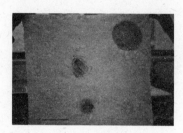

The results were brought to a central point and recorded on a master chart.

This chart shows the results. Remember 'C' means clear, 'S' means shadow and 'H' means heavy shadow. Study the chart for a few moments and see if you can pick out the powders that performed best.

The second test consisted entirely of hand washing. New mixtures were prepared and new samples were used. Each girl hand washed a sample for three periods of five minutes. A judgment of cleanliness was made after each period.

This chart shows the results obtained. Again, which powder do you think performed best? Compare this chart with the previous one. Which powder now seems to you to perform best under both conditions?

To decide which powder offers best value for money we need to know the relative costs. Information about weight of powder in each packet and the cost was collected.

Here are the results. Note first that the recommended retail price was not given on any packet. This information had to be obtained from a publication called *Shaw's Guide*. The guaranteed weight of powder in the packets varied from twenty-five ounces to twenty-nine ounces, although all the packets were the same size. The girls had to work out the cost per ounce in order to compare prices.

Section 2

Materials and Community Development

4
Aspects of Service

The nature of service programmes

There is no set time or age or ability level for the introduction of community development projects. There will inevitably be different emphases and degrees of commitment stemming from the availability of resources and the age and ability of students. Scope exists for eleven-year-olds to undertake minor projects or to co-operate with older students in major assignments. Most work will probably be attempted by the fifteen- to eighteen-year age group, but the whole process may be viewed as continuous throughout the secondary school.

Timetabling

Community development programmes are by no means confined to the once-a-year production of Christmas toys for the local children's home. Neither need they be synonymous with 'end of year' or 'after exams' assignments, although such periods may often be useful in providing time and opportunity for the application of concentrated effort. Instead, if the activity is to be a viable element of the curriculum, continuity of action may be necessary, perhaps by means of sessions drafted into the work at different times of the year.

No set pattern of timing can be suggested since each school will adapt its own resources to the work in hand. Sometimes it may be necessary to complete an operation in a short period of time. It would be unsatisfactory, for example, if a student working on the redesign and construction of an old age pensioner's kitchen left the house with the comment, 'I've got to go back to school for geography now, but I'll be here next week to put the other screw in the wall cupboard.'

Yet there are innumerable occasions when existing timetable arrangements need not be interrupted. Take, for example, a case in which equipment requires designing and manufacturing to meet a need already defined and fully understood by the students. Provided that no short-term deadline had to be met work could proceed on a week-to-week basis as part of the normal timetable allocation.

On a number of occasions it has been found expedient to arrange service projects in conjunction with school-based line production work. Such work in itself may require special timetable arrangements; the factors involved are discussed in Chapter 9.

4.1 School-based production unit making wash-basin cabinets for an old people's home.

It is clear, however, that flexibility is often required if a community assignment is to be entirely effective. It is not always possible to arrange field visits or periods of observation or investigation to coincide with a particular subject time allocation. Neither is it always possible to supervise work when a variety of individual and group activities are being undertaken at a number of scattered bases.

Teachers and subjects

It is sometimes debated whether community development projects spring from subject areas or from needs identified within the community. Provided there is willingness for a group of teachers to work together it is immaterial from where the initiative springs.

Many schools already operate a variety of service projects—supplying flowers for the elderly, chopping firewood for the infirm or having the occasional informal chat with the housebound. Coupled with such activities are many outstanding efforts of young people in raising funds via fêtes and sponsored walks. All these demand time and energy on the part of young people and a willingness to become involved with the needs of others.

Community development work offers a viable means of bridging gaps between school subjects. In fact it is difficult for one teacher to work alone or for one subject to monopolize a project if its full potential is to be realized. The nature of such work calls for abilities that find their roots in many subject areas. For this reason some form of co-ordination within the curriculum is usually required. The role of school workshops may be supportive in achieving some aims; on other occasions materials-based work may be highly prominent or instrumental in helping establish and operate a successful scheme.

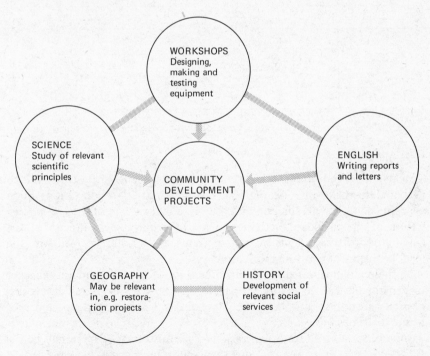

4.2 Possible contribution of subject areas to a community development project.

There is value in having a teacher to co-ordinate work within the school, who is able to liaise with people outside the school with a possible contribution to make. This teacher could also work with students in drawing up schedules and ensure that progress was being achieved.

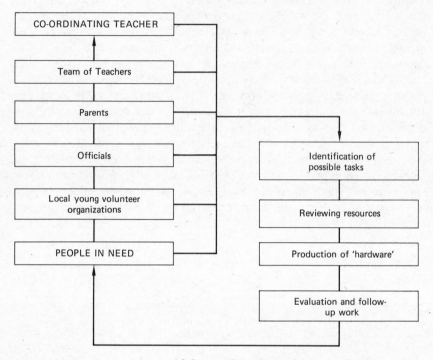

4.3 Community action and the co-ordinating teacher.

Who can help?

Teachers engaged upon a community development project should be prepared to make full use of local resources. Local organizations often welcome contact with students but are not always aware of the *educational* nature of the proposed activities. They also may be unsure about the capabilities of the students or may, perhaps, be too pre-occupied with the legal problems of proposed developments.

In these circumstances it becomes the duty of the co-ordinating teacher to explain the nature of the project to all participants. At all levels discussions are important; in particular, contact between students and professionals is desirable.

In addition to welfare organizations a useful source of help may be the trades unions. On many occasions the local branches may be in a position to suggest sources of expert advice and practical help in a range of projects.

Local resources can include parents who, before they are prepared to offer direct help, may need convincing of the educational benefits of community development projects. It is always wise to gain the written consent of parents before involving students in activities that take them outside the school. (This is particularly necessary where parents may gain the impression that their children are being used as 'cheap labour'.)

When attempting to identify possible themes and to contact people who may be of assistance, local newspaper headlines and editorial comment should not be forgotten. Week by week such newspapers carry details of local matters, needs and developments. From these, students can often make direct contact with a range of people and subsequently undertake a range of design activities.

Perhaps the most important local resource is the local authority. It is usually wise to consult officials in the early stages of planning; their experience in matters such as insurance can often save the school time and money. The main requirement of an insurance policy is that it should cover personal accidents while students are engaged upon community development work. Consideration should, however, also be given to members of the public who may be involved and to clauses on damage and accident to property and equipment.

Themes for community development work

In reviewing the kinds of work that may be undertaken it is inevitable that some will call for greater commitment than others; some may be short, 'one-off' projects while others may be of a continuing or developing nature. Schools should decide on the degree of involvement with which they can cope and plan accordingly.

In many instances it may be necessary to consider the 'political' implications of introducing community development projects into the curriculum. Nowadays there is a growing awareness that it may be educationally beneficial to encourage students to actively participate at all levels in planning, operating and evaluating a range of activities.

Involvement of this kind inevitably results in all forms of research and investigation; at the same time evidence, perhaps some of it of a conflicting nature, may need to be analysed and conclusions formed.

If students are to be aware of decisions made daily on the part of all of us there is need for a questioning attitude; an opportunity for opinions and decisions to be made, based on reliable information. Who really is responsible for the welfare of the old; the suffering; the handicapped? Pollution— whose fault? Who cares? What priority should be given to different needs within society? These and similar questions are likely to develop out of even the simplest practical design situation and teachers should be aware of and prepared for such developments.

Some of the other main areas for community development work are outlined in the following pages. Additional relevant case studies appear in Chapters 1, 5, 7 and 9.

E

4.4 Newspapers may help in the identification of suitable themes.

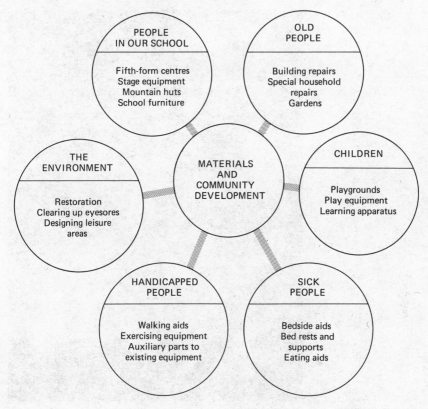

4.5 Themes for community development.

Activities within the school

Distance may be a factor that could restrict, or make it difficult to adhere to, the anticipated schedule. For this reason some teachers prefer to utilize the school itself as a source of prospective activities. Many schools have found that this frequently leads to the creation of new and worthwhile relationships within their own confines as well as providing a range of valuable equipment and amenities that generally improve the quality of school life.

In the past these activities have included: items for use within the school (e.g., games room equipment, special furniture, systems of direction and intercommunication); improvement of amenities in the school playground, playing field or garden (e.g., seats, paths, cold frames); major building assignments (e.g., swimming pool, fifth-form centre, garage, outdoor theatre —see 'Case Study: Building a Garage' and 'Case Study: Building a Fifth-Form Centre').

4.6 Fitting equipment designed and made by students for the school stage.

4.7 Student-built seating for the school playground.

118

4.8 Decorating an old age pensioner's bungalow.

Although such work may be for the school itself schools associated with the Project have found there is scope for students to meet 'outsiders' or to make appropriate visits. At one school, for example, where a building project was undertaken, the process of investigation, design and approval involved contact with school governors, county architects, local building inspectors and builders' merchants. In this and other projects it has been found that while even the most able student will be unable to make all the decisions related to a major project, there is great scope and benefit in helping them to become aware of the total nature of the undertaking. Different teams can usually be established to be responsible for different aspects—to make necessary contacts and to prepare and present estimates and reports to, say, school governors and building inspectors.

Activities outside the school

Greatest scope probably exists beyond the confines of the school, at both local and national levels. Clearly, it is usually easier to co-operate with local organizations, but on occasion it may be necessary to work closely with bases some considerable distance from the school as was the case in the West Riding where two schools undertook a restoration project. (See 'Case Study: Restoration at the Studley Royal Estate'.) Here, both the county architect's department, which worked closely with the two schools involved, and Fountains Abbey, where the restoration work was to take place, were many miles from the schools.

In projects like this communication becomes increasingly difficult to maintain. Frequent visits become time-consuming, hence the necessity for the careful planning of content and the provision for periods of observation and discussion. Surveys and questionnaires often enable the collection of required information for analysis back at school.

The range of possible activities outside the school is almost unlimited. Some of the main areas of work are listed below:

—For old people (designing and making or repairing furniture and other household equipment, painting and decorating, designing and making safety aids).

—For children in nurseries, primary schools and children's homes (designing and making or repairing such items as toys, sand-pits, paddling pools, climbing frames, cages for pets, Wendy houses, etc; designing and making puppets and arranging shows).

4.9 Play equipment for nursery children.

—For hospitals and geriatric units (designing and making or repairing bed-rests, bedside lockers, crutches, wheelchairs, toys and specialized equipment for physiotherapy).

4.10 'Jumbo draughts' for arthritic patients in a geriatric unit.

—For the mentally handicapped (designing and making special aids, equipment for occupational therapy, toys, outdoor amenities, etc; painting and decorating).

—For the physically handicapped (designing and making aids such as wheelchair ramps, electronic aids for the deaf and blind, jigs and fixtures to facilitate the use of tools).

—For the community in general (designing and making equipment for adventure playgrounds or a mobile theatre or exhibition, clearing up choked waterways or other despoiled areas, creating gardens for the blind, or picnic areas, restoring buildings and areas of historical interest).

4.11 A special large-handled mug designed to make drinking easier for spastic patients.

Organizational factors

In any community development project involving contact with outside officials and organizations there are a number of factors that must be considered if good working relationships are to be established and maintained:

Wherever possible co-operate closely with the appropriate officials and organizations. This can help avoid duplication of work already being undertaken by other bodies. It also helps students form continuing relationships and commitments. In some cases this may be essential as part of design evaluation, especially where a piece of 'medical' equipment is at issue.

Always ensure that the 'client' is aware of the educational implications of the work. If this is done the two-way process benefiting both the school and the recipient becomes more effective.

Enable students to make direct contact with the range of personnel engaged upon a scheme. Many problems are difficult to understand if this is not built into the programme.

Keep everyone informed about the progress of the project. Where long-term design and construction work is involved the people on the receiving end may tend to forget about the venture if they are not kept informed. In any case a continuing contact may be of benefit to the students. Remember that 'outsiders' may appreciate a visit to the school workshop to observe work in progress.

Establish codes of contact when making visits. All workers need to be sensitive to the feelings of others. When working with old people, for example, it is vital that the sense of independence so important to the elderly is not destroyed; disturbing their personal belongings may upset them and they may be bewildered at first by being surrounded by young people.

Do not over-commit students, staff or outside establishments. Failure to complete an assignment makes subsequent projects difficult to arrange.

Make arrangements for the official handing over of equipment designed and made by the students. This makes a satisfactory climax to their work and gives them the opportunity to see the equipment in the environment in which it will be used.

Money matters

Teachers frequently complain about the lack of finance to undertake new activities successfully. Community development projects may, however, open up new sources of finance for the purchase of materials.

Equipment designed and manufactured in school workshops is inevitably attractive in terms of cost. The profit motive is absent and allowance does not normally have to be made for overheads. Organizations appreciate this and can often make funds available in order to take advantage of a 'genuine bargain'. Playgroups have been known to acquire as many as five pieces of equipment for the price of one!

With the most expensive outgoing—materials—covered there may still be insurance and travel costs. These may sometimes be included in the overall charges for products, or fund-raising events could be arranged. Engaging students in the planning and organization of such events can itself be worthwhile.

Case Study

A Course in Community Service

The practical experience of one teacher in organizing a community service course for fifty fourth-year students led to this article which appeared in Survey 1. *Examples of the reactions of old people and the students themselves appear on pages 14–15 and 29–30 respectively.*

This project was started as an attempt by four teachers to try to integrate their subjects and at the same time attempt to help our fourth-year students to develop a sense of social awareness and possibly to awaken a social conscience. We realize that any project of this type is largely experimental, but, since none of us are altogether happy with teaching our subjects within the confines of a CSE or 'O' level syllabus we hope something may be gained by ourselves, and possibly by other teachers, as a result of our experience.

We are a two-stream school of 250 students on the outskirts of a small country town ; our fourth year consists of forty-five boys and girls. These are streamed into examination and leavers' classes.

The teachers of handicraft, art, home economics and rural studies, together with a 'team' of students, combined for one day each week to engage in work in the town. It is appreciated that a whole day is rather more than we had even hoped for—in fact this was ideal, but even a half day would have made some of our work possible.

Examination students were involved in community service for two-thirds of the term, the leavers were involved for the whole term.

A rationale

Much of the community of which the school is an integral part is often not known to any extent by the students. Children need to be made aware of their surroundings and to have their horizons broadened. Community service gives ample scope for this—boys and girls leave the confines of the classroom, the workshop or the laboratory and become involved with other members of the society in which they live. The fact that the people they meet are usually the less fortunate makes the impact of this meeting more dramatic.

Although hospitals, old people's homes, infant, nursery and junior schools already have help from both councils and many charitable organizations they may still provide opportunity for community service. Suitable work is often found in the homes of old people, and of those who are sick or disabled. Many of these people refuse Social Security but are quite willing to help in the education of young people. Council property is only maintained structurally and externally—no interior decoration is done and people in these categories cannot afford the materials or have not the physical capabilities to do this work for themselves.

Community service can very easily become a do-it-yourself course in an out-of-school environment. This in itself is not a bad thing as a range of decisions and skills are used which would not be easily practised within the confines of the workshop.

Mixed groups of students are preferable for this type of work. Old ladies are much more at ease where there are girls in the vicinity to make pots of tea, and so on, than they would be with an all-male group.

On the purely practical side, also, girls are able to help with curtains, various sewing jobs, organization of kitchens, and so on, much better than boys.

Starting a community development service project

One of the most difficult aspects of this type of project is making contact with the people needing help. Unless the teacher has long and intimate knowledge of the area close to the school it is very unlikely that the type of people requiring help can easily be contacted. Since travel, complete with tools and materials, from school to the place of work is usually on foot only a small area can be covered. A school bus is a boon for this type of work and widens the scope of the project considerably.

1 Probably the most useful person to give details of people who need help is the council rent collector. He calls weekly at hundreds of houses and is often the only person who ever sees the inside of these homes. In the case of old age pensioners he is their only contact with the authorities.
2 Allied with the rent collector, the housing manager for the council has details of the many people who are on the waiting list for houses and are living in unsatisfactory conditions. The housing manager also has authority to give certain materials for decoration of council properties.

3 A more obvious source of contact are social workers who may be particularly useful where disabled people are concerned—they have lists of the blind, and those who for various reasons have difficulty in looking after themselves.

4 Whether the school has any connection with the church or not, most clergy are able to suggest some people in need of assistance.

5 Solicitors are sometimes able to give help through their knowledge of the courts, bankruptcy cases, etc.

A formal introduction to the householders by one of these is often the easiest, but it should be noted that *NO approach should be made unless the householders concerned have been advised of the visit. Most old people have been warned by the police and social services not to admit anyone they don't know.*

One other important point deserves mention here. It has been found that when an approach has been made to a particular house, a more satisfactory first meeting is made if a woman teacher can be taken along as well. This makes for a more relaxed attitude, particularly with the elderly, and discussions of kitchen layout and various points of personal comfort often require the feminine viewpoint.

To make the initial visit more satisfactory it is often necessary to emphasize to the householder the educational aspect of the project.

As teachers, it is often difficult to appreciate the feelings of fear and distrust which many people have for young people. This is a real problem and can only be alleviated by the attitude of the children themselves.

Finance and materials

When a community development service project involving the renovating, repair and decorating of property is undertaken, considerable quantities of materials and tools not normally found in the school workshop are required. Financing such a project cannot, of course, be done through normal workshop allocation.

1 The local education authority may help with the initial outlay for tools, brushes and rollers. It is unlikely, however, that they will supply the materials to be used on the project.

2 Private school funds may be used for smaller, incidental needs.

3 Organizations such as Round Table and Rotary can sometimes help towards financing a community development project.

Various sources of supplies of materials can be tried as follows:

1 Local building sites—builders sometimes have quantities of surplus decorative materials left from completed work. Plaster, paints, tiles

and wallpapers together with adhesives for floor tiles and ceramic tiles can all be obtained from this source.

2 Paint and wallpaper manufacturers—letters explaining the project sent to as many firms as possible may bring some discontinued stocks.

3 Local suppliers—paint and wallpaper shops: cheap or discontinued lines. Builders' suppliers: glass, plaster, putty, timber and mouldings. Paint and paper wholesalers: damaged stock. Drapers shops: curtain material, curtain tape, etc.

Course content

At an early stage in the planning there should be a meeting of the team of teachers and, if possible, the head teacher and the subject organizers. At this meeting can be discussed the aims of the project plus any problems likely to arise.

Stage I. Whether the project arises as a result of a teacher's decision or the students' selection, a necessary preliminary to any investigational or practical work is an introductory lesson involving all the teachers and the complete group of children.

It is important that the children be given some idea of the people they are about to visit; any eccentricities of appearance or manner should be explained. At this stage the students should discuss, and therefore become aware of, the possible kinds of work they may undertake.

Stage II. Following this lesson the children usually need to be split into small groups to go with their teachers for an exploratory visit to their group project houses. There they should be introduced to the householder so that they can talk about the jobs that need doing. Wallpapers, paints and colour charts can be taken and discussed in this period with the householder. This seemed, in our experience, to be the best 'ice-breaker' both for the students and the individual householder as we found both seemed to be in awe of the other in the initial stages.

Stage III. When the plan of work has been agreed upon by children, householder and teachers, the various tasks can be allocated for the next week's work. Any potential snags can be discussed by the group as a whole and the whole plan can be written up by the students in their 'record of work' books.

Stage IV. Before work in the house proper is started, each group can be equipped with tools and materials from the central store. At this stage some team teaching can be done with teachers advising on soft furnishings, kitchen layout, colour schemes, and minor structural problems.

Stage V. Here is a good place to show films on a variety of techniques—film strips and loops being particularly useful.

Many of the larger manufacturers are willing to send their technical advisers and demonstrators to talk to the children—these are professional people and their work is usually of a high standard. Their one fault is they are often not used to a younger audience and tend to be too technical and advanced for the average student.

Stage VI. Work on the house can now be undertaken. The splitting up of a group into various jobs sometimes leads to friction if care is not taken. Boys seem to work better and more consistently when working with girls.

Where a new problem, technique or process crops up all work can cease for a few minutes while the group is given a brief demonstration. This seems a more satisfactory method of dealing with the many and various problems than by giving too many technical talks before work starts.

Stage VII. As work on the decorative side progresses the more specific skills learned at school can be brought into play—boys can fix cupboard doors, repolish and repair furniture, girls may cook meals for the householder, sewing machines can be brought to the house and curtains made or repaired on the spot. Upholstery can be washed and repaired and major household cleaning tasks can be undertaken.

Stage VIII. When all the physical tasks have been completed the less tangible work may carry on. Some children may wish to keep in touch with the householders—occasional visits, small gifts, but most of all some interest in them can be shown. Many students may wish to look upon the house as their adopted property and to continue their work in their free time in the evenings and at weekends.

Case Study

Restoration at the Studley Royal Estate

The Studley Royal Estate comprises Fountains Abbey, Fountains Hall, the Studley Royal Gardens and the Deer Park with its 450 deer. It was bought by the West Riding County Council in the late 1960s to avoid commercial exploitation and to provide a public amenity as a possible alternative attraction to the Yorkshire Dales. The estate covers 640 acres and has a boundary perimeter of approximately seven miles.

In the early part of 1968 two schools in the West Riding received a tentative request from the County Council for help in restoring certain parts of the estate. These schools, Aireville County Secondary, Skipton, and Bingley Beckfoot Grammar, decided to collaborate on certain aspects of the work, despite the fact that they are fifteen miles apart and each twenty-five miles from the estate. Their aims in taking on the work were expressed as follows:

Apart from the social community service aspects the project afforded an opportunity for the staff and students of both schools to meet and discuss common problems. Some of the aims we established were:

1 to provide an opportunity for students to develop the ability to identify a need and take the appropriate action necessary to meet it;
2 to provide an opportunity for students to develop an interest that might otherwise have remained undiscovered;
3 to develop their curiosity and awareness of the real stuff of history and science;
4 to provide an introduction to the systematic collection of information;
5 to enable students to gain valuable educational and social experience by learning to work and serve together.

Plans and preparations

Progress reports on the work appeared in *Survey* 3 and *Survey* 9. The quotations which appear in this case study are taken from these articles.

129

The preparatory stages in which we sorted out the ideas, and compiled them in a logical sequence, began with a series of meetings throughout the winter of 1968/9. Despite the weather five meetings were held and we decided to contact the Deputy County Architect and arrange a preliminary visit to the estate.

At the same time we decided that we would invite other departments within our schools to take an interest in the project with a view to calling on their specialized knowledge as required during the work.

The preliminary visit was made in April 1969. The party consisted of the Deputy County Architect (Mr W. T. C. Walker), the Deputy Headmasters of both schools, the Heads of the Craft and Design Departments, and a woodwork and an art teacher.

Mr Walker began by giving an historical and geographical account of this fine estate. On the tour which followed, various objects that were in need of restoration were pointed out and photographed. The problems involved were discussed and details of the work noted.

This was, of course, merely the beginning of a series of projects that was likely to extend over several years. This continuing concern for something so valuable to the community as Fountains Abbey appeared to us to be a most important educational factor. Time was to be of no account in carrying out the work.

The visit enabled the two schools to identify a number of tasks involving the replacement of some items which were in an extremely dilapidated condition and others which no longer existed. An initial list of projects was drawn up that involved designing and making the following items:

1 a large semi-circular grille over the archway at the main entrance to the park;
2 large double entrance gates;
3 a wooden gate at the entrance to the churchyard (figure 4.12);
4 weather vanes on top of the Fishing Tabernacles;
5 a small round Garden Temple by the Chinese Gardens;
6 a wooden deer-gate (figure 4.13);
7 a set of six garden chairs in Chinese Chippendale style;
8 a section of wrought-iron fencing;
9 a safety rail around a high-level Chinese garden;
10 three pairs of large wrought-iron gate hinges;
11 railings at the canal gate (figure 4.14);

These tasks were examined in the light of each school's expertise and facilities. Finally, Aireville school took responsibility for items 2, 3, 4, 10 and 11, and Bingley Beckfoot school responsibility for items 1 and 7. It was intended that they should jointly undertake work on item 5.

Once these projects had been established each school set about selecting the students who were going to be involved. The next step was to organize a general briefing and combined visit of both schools to Fountains Abbey. Subsequently, a large display was set up in each school of large-scale maps showing the Estate boundaries and detailing the selected tasks each department would tackle.

4.12 The churchyard gate was in a poor state of repair and showed signs of decay.

4.13 The new deer-gate, made by the students.

4.14 The new canal gate railings

The nature of the restoration work

An extremely important concern in the work undertaken was that the items made should as accurately as possible reflect the original. In some cases the County Architect's Department supplied drawings (full size and scaled) indicating the siting of the item, its overall dimensions and its appearance.

At first sight it might appear that providing students with drawings of this sort is in contradiction with many of the important requirements of a problem-solving activity. In fact this is not the case, since the drawings were mainly of those items for which fairly extensive book research and a specialized knowledge of contemporary styles were needed. Wherever possible the students undertook research themselves (see figures 4.15 and 4.16). In addition, the architect's drawings, even when supplied, did not specify particular forms of construction; all decisions regarding construction, the selection of materials and manufacturing techniques were left to the schools. The schools were also able to amend the drawings if this was dictated by technical necessity.

The students made their decisions in discussion with the teachers. Occasionally the work demanded facilities that the school did not have, so links were established with local firms who were able to assist with

4.15 On-site measurement for the canal gate railings.

4.16 Checking measurement for the deer-gate.

specialized tasks. Materials were bought by the schools themselves with money provided by the County Council.

Much of the work was repetitious: several identical components were required, or parts had to be formed to similar radii. This was turned to advantage by the schools and the design of jigs and tools—some reasonably complex, others quite simple—provided much of the intellectual and creative challenge of the work.

Other important areas of educational benefit included the need to prepare detailed working drawings, the opportunity for model-making (see figure 4.17) and the production of accurate casting patterns made of wood.

4.17 Model of canal gate railings.

The scale of the work

Almost all the items made were on a larger scale than is normally tackled in a school workshop. For this reason most jobs were undertaken by teams of from two to five students rather than by individuals working alone.

The need for student teams is evidenced by the scale of the work carried out in the construction of the canal gate railings. A number of eight-foot lengths of 32 mm square-section steel had to have finials forged directly onto one end—an undertaking of too great a magnitude for a single student.

The teachers felt that the scale of the work was a distinct advantage, partly because it gave a 'man-sized' quality to the project, partly because it emphasized the real—not contrived—nature of the tasks, and partly because of the additional problems it raised for the students to solve.

The students and their work

Both schools decided that the work was suitable for students of all abilities. Slides taken by the teachers were used to introduce groups of fourth-year students to the Studley Royal Estate. They were also supplied with a number of standard guides. Having declared their interest in the project the students visited the estate and the specific problems mentioned above were pointed out to them.

The concern of the groups on their first visit was to establish the parameters of the problems which faced them. Where through neglect or age wood had rotted or iron rusted away, how could it be replaced? If the original had disappeared, what had it been like? How had it been constructed? Where could they find out more about it? Could a replacement be designed? Could modern techniques of finish and construction be employed? How could fixings be made between wood and stone? How could metal fittings be secured to stone? And so on.

The students quickly appreciated the value their work could have to the community and accepted their part in the undertaking not merely with enthusiasm but, as time went on, with a sense of purpose and almost dedication.

It was fortunate, perhaps, that this was so. The products they were to construct, because of their historical importance, had to be of the highest quality and expensive materials were being used.

Early on it was decided that the students' projects should be considered part of the normal 'O' level or CSE examination work (if they were involved with these examinations at all), and not only was their practical work to be submitted but the opportunity was taken to use the Estate—its history and its many specialized aspects—as the focus for the required extended essays.

As an aid to the continuous assessment of the students' progress each one kept a diary recording the work undertaken in the practical lessons and the information gained from each visit to the Estate.

The information required for the work itself and for examination purposes was gathered in a variety of ways: from libraries and guide books, from the architect's drawings, from details of remaining items of original work, by talking to the estate workers and their foreman, the forester, the Ministry masons working on the abbey, by photographs and measured drawings. On at least one occasion the students made a full-size mock-up of the item under construction and took it to the estate to try it in position.

One spin-off from this kind of activity was their increasing ability to understand orthographically projected drawings. They understood much more readily the architect's elevations when able to compare them with the real thing.

Visits were made to the estate by the working parties as necessary, using the school minibus. Additional visits took place during half-term holidays. With the exception of one item which was worked upon after school hours on two evenings per week, all the work undertaken was completed in the normally allocated workshop time.

The following accounts of some of the projects that were tackled by the students may give some indication of the kinds of design work that were involved.

Wind vanes

The production of six identical wind vanes was undertaken by a team of four boys over a period of four terms. The architect's drawings were amended at the beginning of the project to provide greater structural strength. Much of the early discussion was dominated by the problem of securing each pair of vanes to the central support collar. The first idea was abandoned because of the difficulty in shaping semi-circular channels to fit the support; the vanes were to be made of 2 mm thick copper.

The second idea, which required the use of a separate collar made of standard gauge copper, was also rejected because the thin wall of the tube was felt to lack strength.

The students then investigated the possibility of using a solid copper rod with the centre drilled to fit the support. This, too, was abandoned because of the waste involved and the difficulty in drilling the hole accurately.

Finally they decided to cast a collar of the required form. But the school did not have facilities to cast copper. This led to the first contact with a local foundry. An initial visit was arranged and the team of boys were shown the techniques employed : they found out how to make the split patterns they would need.

On a day when the foundry was normally closed the team, led by the foreman of the casting bay, completed the necessary processes to cast the six collars. (See figures 4.18–4.22.)

4.18 Centre pattern and mould for the wind vanes.

4.19 Pouring the metal at the foundry.

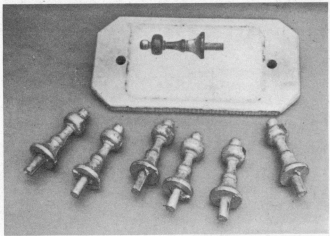

4.20 Finial pattern and castings.

Meanwhile, sheets of copper had been shaped by hand to the required profiles. The boys were now faced with the problem of how to join them to the collars. After examining a number of possibilities they decided to machine grooves to receive the vanes on the outer faces of the collar. This operation, too, was beyond the resources of the school so a local mill-wright was approached. The team spent another complete day in the mill-wright's workshop, working under the superyision of an old boy of the school.

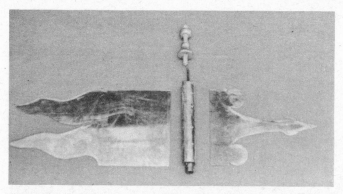

4.21 Wind vane prior to silver soldering.

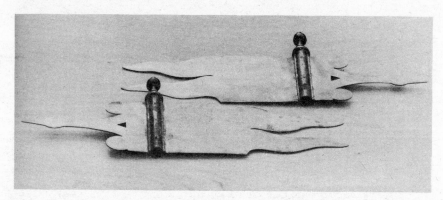

4.22 Assembled wind vanes.

The actual attachment of the vanes to the collar was the subject of considerable investigation. At first the students did not appreciate how much heat the copper would absorb. It was only when the largest oxy-acetylene apparatus available was used that sufficient heat was generated to run the silver solder into the joint.

Main entrance grille

The production of a grille for the main entrance was a much larger-scale undertaking. Some indication of the problems encountered is given in the following account:

Our task was to measure the main archway in preparation for the construction of a semi-circular grille. The Estate staff had erected scaffolding prior to our arrival and as we looked up we were struck by the scale of the work. Perhaps half a ton of metal would be used to make the grille. Had we bitten off more than we could chew? We also became aware of our temerity in adding to something which had already stood without our assistance for several hundred years. Without doubt our group of five boys appreciated that they were fortunate to be taking part in this work and were eager to get started.

After an initial survey of the archway we climbed the scaffolding to examine the masonry in greater detail. We noticed that a deep channel, perhaps 10 cm wide by 7–10 cm deep, was chiselled underneath the archway running the full length of the span. We were all fascinated. There appeared to be no reason for it; it could not have been used in any way to support the grille. We discussed this together, teachers and boys each contributing their own theories. The final consensus of opinion was that the measurements for the grille were taken by the blacksmith either from a drawing or from the archway just after completion, and by the time the grille was made the archway had settled under its own weight such that its dimensions were slightly less than originally intended. Hence the chiselling of the channel to allow the too-large grille to be inserted.

This time there was to be no mistake. Careful measurements were taken by the boys and these were transferred to several sheets of hardboard. A template was constructed there and then and tested under the archway for accuracy. Once a fit had been achieved the template was taken back to school in sections and re-erected ready for the work to begin.

A team of four boys, assisted by our workshop technician, are now engaged on making the grille. Before construction could start they had to consider how the metal was to be bent and manipulated (some of it is 75×6 mm in cross-section). This necessitated the design and construction of jigs and bending wrenches, including a lathe copying device for turning spacers. Here was the really creative side of the work; the repetition came later.

4.23 A hardboard template for semi-circular grille is checked for accuracy.

139

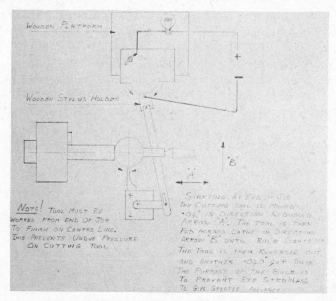

4.24 A lathe copying device.

4.25 Architect's drawing of grille.

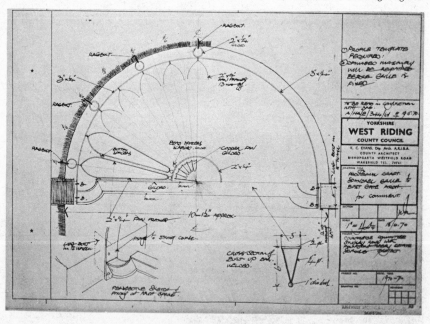

At the time of writing the grille is almost complete and will soon be placed in its intended position.

'Chinese Chippendale' chairs

Another rather unusual project began with an interesting discovery . . .

Shortly after our visit to carry out preliminary measurements on the grille we made a further excursion to the estate, this time to the coach house to inspect a garden chair of which we were to make copies. At first sight we were not impressed. It looked as if it might have been part of a job lot in a jumble sale. But after the Deputy County Architect had contacted the Victoria and Albert Museum we realized that our first impressions were wrong. Here is an extract from the Museum's letter:

'These chairs are of great interest and look just the sort of thing that would have furnished garden architecture between about 1740 and 1760. Such chairs usually have cane seats, and we have never seen ones with lattice before . . . it is very nice to think that you will be reproducing these chairs for the Studley Royal buildings.'

4.26 The original garden chair which was to form the basis for four reproductions.

At present four boys are engaged on this project, working in pairs but making a chair each. Full-size working drawings were made from the original chair. These are being followed meticulously in an effort to ensure that our reproductions are as close to the original as possible. Two of the chairs, will form part of the boys' GCE or CSE course-work.

The fact that the chairs have an historical importance, allied to their status as examination pieces, has been encouraging to the boys who have continued to show great interest in the work. Perhaps this has been further reinforced by the knowledge that their names, as makers, will be on plaques fixed to each chair and that these will be on view to the public.

The contribution of other departments

An area of work as rich as this naturally provides many opportunities for links with other subjects. The possibility of forming such links was discussed at an early stage and many teachers identified ways in which work at the Estate could contribute to their own studies, or ways in which the special qualities of their subjects could contribute to restoration work.

For a variety of reasons most of these possibilities were not developed. One project that did materialize, however, was a constructional survey of the Temple of Fame undertaken by the mathematics department at Aireville School.

The Temple of Fame

This small temple, shown in figures 4.27 and 4.28, is in a dangerously dilapidated condition, three of its columns supported on makeshift brick pillars. It is fenced off from the public.

It was proposed that the existing columns and the brick pillars be removed and new ones made. Since it was impossible for the school to dismantle it to record its dimensions, the task of surveying the temple was undertaken by the mathematics department. In this way the data could be collected accurately and safely.

The survey was reported as follows:

How the information was gained

1 *Diameters and thicknesses of base sections.* By simple measurement with a tape measure.
2 *Heights and curvatures of supporting columns.* The heights were measured by using an extending stick and a plumb-bob.

The curvature of the columns was discovered by measuring a

4.27, 4.28 The Temple of Fame.

succession of circumferences, working back to diameters and then plotting the results to scale on graph paper.

3 *Details of configurations at the head and feet of the columns.* By observation.

4 *Details of the surrounding 'crown' above columns and below the dome.* By observation.

5 *Overall height of the building.* Three methods were employed:

    a A simple theodolite was made from an ex-RAF Astro-Compass already available in the mathematics department.

    b A mariner's sextant—also to hand in the mathematics department.

    c Measuring shadows caused by the sun when its altitude gave a reasonable chance that the sun's rays were striking the top of the dome and not much beyond. The height was then calculated using trigonometry and similar triangles.

6 *Radii of curvature of outer shell of dome.* There was no safe way of finding these on site so sufficient widths and heights had to be taken to enable us to draw to scale and then to find the centres and radii of curvature by doing a little geometrical construction.

7 *Radii of curvature of inner shell of dome.* A great deal of computation took place in the drawing stages, particularly when dimensions were transferred from one scale to another. When things didn't fit some rigorous checking had to be done.

These dimensions were used to produce a number of drawings of the temple from which was made the excellent wooden model illustrated in figure 4.29.

Benefits to the students

The benefits to the students have been extensive and varied. In personal terms, as well as educationally and socially, they seemed to have gained enormously from the type and scale of the undertaking. The technical problems encountered promoted a great deal of interest and individual contribution.

The students placed a high value on the work they did, not only because of its intended siting, but because they were aware of the contribution they were making to the preservation of an important part of our architectural and historical heritage. This aspect took precedence in their minds over the fact that their work would be part of their examination submissions.

The projects have been demanding in terms of planning and time, but their success, both educationally and in practical results, more than compensates for the efforts of teachers and students. One of the teachers had this to say about the work:

What has all this meant to the school? An awareness has been generated that there is a need to preserve, restore and improve our environment and thus raise the quality of our lives and the lives of others. More specifically, a group of students are actively involved in a community service project in which they feel proud to play a part. We also think that we have produced an effect on the rest of the school and its curriculum. There is evidence of a spillover of this interest into the courses we have planned for our fourth-year non-examination students.

Already flourishing are activities concerned with forestry, hospital work (constructing a garden and rockery for the patients), toys and equipment for primary schools and play centres, improvements to the school environment (garden seats and an aquarium for the main entrance) and community service work with the old and infirm.

In an automated society with the inevitable increasing amount of time spent at school the future may well demand that a greater proportion of the curriculum be devoted to social education and education for leisure. I believe that the kind of work in which we at Bingley Beckfoot and Aireville have been involved will have an increasingly important part to play in the education of young people.

4.29 Model of the temple.

5
Designing for the Old and Infirm

The potential of work for the old and infirm

The design and manufacture of equipment for the handicapped and disabled offers wide scope for a community development project.

The potential may be illustrated by considering some of the problems related to confinement in a wheelchair. Apart from moving about and getting his wheelchair in and out of buildings and up and down steps, a disabled person may need suitable working surfaces and storage units. There are also problems associated with toiletry and recreational activities. All such needs have practical design elements that can be readily identified.

Whatever the extent of the individual's handicap—whether he is completely immobilized or has less severe restraints on his movement—there are similar needs to be met. Common problems include the inability to hold cutlery or pens, turn on taps, prepare food or turn the pages of a book.

Physical handicap is not limited to one age group, but age itself does tend to bring a stiffening of joints with the attendant difficulties of movement and manipulation. Even old people who may be termed 'active' usually require some form of practical help from time to time. Indeed, this area of work probably provides the most common form of social service work in our schools today.

In recent years there has been a growing awareness of the need to provide a range of welfare facilities for old people. Local authorities now set aside large sums of money to build accommodation for the elderly. Even so, despite a rapid increase in their numbers, 'long stay' geriatric hospitals and geriatric day hospitals* find it difficult to meet all the day-to-day needs necessary to the comfort of old people or to provide all the essential equipment required for effective physiotherapy.

Wide scope exists here for senior students in secondary schools to meet

*See *The Geriatric Day Hospital*[21] for information on the recent expansion in this field.

146

some of these needs and design and make some of the necessary equipment.

Many schools have established some form of contact with local geriatric units. Usually such links have been made via a particular subject area in isolation from the rest of the curriculum. For example, social studies schemes have been set up whereby students visit a geriatric hospital to talk with the old people. Already students supply flowers and plants to decorate the wards as part of rural studies. Many craft departments undertake to repair broken equipment. All such work has its value, not least for the old people.

But the value to the students can be much increased by careful planning.

Intellectual values

Through work with a geriatric unit students are provided with opportunities to express themselves in several ways—intellectually as well as through manual skills. They may become involved in problem-solving situations which allow the development and application of a range of intellectual qualities. There is considerable scope for the application of the design process as outlined in *Materials and Design: A Fresh Approach*[2].

Social values

In their practical work students will be required to recognize and deal with the special needs and problems of old, and possibly sick, people in a geriatric unit. They will need to develop understanding and sympathy if they are to arrive at valid solutions to these problems.

In this way they may come to understand more about the place and function of our social services and their attitudes towards the old may be formed or modified. At the same time there is scope for students to come into direct contact, not only with the old folk, but also with doctors, nursing staff and the personnel responsible for administration.

The aims and objectives of work with a geriatric unit

The linked aims and objectives diagram (figure 5.1) may be useful in helping to determine the goals of a geriatric project. It is by no means complete but serves to illustrate the importance attached to the different experiences that a teacher may wish his students to undertake.

It will be noticed that several of these aims are fairly specific in terms of student performance. This is necessary if some meaningful evaluation is to take place. Work may often have to be based on more general aims, but the nature of these is usually such that it is difficult to observe the intended outcome of the course.

It is frequently difficult to be precise about the values attached to certain activities, but it is possible to introduce some degree of objectivity if an attempt is made to identify the action expected of the students when working towards or attaining the aim in question.

It may also be found that when planning an entire course a series of linked specific statements may be more valuable in practice than a general

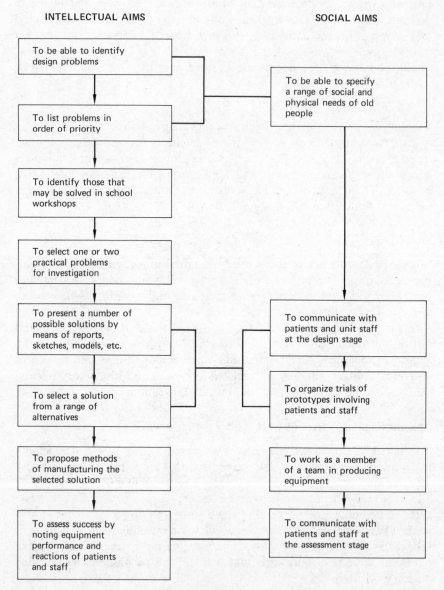

5.1 Some linked aims and objectives that may be appropriate when developing a geriatric unit project.

description of course content. For example, it could be stated that 'students will be expected to present evidence relating to the history of the geriatric unit, draw up lists of the reasons why patients were admitted to the unit, prepare outlines of a series of specific practical needs of the patients,' and so on.

One fact that should be stressed at this point is that these intellectual and social aims are of prime importance. Although the equipment produced can prove extremely useful to the patients it is vital that the students are presented with a real problem-solving situation offering scope for the application of intellectual skills and the development of social awareness.

Studying the needs of the patients

When studying the needs of old people who are sick it is necessary to understand that methods of nursing have changed considerably during recent years. In the past patients were often confined to bed; nowadays they are encouraged to get up and move about the hospital. Formerly they needed little more than a bed, a locker and a chair for visitors; now they require tables, armchairs, wheelchairs, walking aids and storage space for their clothes and equipment.

As a result of their patients' increased activity the nursing staff also require a wider range of equipment—occupational therapy apparatus for example.

Following a general appraisal of a geriatric unit by the students, a teacher may find it necessary to introduce topics which in themselves may lead to definite design problems. It may be necessary to outline specific elements in the requirements of patients and staff. The nature of some of these may be summarized as follows:

—lifting;
—feeding;
—dressing;
—exercising;
—storage;
—movement of equipment.

These requirements may best be realized by students by arranging a visit to a geriatric unit so that they can observe the actual situation. Such visits must be carefully planned to avoid inconveniencing hard-pressed hospital staff and at the same time ensuring that on a first visit students are not confronted with severe cases of handicap or deformity; young people often find such cases difficult to cope with, and only after a period of getting to know a hospital or home are they able to accept situations which at first may have repulsed them.

149

It could be pointed out that many of the changes in nursing techniques that have taken place in recent years were not taken into account when the hospital was originally designed. This may not, of course, be applicable to a new, purpose-built hospital, but unfortunately, despite an improving situation, these are still the exception rather than the rule. Old and converted buildings are still very common.

Since new equipment frequently has to be accommodated in less than adequate space an additional aspect of design work becomes apparent. The proximity of physiotherapy areas in relation to wards or bedrooms, the positioning of rest areas, lounges and toilets, and so on, could provide starting points for useful studies of the movement of patients and staff around a building.

Students should be able to appreciate and deal with these problems if they are encouraged to obtain at an early stage the opinions of the nursing staff on such questions as:

1 Will the usefulness of an article justify the space it takes up?
2 Can the article be used for more than one purpose?
3 Can it be dismantled for ease of storage?
4 Is there any 'unused' space that could be put to good use?

All these points, and many others, could be incorporated into the students' investigational work. This forms an important aspect of identifying and solving problems and will therefore require careful planning. Before attempting to gather information students should be encouraged and helped to prepare sequences of definite points to be studied.

What can be done?

If the introductory stages of the project have been planned and executed carefully the students should have a basic knowledge of the needs and problems of the old and should be able, with a little well-directed assistance from the teacher where necessary, to recognize specific needs which they are able to tackle. A brief outline of the kinds of activities that have been found to be appropriate may, however, be useful at this stage. This list is, of course, by no means complete; many design problems may arise from the highly individual requirements of a particular patient or a particular hospital.

Typical problems that students tackle include the design and manufacture of:

1 specialized recreational equipment, e.g., dominoes for use by the blind, device for displaying a 'hand' of playing cards, draughts for use by patients with arthritic hands (see 'jumbo draughts' in 'Case Study: A Geriatric Project');

150

2 bedside lockers, bed-rests, reading rests (perhaps with a device for turning pages);
3 small table that may be used by a patient confined to a wheelchair;
4 electronic aids for the deaf and blind;
5 device for retrieving fallen objects for use by patients who are unable to bend or are confined to a wheelchair;
6 aids for patients in wheelchairs, e.g., devices for opening doors, ramps, fitments to enable patients to keep their personal belongings to hand, methods of motorizing and steering a wheelchair;
7 walking aids;
8 device to enable patients to get into and out of a bath unaided.

Preparing the design brief

Once a particular need, or group of needs, has been isolated and the necessary investigation work has been carried out the students will have to draw up a design brief. While many of the factors involved will be peculiar to a certain problem there are some points that are more widely applicable. For example:

—nurses are not always mechanically minded, nor are most patients, so adjustable or moving parts must be easy to operate and ideally it should be impossible to use the equipment incorrectly;
—equipment involving movement will almost certainly have to operate silently;
—portable equipment must be easy and safe to move;
—all apparatus must be easy to clean;
—'long stay', 'short stay' and day hospitals may have different requirements;
—it is usually necessary to make a balance between the domestic and the clinical aspects of hospital life.

Aspects of organization

There are several possible approaches to a geriatric project, but whatever approach is taken it is clear that a sequence of events will have to be planned. The initial aims must be borne in mind and opportunities for students to attain these aims should be built in. It may also be necessary to consider what forms of assessment will be needed at various stages of the work.

A teaching team

For the project to offer the maximum educational benefit students should be provided with opportunities to acquire a *total vision* of the proposed

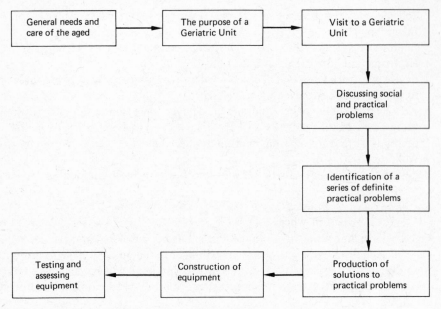

| General needs and care of the aged | → | The purpose of a Geriatric Unit | → | Visit to a Geriatric Unit |

Discussing social and practical problems

Identification of a series of definite practical problems

| Testing and assessing equipment | ← | Construction of equipment | ← | Production of solutions to practical problems |

5.2 Organizing a geriatric project—a possible approach.

activity rather than their involvement being restricted to their own particular area of work. If the stated aims take this need into consideration it usually becomes clear that the attainment of a full range of experiences relies on the establishment of a guidance team. Such a team may consist of teachers from a range of subject areas, nursing staff from the geriatric unit, a physiotherapist, a geriatric doctor, local council officials and the patients themselves.

The value of a team approach in relation to the objectives stated may be illustrated by considering one of these objectives—that the students should be able to specify a range of social and physical needs of old people. This is clearly desirable if students are to make a purposeful selection of problems which can be related to workshop activities. To guide the students towards a situation in which they are able to attain this objective the views, experience, knowledge and expertise of the full team of teachers and others may be required. It is clear that a workshop-based teacher could not hope to cover all aspects of this objective alone; lack of time alone would probably rule this out. The social studies area of the curriculum may best incorporate periods devoted to surveys and analyses of the incidence of certain problems, while, say, the history teacher could trace the development of a range of social and physical needs and ways of meeting them.

Figure 5.3 shows the possible contributions of a teaching team in terms of the typical school subject areas. Exactly what is covered will naturally depend upon the inclinations and abilities of the teachers and students. The important point is that the group of teachers should work as a team, drafting in the help of 'outsiders' where necessary—for example, in identifying and helping students set realistic limits to the work.

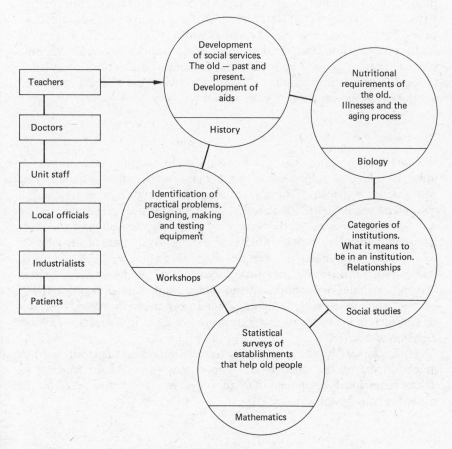

5.3 The possible contributions of a teaching team.

Time allocation

How the planned sequence of events is fitted to existing or modified time-table arrangements will depend on such factors as the flexibility of the time-table, how urgent or complicated the work is likely to be, and whether 'outsiders' are willing to assist with the programme.

At one extreme it may be possible to allocate a block period of time in which to undertake the entire project. Alternatively, and at the other extreme, it may be possible to work with a class following a normal 'periods' timetable. In the latter case teachers would make their particular contribution as the class rotated. In both cases it would be necessary to ensure that the required teachers were available at the appropriate time.

Clearly, the conventional form of timetabling would ensure a prolonged project, which may sometimes be advantageous. Nevertheless, the rapid production of a number of similar items of equipment on a production line basis could offer several educational benefits and this may require a blocked period for the practical work. The way in which the estimated time required for the project is fitted into the timetable—as a concentrated block, a variable block allocation, regular periods with a concentrated block for completion or regular periods throughout—must be resolved by the teachers concerned in relation to the situation in their school.

Assessment

We have already stated that it is necessary at the planning stage to bear in mind what kind of assessment of the students' work will be required. This will depend on the stated aims of the work. Some aims may be terminal in nature and will have to be assessed at the end of the project. Others may be assessed more readily at earlier stages. For example, the ability of a student to communicate with patients when determining, say, the size of a handle for some piece of equipment may best be judged at the time at which such work take place. Furthermore, continuous assessment of a particular ability may indicate rates of development and expose transitional difficulties. It will be clear from these examples that ongoing forms of assessment may have to be considered. Problems of assessment are discussed in *Education Through Design and Craft*[11].

Self-assessment by the student is extremely important. This will need to be considered by the teachers and opportunity provided for students to deliver completed equipment and to judge results by the reactions of patients and hospital staff.

Case Study

A Geriatric Project

The geriatric project described here was undertaken by a class of fifteen boys of average ability. They started the work in their third year and continued into the first term of the fourth year.

The starting point

The project arose as a result of the interest of several members of staff in students' attitudes towards old people. 'If', as one teacher said, 'our students are developing healthy attitudes towards old folk, what is it that we are doing which fosters this? On the other hand, if children are indifferent or react negatively to pensioners, what should we be doing about it?'

This is where we started. We did have a suspicion that our students' awareness of the needs of old people was not as positive as we might have hoped. We also had in the back of our minds that there was a geriatric unit conveniently situated less than a quarter of a mile from the school if we decided to develop work in this field. For some time senior students had regularly visited the unit to take flowers and talk to the old people. But it seemed to us that there was scope for forming additional worthwhile links between the unit and our workshops. Here was a real learning situation which could involve workshop skills with opportunities for the development of both intellectual abilities and social attitudes and which could benefit both students and patients.

Determining the initial attitudes of the students

Before much planning could take place it occurred to us that we should know something fairly positive about the knowledge and outlook of our students with regard to old people. In order that our results should be valid we proposed to canvass a cross-section of students throughout the school.

155

The best way to collect the necessary information for analysis seemed to be by questionnaire. As we were not too familiar with the techniques involved we decided to conduct a trial survey (dealing with attitudes towards television). This enabled us to check our own skill in wording questions and also served to acclimatize students to filling in forms. The trial was of great help and ensured that elementary blunders were avoided on the final questionnaire. We were quick to spot the advantage of a 'yes/no/don't know' response and prepared our questionnaire on this basis.

Elements of the questionnaire

In preparing the questionnaire we tried to incorporate an optimum number of questions that would give enough data for analysis yet not present the students with the boring task of completing an almost end-less list. In fact we used thirty questions, as we had discovered from the first questionnaire that this was a reasonable number for the children to cope with in the allotted time.

We also needed to bear in mind that the results would have to be analysed. This involved weighting the responses. To simplify this, statements were paired—one, judged to be pro-old people, would be matched with a second statement that might be thought to contradict it. Obviously, we had to use some subtlety here; the pairs of statements had to be worded differently and were not placed close together in the questionnaire.

After the expenditure of much spare time we were finally able to draw up a satisfactory questionnaire consisting of thirty statements, fifteen of which were deemed to be pro-old people coupled with the same number of polar opposites designed to counter them. If a student was consistent in his answers (and if the statements really were related in the way we hoped they were) he would tick the 'yes' column for one statement and the 'no' column for that statement's pair.

This division of the statements into equal numbers 'for' and 'against' made weighting simple. We gave the same score of two points to a 'Yes' to a pro-old people statement or a 'No' to an anti-old people statement. A 'don't know' gave one point and the other two ways of responding yielded no rating. If a statement was left unanswered for any reason one point was given as though the 'don't know' column had been used. If we had given no score in such instances this would have shown in the analysis as an anti-old people response. The maximum score possible was 60.

Nowadays all kinds of suggestions are made as to how we can provide for old people in our community. To give some idea of possible requirements it would be helpful if you, as a young person, would complete the following questionnaire. All you have to do is to place a tick (✓) in what you think is the appropriate column. Thank you for your co-operation.

		Yes	No	Don't Know
1.	It would be a good idea for school societies to organize meetings with old people.			
2.	As you grow older you find new interests to replace those you can no longer follow.			
3.	Old people try to tell us that they have done a lot to make life easier for us, but they frequently exaggerate.			
4.	It is better for people who require special help to live away in a special home rather than in the family home.			
5.	Those who go around painting pensioners' houses are usually 'goody-goodies'.			
6.	Old people are too bad tempered to get on with anyone.			
7.	Teenagers must realize that people may need extra help as they grow older.			
8.	Life will still be worth living when I am a grand-parent.			
9.	Old people should not try to tell us what to do.			
10.	Many old people can take a great interest in life despite their years.			
11.	Grey hair can make people look dignified.			
12.	Once you are over fifty you are too old to really enjoy life.			
13.	We owe a great deal to those much older than ourselves; so we should do our best to do something for them.			
14.	Old people always live in the past.			
15.	Old people who need special help require their relatives around them.			

5.4 Page 1 of the questionnaire showing the first fifteen questions. Note, for example, 'paired' questions 4 and 15, 10 and 12.

Results of the questionnaire

Analysis of the responses to the questionnaire suggested that as students moved up the school they became less inclined to think about or help old people.

This appeared to be a definite tendency, so one of our tasks seemed to be to arrest this by enabling our students to gain an understanding of what it means to be old and to become aware of general and specific physical and social needs of old people.

Now that we had proved that there was a real need for a meaningful link between the school and the local geriatric hospital, we were able to go on to formulate a set of linked aims and objectives similar to that outlined in figure 5.1. Our next step was to consider how the work was to be organized and, in fairly general terms, what the content of the project should be.

Teachers and timetables

General responsibility for the project was in the hands of two craft teachers. However, the activities relied very much on a team approach with contributions from a number of subject areas. These contributions were generally as illustrated in figure 5.3. It should be noted that valuable assistance was received from 'outsiders' such as doctors, nursing staff and local officials.

The timetable was rearranged slightly to accommodate the practical work that we anticipated would develop. Instead of the class undertaking their two double periods of workshop activities on different days provision was made to allow a full morning for the work. Some adjustment was also made to ensure that two craft teachers could be available for the whole morning. Before long, Friday mornings became known as 'Geriatric Project Mornings', although work at other times of the week in other subjects became a feature of the undertaking.

The plan

We did not intend to draw up a rigid plan for the students to follow. We felt that it was essential that they should be allowed to look at the situation, recognize the needs and problems of the patients, carry out their own investigational work, formulate their own solutions, and so on.

This was an open-ended situation that demanded a flexible approach. The following plan appeared to satisfy this requirement. It was divided into eight stages:

1 talk and slides on general needs and care of old people;
2 lecture on the purpose of a geriatric unit;
3 visit to the local geriatric hospital;
4 discussion of the social and practical problems found in the hospital;
5 identification of a series of practical problems;
6 production of solutions to practical problems;
7 construction and testing of equipment;
8 assessment of equipment in the hospital.

'Behind the scenes' contact was made with officials at the hospital before work started and it was encouraging that doctors, nurses and patients readily grasped the reasons for the students' involvement. There was never any cause during the project to suspect that the activities involved anything other than a two-way process. The hospital staff and patients were pleased with the work that was done but at the same time everyone was anxious that the students should benefit educationally.

First steps

The students' first introduction to the broad area of work in which they were to be engaged was via a talk, illustrated with slides, on the general needs of old people. This was followed by a visit from the local consultant geriatrician. He gave the students a stimulating talk, well illustrated with slides and charts, which set the tone for their subsequent involvement. Methods of nursing have changed rapidly in recent years and, although facilities are not all that one would wish, the sharp contrast between the conditions of, say, fifty years ago and those of today greatly interested the students.

The talk also introduced them to some of the ailments of old people and the importance of physiotherapy in keeping old folk active.

Discovering the problems of the patients

The slides and talks so far had acted as a general introduction to the nature of a geriatric hospital and the needs of the patients. The next step—a visit to the hospital—would reinforce this knowledge with some first-hand experience and also enable the students to encounter and begin to understand some of the more specific problems of old people.

The students' first visit to the hospital boded well for the rest of the project. Their work was to be centred on the physiotherapy unit and they took a great interest in the facilities available there and the general organization of the hospital as a whole. This interest is perhaps best illustrated by listing some of their comments and questions:

—'What's physiotherapy mean, sir?'
—'What does a consultant geriatrician do?'
—'It's different from an ordinary hospital.'
—'Where are their real homes?'
—'Some of the equipment could be better.'
—'They aren't very strong.'
—'Can we design a walking frame?'

The physiotherapist helped the children to analyse several common requirements of patients. Factors such as lifting, feeding, dressing, exercising and the movement and storage of equipment were illustrated by examples taken from the normal daily routine of the hospital. After further discussion of these factors—the practical problems—and the interrelated social problems the students were ready to identify and investigate a series of specific practical needs.

Starting to tackle design problems

The students were now in a position to identify the shortcomings of some of the existing equipment in the hospital and the need for a number of additional pieces of equipment. Figure 5.5 will give some indication of the extent of the problems that were tackled.

What this chart does not do is indicate the responses of the students when discussing with the physiotherapist and patients these shortcomings and needs. How critical they were of some of the design features of commercially produced apparatus—and the hospital staff agreed with them! We thought that communication between students and patients would be difficult to establish, but once students had decided upon the problem they were to tackle, and the old people had realized that they were *doing* something, communication became easier.

Before long a range of design briefs had been drawn up for either the modification of existing equipment or the design of new apparatus and the workshop facilities began to put to good, practical use.

Students usually worked in teams and moved freely between the school and the hospital on Friday mornings. Without fully realizing it, one group became deeply involved in ergonomics when looking at the difficulty patients encountered when trying to use the interchangeable handles on exercising springs. Another aspect of ergonomics was dealt with by a group of students who noticed that patients suffering from arthritis of the hands found great difficulty in grasping conventional draughts. They developed a design for 'jumbo draughts' which are now in daily use in the hospital.

Many of the items of equipment outlined in figure 5.5 are illustrated and described in more detail in the following pages. The development of

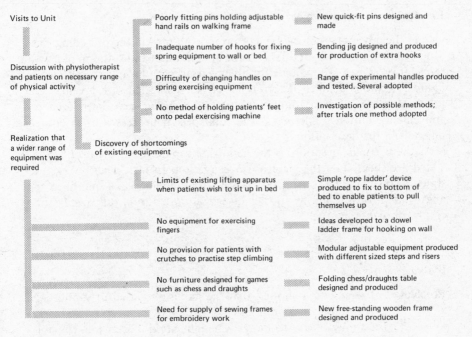

Visits to Unit		Poorly fitting pins holding adjustable hand rails on walking frame	New quick-fit pins designed and made
Discussion with physiotherapist and patients on necessary range of physical activity		Inadequate number of hooks for fixing spring equipment to wall or bed	Bending jig designed and produced for production of extra hooks
		Difficulty of changing handles on spring exercising equipment	Range of experimental handles produced and tested. Several adopted
		No method of holding patients' feet onto pedal exercising machine	Investigation of possible methods; after trials one method adopted
Realization that a wider range of equipment was required	Discovery of shortcomings of existing equipment	Limits of existing lifting apparatus when patients wish to sit up in bed	Simple 'rope ladder' device produced to fix to bottom of bed to enable patients to pull themselves up
		No equipment for exercising fingers	Ideas developed to a dowel ladder frame for hooking on wall
		No provision for patients with crutches to practise step climbing	Modular adjustable equipment produced with different sized steps and risers
		No furniture designed for games such as chess and draughts	Folding chess/draughts table designed and produced
		Need for supply of sewing frames for embroidery work	New free-standing wooden frame designed and produced

5.5 Developing and solving design problems.

new handles and hooks for the spring exercising equipment has been dealt with at some length as it is felt that this is an excellent example of the rich potential that can exist in a relatively simple problem in developmental design. The range of solutions that were generated and realized admirably illustrates the nature of the divergent and far-ranging thinking that this kind of problem-solving can encompass.

Testing solutions

Throughout the work students made frequent visits to the hospital to check the validity of proposed solutions and to try out prototypes. After a while, staff and patients expected students to wander in at any time during the Friday morning sessions.

Because of their total identification with the old people's problems, students soon became able to conduct their own small-scale enquiries. They would take a partially completed solution to the hospital and outline the idea before putting it to some sort of test with the patients. Accordingly, the students found themselves delegating or accepting responsibility for presenting individual designs in readiness for next week's visit.

*   *   *   *   *

Results of a geriatric project

One of the advantages of the type of project outlined in the preceding Case Study is the opportunity it offers for the investigation and solution of a wide range of problems. The kinds of problems dealt with have been outlined in figure 5.5, more detailed descriptions of some of them are given in the following pages. The headings **problem** and **solution** have been used for convenience although factors of the total design process are, of course, inherent in the descriptions.

As the original 'situation' is the geriatric hospital itself, the problems as stated are themselves the result of investigation. In fact, each problem as stated below could be considered as a design brief, albeit in a simplified and abbreviated form requiring further investigation before a full specification can be drawn up.

Walking frame fixing pins

Problem Investigation showed that the fixing pins used to support the adjustable hand-rail on the patients' walking frame had a number of shortcomings. The pins fitted loosely into the holes in the support bar and were kept in position solely by the weight of the hand-rail. The students felt that this was insufficient and that there was a danger of the pins working out of the holes and the hand-rail dropping out of position. They therefore decided to design a new type of pin that would fit more firmly and incorporate an easy-to-operate retaining device.

Solution A set of stainless steel 'quick-fit' pins were designed and made.

Spring exercising equipment

Problems Study of the spring exercising equipment used by the patients to strengthen arm and leg muscles revealed a number of areas for improvement:

1 there was an inadequate number of hooks for fixing the springs to the wall or bed;
2 if more than one spring was connected between a single hook and handle (to provide increased tension) the coils tended to become entangled;
3 the method of attaching the spring to the handle was such that patients found great difficulty in removing the handle in order to change the spring.

162

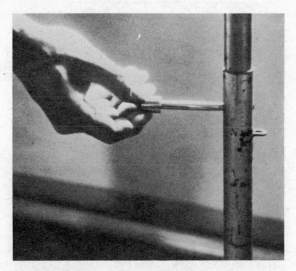

5.6 Support pin that vibrated loose on tubular steel walking bars.

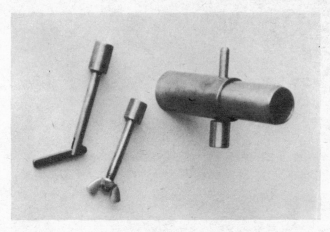

5.7 Simulation of the problem and suggested solutions.

Solutions　No really creative thinking was involved in the design of the simple hook but the students soon realized that as a number were required a jig would be needed to simplify construction and ensure that they were of uniform size and shape. A jig was therefore designed and made incorporating a pulley and lever arrangement for ease of operation (figure 5.10).

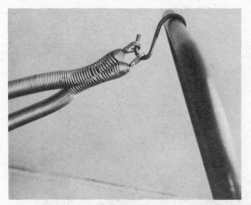

5.8 Exercise springs became entangled when a single hook was used.

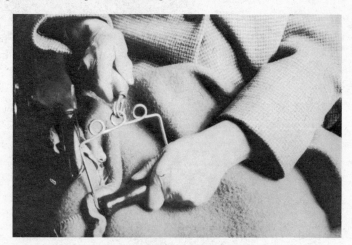

5.9 Old folk found difficulty in changing springs.

5.10 Jig devised by students for producing hooks to be used with single exercising spring.

Bearing in mind the problem of the springs becoming entangled, the students decided that although the hooks would be acceptable when a single spring was in use some provision would have to be made for keeping the springs separate when two or three were attached. The final solution (figure 5.12, top right) consisted of a steel tube with a long screw through the centre and incorporating three slots. The clip-ends of up to three springs can be inserted into the tube through the slots and when the screw is passed through them and screwed home they are held firmly in position in such a way as to avoid tangling.

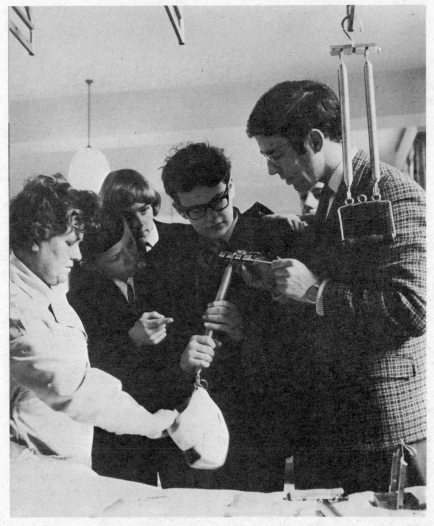

5.11 Discussion of problems and solutions in real situation.

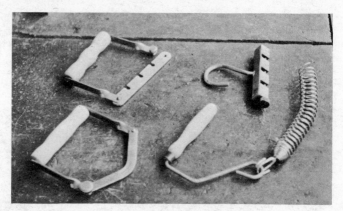

5.12, 5.13 Range of solutions to overcome problems.

It is interesting to note that the group's initial idea of using a round tube was rejected in favour of a square tube after tests proved the latter to be stronger. They were able to indicate why this should be so.

Ergonomic consideration had to be taken into account in the design of a new range of handles as they would have to be capable of being used and interchanged by patients with weak and sometimes arthritic hands. The simplest, most basic answer is shown in figure 5.13, bottom right.

The above solution, although ideal when only one spring is used, is not suitable when more than one spring is needed. The handle illustrated in the top left-hand corner of figure 5.12 satisfies both the requirement of ease of interchangeability and that of separation of the springs. This idea was triggered by a boy noticing the clip on his duffle bag and realizing its possible application to the problem he was working on.

166

The next solution, shown in figure 5.12, top right, was also inspired by an article commonly found in schools.

The wooden hand-grip can be removed by operating a catch mechanism similar to that used on a geography map roller. The metal 'U'-section can then be slipped through the clip at the end of an exercising spring and the handle replaced.

Again, this handle was only suitable for use with one spring. It did, however, have a versatility that made it a useful addition to the range. The fact that the hand-grip was removable soon led the boys to realize that it could be interchanged.

This resulted in the design of a foot-rest which could replace the hand-grip allowing the device to be used by a patient to exercise arm and leg muscles together by placing the foot-rest under his foot, attaching a handle to the opposite end and pulling.

The design illustrated in figure 5.14 was chosen by the old people and the hospital's physiotherapist, after trials of all solutions, as the most successful general purpose answer to the problem, although the others were retained and are still in use. The notched bar unscrews and pivots to allow up to three springs to be fitted. One point of interest is that the captive screw holding the notched bar was designed after examination of a camera case retaining screw.

5.14 The solution the old people considered to be best.

Foot exercising equipment

Problem   One group of students noticed that patients using the foot exercising machines had difficulty keeping their feet in position on the pedals. As a slip could—and on occasions did—result in painful bruising of the ankle or instep, they determined to investigate the possibility of fitting some form of device which could prevent this.

Solution   Their first solution was probably the most obvious answer to a problem involving feet slipping from pedals—a device based on the toe-clips favoured by racing cyclists and schoolboys. Tests proved that this was not an ideal solution as the feet were not held securely enough. Solutions involving tying knots or buckling straps could not easily be handled by the patients.

Finally, the students arrived at the device illustrated in figure 5.15. This incorporated a fairly new material, Velcro (often used for the fastenings of driving gloves), which 'sticks' to itself under light pressure, holds firmly and yet can be undone quite easily—properties which make it ideal for use by old people who find difficulty in handling conventional fastenings.

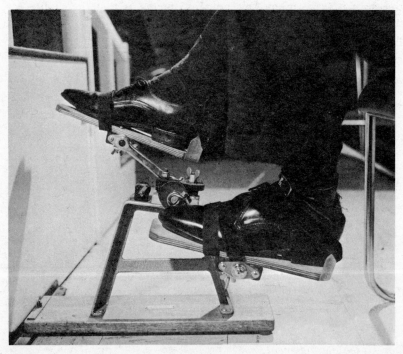

5.15 Solution for preventing old people's feet from slipping off pedals of exercising apparatus.

Finger exercising equipment

Problem   Although equipment was provided for exercising arms and legs there was no piece of apparatus designed specifically for exercising the patients' fingers. Students, after consultation with the physiotherapist, felt that there was a need for such equipment to supplement the function of needlework and basket-making in this area.

Solution   A small ladder device was designed and made (figure 5.16). By 'walking' their fingers up the rungs patients are able to exercise their fingers and shoulders. The rungs are numbered and several patients took pleasure in comparing their 'score' with the previous day's attempt, as through continued exercise they were able to raise their arms a little higher.

5.16 Students designed, constructed and assessed a finger exercise ladder.

'Jumbo draughts'

Problem   Due to arthritis of the hands many patients had difficulty handling conventional draughts pieces.

Solution   A group of students designed and made a set of giant-size draughts with a table to match. The shape of the pieces was the

169

5.17 'Jumbo draughts' help crippled hands become active.

result of their investigations into the problems encountered by arthritic patients in grasping objects.

The success of this solution is illustrated by the equipment's popularity with the draughts-playing patients. One point of interest is the provision for forming 'kings'. The pieces are reversible and on the base of each is a letter 'K', burnt into the wood by means of a metal die.

Step climbing equipment

Problem Students observed the difficulty the old people had in negotiating steps and stairs. They found that the existing walking frame (mentioned above in connection with the design of new fixing pins) had no real provision for patients to practise climbing steps. A small, narrow step could be fitted between two of the hand-rail supports, but this was not very satisfactory. For example, it was not wide enough to take the tripod type of walking stick and did not give experience of negotiating more than one step at once or steps of different sizes.

Solution The basic idea of a step exercising frame with varying step sizes was fairly simple. Not so simple were the problems that had to be dealt with in translating the idea into reality. The frame had to be robust and rigid, but it also had to be reasonably light and compact to enable it to be moved by the nursing staff and stored.

Other points to be considered were the overall dimensions—particularly in view of the necessity to incorporate different step sizes—the surface finish of the treads, and the need for the height of the handrails to be adjustable.

The problem of combining strength with ease of movement and storage was solved by making the frame in three sections. These simply slotted together in use; various methods of interlocking were experimented with but the students discovered that the slotting arrangement, together with the weight of the sections, was quite sufficient to keep them in place.

The group sought specialist advice when considering what material to use on the step treads. They wrote to a local factory, Ferodo Limited, outlining their problem and received details of non-slip materials. They visited the factory to find out more about the material and shortly afterwards requisitioned a quantity of step-edging angle strip and a roll of rubber non-slip tread material.

The same group also decided that some of the metal parts on the frame should be sprayed rather than painted by brush. This simple decision turned into an experience for the whole class.

A visit was made to the local factory of the British Domestic Appliance Company to study industrial finishing techniques while the metal fittings were being coated by a process of electrolysis dipping. In addition to the usual benefit of an industrial visit there was an added value here as the students were looking at the processes with a particular problem in mind. They could appreciate the validity of commercial techniques by relating them to problems they had met themselves.

A further benefit of this visit was to another area of work in the project. The students working on the spring exercising equipment problem (see above) had a quantity of special hooks chromium plated.

Once coated, the metal fittings were to form part of the hand-rail supports. The wooden hand-rails bolted on to these square metal tubes which fitted over wooden uprights. The uprights were drilled at regular intervals and matching holes in the metal tube enabled them to be raised or lowered as required and locked in position with a fixing pin.

Conclusions

As a result of the year's activities several useful pieces of equipment were designed and made. A wide range of possibilities, in terms both of solutions and of further work, was uncovered.

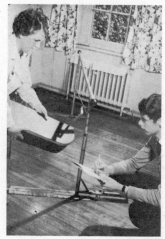

Design process for step climbing equipment

5.18 Old man on stairs (situation).
5.19 Existing equipment (situation).
5.20 Students investigating stairs (investigation).
5.21 Model equipment (solution).
5.22 Students in factory watching finishing (realization).
5.23 Completed equipment in use (evaluation).

The responses of the students showed a depth of investigation their teachers had not always anticipated. Nevertheless, the planned course of events produced design work, documents (such as *A Short History of the Conway Geriatric Hospital*) and equipment that suggests the involvement of students in work for the old that has potential far beyond the activities normally associated with school workshops. Students became aware of the organization of the hospital, were able to communicate, even with the most difficult patients, and eventually showed an eagerness to help improve the lot of the old folk who were confined to the geriatric unit.

The final questionnaire answered at the end of the year clearly indicated an improvement in the attitudes recorded earlier.

Students' answers to the questionnaire

As work progressed students' reactions to the project were sought. Some of their responses to the statements in a questionnaire distributed half-way through the project are given below.

1 To me the main value of the work was:
   —(Only one boy wrote about aspects of the craft work whereas twelve spoke of the value of making things for old people.)
2 During the course I have been interested in:
   —(Eight mentioned aspects of the work. Two just said 'everything'. Five mentioned the old people in their observations, implying that they could see the use of what they had done. Seeing the old also interested some.)
3 During the course I was not interested in:
   —(Five left this blank. Others said that all the work was interesting. Some just mentioned a few aspects of their craft work which had not interested them. None made any mention of the old people that they were dealing with.)
4 I was unhappiest when:
   —(Five mentioned the time they first saw the old people, many of whom were bed-ridden. One went on to say that this initial impression wore off as they saw more of the patients. Six complained about certain aspects of their work. One said that he had expected at first that he would miss making things—presumably meaning for himself—but that now he prefers making articles for the hospital.)
5 The point that interested me most was:
   —(Five mentioned aspects of their work. Eight spoke of the old people and said that seeing them was important. Two felt that their visit to the Ferodo factory was the most important aspect of the project.)
6 You are now half-way through the course. Do you want to continue with it or not? If not, say why.
   —(All said that they wished to continue.)

7 Do you like the way metalwork and woodwork have been taught during the course? Is it better than the usual woodwork/metalwork lessons? Give your reasons.

—(One said 'not really' but all the others said that the work was more interesting and that they did more than they would otherwise have done. Other interesting points made were that the atmosphere was more informal, that the work was of value to someone else, and that the keen interest of the teachers was noticed.)

Further observations

During the work it became clear to the teachers involved that there is great potential in a geriatric project. In addition to those factors dealt with in the aims and objectives section of this chapter there is the advantage that the amount of work that could be done is virtually unlimited.

Much commercially available equipment does not meet all the requirements of a specific situation. Each patient is an individual and ideally requires apparatus designed to suit his particular needs.

Although the students were involved in tackling quite a wide range of design problems at the hospital there is still plenty of scope for future groups to investigate and solve problems.

Two possible organizational problems should be mentioned.

First, it is important to explain to hospital staff that the students will not just be making things to order. It is too easy for them to be reduced to carrying out simple repair jobs or turning out dozens of frames to enable the patients to make stools or baskets as occupational therapy.

Second, steps should be taken to ensure that students do not come into contact with some of the more distressing cases in the hospital. In the project described the physiotherapist was always present with the students at the hospital and was able to see that this did not happen.

Case Study

Students' Reports on Geriatric Project

The following extracts are from the reports of fourth-form students engaged on a community development project in a secondary school in Northern Ireland.

The first two extracts describe how the project got under way and outline some of the problems encountered in designing and manufacturing walking aids for old people.

Designing walking aids—(1)

This project was started after the woodwork teacher, Mr Maguire, showed us some slides of a school in England who made things for some old people and a nursery. Afterwards we decided we would undertake the project and we started after Christmas. First we got into groups for metalwork and woodwork. These were then split up into smaller groups. Some were to make things for an old people's home and the others were to make things for a children's home. I was in a group to make something for the old people.

As we did not know what would be needed a visit was arranged. One Thursday morning we went up to the old people's home. Some were to see the old women and the others were to see the old men. I went to see the old men. We were shown into a room where there were several old men. We asked what their greatest needs were. We were told they wanted walking aids. The old men said that when they applied to the Welfare for walking aids they were told they could only get wheelchairs. But one of the nuns told us that the men were too young for wheelchairs. So this was our problem. To design and make several walking aids.

When we returned to school we got down to designing some walking

175

aids. Another visit was needed to get door measurements and some others. Four days later we borrowed a bending machine and started making the walking aids. But that was not all because we came up against some more problems which had to be ironed out. This meant another visit to the home to find out if the aids were to go upstairs and where were they going to be stored. We asked the nun and she told us the men would keep them in their rooms downstairs.

The next problem was getting some rubber feet. After many 'phone calls we found a shop that we could get them from. So we went and got them. These were fitted and a few finishing touches done to the walking aids and they were ready.

Designing walking aids—(2)

This project was taken on by the metalwork and woodwork departments and was arranged mainly by Mr Maguire who got the idea after showing us a film about how schools made things for old people and children in homes. Then different groups were arranged who went to see the children and old people in Nazareth House and Nazareth Lodge. The purpose of this was to talk to them and get some idea of what needed making or fixing. Our group saw the old people and found that many of them found it hard to walk. This was because the Welfare would not supply them with walking aids. So we decided to try to make them some walking aids. We started just after Christmas and were hoping to be finished before Easter.

Mr Donnelly, who was in charge of the metalwork section, got a bending machine and a good supply of aluminium tubing. During this period we were drawing and planning how to make the walking aids— what size they would have to be and how we were going to put them together. The old people's home had lent us the one walking aid they had so we could get some ideas from it and get rough measurements.

After all this planning we decided that we were ready to start making something. We tried a mock-up first but it didn't turn out too success-fully, but then we got the idea of it and started measuring and bending. If we were going to weld the parts together we would have to make some sort of stand to keep it steady. Welding is a hard job but with aluminium it was even harder because it melted quicker. But with the help of Mr Anderson, an expert welder, we couldn't go wrong.

Now we had to get some sort of rubber feet and handles so we all started investigating. We found a shop that sold them so we took off down town and bought sixteen. But we could not find any handles suitable for the job. So then it was Mr. Donnelly's turn for some quick thinking. He suggested we should use bicycle handgrips. We fitted these, cleaned the walking aids up and tested them out for size and strength. They turned out to be perfect. We will shortly be taking them up to the home.

Another group of students designed and made a number of footstools. Here one of them relates how their work was received by the patients.

'A ray of sunshine'

A couple of months had passed since our initial visit to the old people's home. Many an hour had been spent at the drawing boards trying to find the perfect design for the various groups. Many an hour had been spent putting these ideas and designs into operation. At last, however, after being delayed for a few weeks because of the Easter holidays, the big day came.

This was the day when we would attempt to put a ray of sunshine, as it were, into the hearts of a small percentage of people not as lucky as ourselves. We would attempt to put a ray of hope into the eyes of these people, to let them know that people still think of them, to let them know that they have not been abandoned. In general we were attempting to make these people happier than they really are.

It was a Thursday morning when all the jobs were gathered together and we set out on foot up the Ravenhill Road. At the very top was the modern building of Nazareth House. We were met at the gates by the Sister-in-charge who greeted us and led us through the corridors to a very neat and tidy waiting room where many old people were enjoying their morning nap. Some read the daily paper while others sat on their own in a daze taking notice of no one. Our entry was greeted by curious looks as many old folk had forgotten that we had been to see them two months ago.

The more talkative women came forward and introduced us. After the introductions we distributed the foot-stools that had been made by our group and the old people tried them out. They said that the stools were the best of all the things that had been made. This was, of course, a known fact to our group beforehand.

After all the equipment had been presented and tried out and everyone was satisfied our teacher took some photographs, first of the old people on their own with the equipment and then of the whole class together. Many were very excited at the possibility of being in the papers. To round off a most enjoyable morning we got a cup of tea with cake, which went down very well indeed. As we left we heard the comment, 'All we can do is pray for you.' This made everything worthwhile.

177

At the investigation stage the students were encouraged to look closely at the needs of the end-user so that they would be able to produce a full and satisfactory design specification. One group drew up the following list of six requirements for the design of a bed-rest.

Qualities of a bed-rest

We decided to make a bed-rest. Six qualities were needed:
1 it had to be easily stored;
2 it had to be comfortable;
3 it had to have at least three different heights;
4 it had to be portable;
5 its height had to be easily changed;
6 it had to be compact when folded.

In about two days the design had been completed on paper. It was now necessary to make a sectional prototype to see if it would work. We found a few points of trouble, e.g., balance and maximum height and compactness when folded down.

6
Designing for Play

The range and depth of the work that may be based upon the topic of 'play' is considerable. It offers scope for many valuable links with other subjects in the curriculum. In fact, such is the potential of this topic that a teacher's first problem may be to decide which of the many areas of work will be of most value to his or her students—bearing in mind the limitations of the timetable.

An approach to play

Clearly, the value of this work will rest partly on the opportunities it may offer for students to recognize and solve problems through the application of the design process.

Accepting that a design approach will satisfy a range of intellectual and social needs it becomes necessary to consider *how* the activity may be built into the school programme and *what* the students should do. The answers to these questions will be related to the age and ability of the students, although it is worth remembering here that the scope of play is such that it may be an appropriate theme of study at any stage of secondary education.

Consideration of what will be attempted will probably suggest how the work may be undertaken. Initially it will be necessary to help students to realize that play is a natural form of human behaviour, that it is crucial to the development of an individual's ability to perceive and handle materials and objects, to understand and communicate, and to form attitudes and responses to people and things. It is clear that this work could involve psychological and sociological studies, although of necessity at a superficial level only, except perhaps in the sixth form where deeper studies could be encouraged.

In the practical subjects the main emphasis may be on the design, construction and evaluation of play equipment. Such activity lends itself to a variety of approaches but the following represent some of the fundamental factors that require consideration.

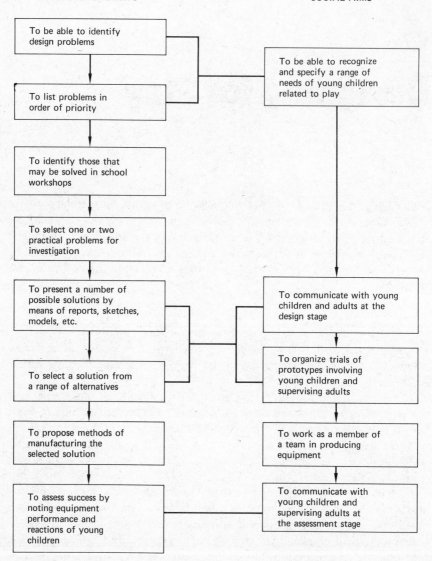

6.1 Aims and objectives.

Forms of play

It will be necessary for students to appreciate that play can take different forms. Various systems of categorization may be drawn up, from a simple division into 'strenuous', and 'non-strenuous' activities, to more sophisti-

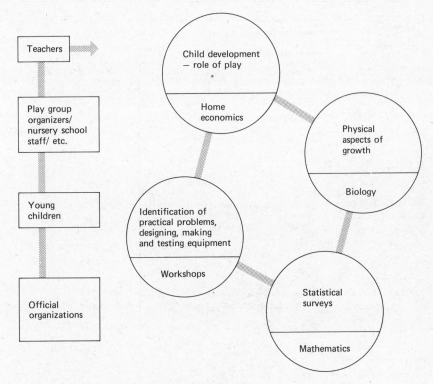

6.2 Possible contributions of a teaching team.

cated systems which categorize play in terms of the way it assists child development—e.g., physical, intellectual, emotional, social—and the nature of the activity itself—imitative, competitive, and so on.

Some teachers may find it helpful to draw up a system of classification during class discussion. Such a system is bound to be rather limited; play is not easily categorized and any particular activity is almost certain to include aspects of several categories. Nevertheless, the simplest system can help students develop an awareness of what play involves.

For example, the basic categories illustrated on the left-hand side of figure 6.3 could be introduced and the remaining columns developed by drawing suggestions from students.

Watching children at play

For students to become aware of the significance of play some form of observation and investigation will be required. Many schools begin by introducing the subject with a filmstrip and then follow this up by taking students to a play group or nursery school to observe actual play situations.

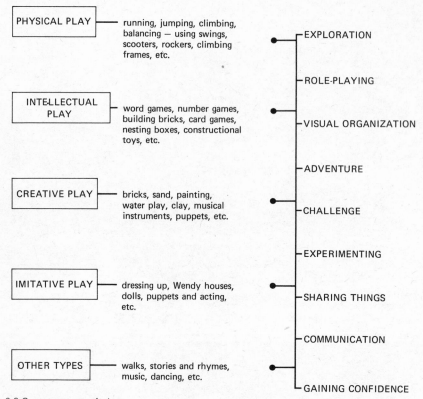

PHYSICAL PLAY — running, jumping, climbing, balancing — using swings, scooters, rockers, climbing frames, etc.

INTELLECTUAL PLAY — word games, number games, building bricks, card games, nesting boxes, constructional toys, etc.

CREATIVE PLAY — bricks, sand, painting, water play, clay, musical instruments, puppets, etc.

IMITATIVE PLAY — dressing up, Wendy houses, dolls, puppets and acting, etc.

OTHER TYPES — walks, stories and rhymes, music, dancing, etc.

EXPLORATION

ROLE-PLAYING

VISUAL ORGANIZATION

ADVENTURE

CHALLENGE

EXPERIMENTING

SHARING THINGS

COMMUNICATION

GAINING CONFIDENCE

6.3 Some aspects of play.

A suitable filmstrip, *Playthings*[7], is available in the Design and Craft Education series.

Details of local play groups and day nurseries and the name of the area play group organizer may be obtained from the local Social Services Department.

Establishing a school play group

In some regions, it may be difficult to arrange visits to organized establishments, although there are signs that their number is increasing. It may also be possible for students to observe young children in their own or a neighbour's family, or they might visit local parks and play areas. An alternative which has considerable scope is the establishing of a play group within the confines of a secondary school where members of staff or local residents can leave their children for short periods at regular times each week. The potential, and problems, may be illustrated by this account of the experience of one home economics teacher (overleaf):

182

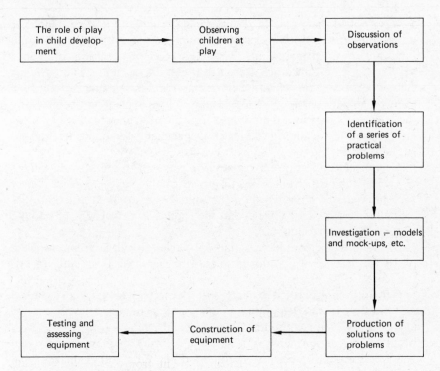

6.4 An approach to organizing a play project.

6.5 Where to see children at play.

It was decided that if we made the modest charge of $7\frac{1}{2}$p per child per afternoon we should soon accumulate enough funds with which we could buy some toys and equipment. This simple economic decision could have led us into legal difficulties, for since the Nurseries and Child Minders Act of 1948 and the Health Services and Public Health Act of 1968 (Section 60), anyone looking after children for payment will be breaking the law unless they and the premises in which the children are cared for are registered with the Local Health Department. We had, therefore, to succumb to the rigour of 'official registration'.

A letter of application for registration was sent to the Medical Officer of Health. The church hall was inspected by the Senior Medical Officer for Maternal and Child Health. The toilets were declared fit (so long as we could supply paper towels) and the room was declared large enough to take twenty-five children.

One adult helper would be required for every five children but we were pleased to learn that a senior girl could be classified as an adult in this capacity.

A fire officer also called to check that the electric sockets were switched and shuttered and that a fire blanket and extinguisher were readily available. We had to promise that the children would not have access to the kitchen area which was to be banned during the playgroup session. But it was not until we received a first aid kit and a potty from the local clinic that our premises actually became 'registered' and we were ready to enrol our first customers.

At another school the same problem was tackled in a slightly different way:

We decided to include a year's course on 'Child care and development'— the extension of a term's course we have been running for some time. To make the course meaningful we wanted to have real children in the school so our students brought toddlers to school for play activities during one term. After first getting the headmaster's permission to run the course we then notified all parents by letter; after having these letters signed and returned to us we obtained written consent from the parents of the toddlers.

For this series of lessons on play one class of girls is divided into five or six groups with three or four girls in each. While one group acts as play leaders, another works on an assignment such as 'buying toys' (during which they may visit toy-shops if they wish), and the remaining groups are responsible for collecting the children and returning them home.

In the multi-purpose room where we 'entertain', sewing machines and other pieces of dangerous equipment are locked away before the children arrive. Although I doubt whether any young child would reach (or even see) the gas tap I turn all gas off at the main; the electric sockets, though shuttered, are also turned off.

Our play activities are not extended outside since we have no safe restricted area. There is an outside door nearby in case fire should make an urgent exit necessary. . . . During our play sessions I stay fairly close to the door to prevent escapes and to regulate visits to the lavatory.

6.6 A school play group.

Planning for observation

Wherever the period of observation is undertaken it is advisable to ensure that a range of fairly specific factors is covered. This may entail the preparation of a list of key questions for use by the students and the formation of teams to concentrate on particular aspects of play.*

Many students feel more at ease if a 'survey approach' is applied initially. This helps them overcome any feeling of strangeness they may have on first mixing with a group of young children. Such surveys could include analysis of the space available, the range of equipment supplied, and the number and

*The booklet *You Are a Designer*[8] has been developed to help students tackle design problems in a structured way.

age of the children using the play area. This type of approach can quickly lead into more fundamental aspects of how and why children play.

By watching children at play and, where possible, helping to organize a play group, students should be able to build up a picture of the role of play. This may be reinforced by bringing together the information they have gathered. As well as using data that has actually been recorded it may be beneficial to probe impressions gained and observations made by the students but not recorded; this may best be done through discussion.

The students' responses

Given reasonable conditions most students are at least capable of compiling lists of materials and equipment found in a play area and noting the kinds of games the children prefer to play. Identification of these factors may lead to a variety of design problems ranging through:

—repairing broken toys;
—modifying or developing existing equipment;
—producing new equipment for existing communal play areas;
—producing equipment for use by individual children within a family setting;
—establishing new play areas.

Examples of the ways in which individual schools have tackled these design problems are given in the case studies in this chapter.

Design factors

The majority of the factors that students will need to consider at some stage during the design process are given in *You Are a Designer*[8]. Nevertheless, there are a number of additional points relating specifically to this area of work which may have to be taken into account. They include:

—overall safety (e.g., certain types of toys are covered by British Standards and their construction will need to comply with these);
—the extent of supervision;
—regulations governing the amount of space per child.*

The construction of adventure playgrounds and similar outside play areas may necessitate the consideration of such additional factors as:

—possibilities in the use of existing natural resources (e.g., slopes and trees);
—boundary fences;
—site construction.

A number of books dealing with play and related subjects are listed in the bibliography. Some of these may be suitable for use by students during their investigation work.

*See *Standards for School Premises Regulations 1959*[22] for guidance.

Case Study

Play in a Child Care Course

The design and construction of play equipment forms an important part of this two-year course for fifth-year non-examination girls. The first year is devoted to the theme of 'Child Care'. The following extracts from the course syllabus illustrate how the practical design work forms an integral part of the course as a whole.

The course syllabus

Five hours per fortnight are time-tabled for the course, including one two-hour practical session. One term each is spent in the needlework department, the home economics department and the technical department.

Work in the **Needlework** (textiles and dress) department may be divided into three main areas:

(a) THEORY AND DISCUSSION (to form an illustrated project)
1 Aspects of textiles and dress relevant to child care.
2 Safety factors related to articles and garments.
3 The layette—design and suitability of fabric for needs.
4 Clothes for toddlers' everyday activities—design and suitability of fabric.
5 Toys—design and suitability of fabric.
6 Furnishing a nursery.

(b) PRACTICAL WORK
— *Design and construction* of soft toys, layette, toddlers' clothes, bedding, nursery pictures and friezes involving:
1 Choice of article.
2 Aspects of design.
3 Designing the article, garment or toy.

4 Making the pattern.
5 Making the article, garment or toy.
6 Evaluation of the finished product.

— *Experiments* to assess the qualities of natural and man-made fabrics for crease resistance, washability, wearability, inflammability, water resistance, dirt resistance.

(c) VISITS TO SHOPS
    1 To ascertain prices of articles, garments and toys to compare with cost of home-made ones.
    2 To assess qualities of bought articles compared with home-made ones.

In the **Home Economics** department other aspects of child care are developed:
(a) *Films* are used to illustrate various aspects of the work. These include *Family Album, Every Baby a Wanted Baby, To Janet a Son, $\frac{1}{4}$ Million Teenagers, Their First Year, From Cradle to Family Meals* and *Your Children's Play.*
(b) THEORY AND DISCUSSION
— *Child Development*
    1 The following family situations are discussed in home economics and acted out during the students' drama classes:
        (i)   the two-parent family and a stable home;
        (ii) an unhappy home;
        (iii) the young widowed mother;
        (iv) handicapped children;
        (v) adoption.
    2 Baby's needs and requirements.
    3 Baby's routine.
    4 Baby-sitting.
    5 Child development.
    6 Habit and character training.
    7 Accidents and ailments.
    8 Safety and first aid.

— *Children at Play*
    1 Childhood memories.
    2 Child study.
    3 Play groups.
    4 A playroom.
    5 The school playroom.
    6 How and why children play.

7 Kinds of play.
8 Child development and play.
9 Stages of play.
10 Choosing and buying (or making) toys.

Various teaching aids are being developed to support this area of the work. A booklet dealing with the role of play in child development has been written and duplicated. This booklet is aimed at average and below average students, and has sections on 'How children grow and develop —from birth to four years old', 'Children at play—how and why children play, what play should offer, etc', 'How play helps growth and development—the right toys for the right age', and 'Choosing and buying toys'.

Work sheets have been produced to support appropriate sections of the booklet, and a slide sequence is being compiled to illustrate it.

(c) PRACTICAL WORK
   A *Baby Care:* bathing, feeding, changing, washing clothes.
   B *Food Preparation:* weaning, toddlers' meals.
   C *Play Group Activities:* students bring toddlers to school and assist at play groups.

Work in the **Technical** department may also be divided into three main areas:

(a) THEORY
   1 Factors in the design of toys and nursery equipment: function (suitability for age and purpose), appearance, construction.
   2 Basic tools and processes.
   3 Materials: wood, metals, plastics, paint.
   4 Fabrication techniques.

(b) PRACTICAL
   The students are each involved in the design and manufacture of up to four items of play equipment for young children. (A description of this area of their work is given below.)

(c) PROJECT
   Choice of topic on some aspect of the subject, e.g., trees, basic tools, construction in wood, toys through the ages (1800 to the present day).

The students were introduced to play during their work in the home economics department. Through films, discussion and the introductory booklet outlined above they began to form an understanding of its role in child development. This theoretical approach was backed up by a visit to a local play group and their work with the group which had been set up within the school.

At each stage of the design process the students were given a series of simple key questions:

1 Describe your visit to the play group: the organization—the helpers —the children—what they played with—what was said—what you learnt.

2 Describe the toddlers' play activities at school in the same way.

3 Make a list of playthings you think you could make on your own or with some friends.

4 Choose which you would like to make and say why.

At the end of this first stage each student had a clear idea of what she wanted to make:

I will make a clock because it is quick and will help the children to use their brains and help them tell the time. Also, I didn't see one in the play group.

I will make a slide, because they get excited sliding down it and it helps to make them confident.

A boat because it is something to float in water. They like playing in water.

I would like to make a jigsaw puzzle because it is very educational and I would like to make a wheelbarrow because it will help young children to walk.

Investigation

1 Write down who will play with your toys: boys or girls—age—one or many.

2 What size will it have to be? Consider the size of the children, what the toy needs to do, and so on.

3 Will the toy be used inside or outside? How will it be stored? Will it have more than one use?

4 What will it look like? (Describe its colour, texture, shape, and so on.)

5 Will it need to be strong, or light, or have any other special feature?

Specification

1 Describe in detail what your toy must be and do.

2 Draw a diagram of the toy you have decided to make.

The hobby horse must be the right size for a small child to play with. It must not have any rough edges for small children to hurt themselves. It must not have any nails sticking out of the sides.

The clock hands must not fall off or be too loose and the numbers must be big enough to be noticed.

I will use bright colours because children respond to bright colours.

(The jigsaw puzzle) is blocks of wood cut into shapes which then can be put together, describing itself to the children who play with them. They must be the correct size otherwise they will not go into the shape designed.

To have a correct plan of our wheelbarrow you must work it out so that it is not too big for the child to carry along or to push along. The handles must not be too long or too thick or too high. Because if the handles were too high the child might not be able to reach. Also the barrow itself must not be too deep, because if it was too deep the child could fall and hurt itself. We made the wheelbarrow because we thought it would help them to walk along and give them some thought of adventure.

Solutions

1 Draw all the pieces you will need to make the toy. Put measurements on and describe each piece. Say how much each piece will cost.
2 Write down the things you will have to be able to do to make the toy.

Realization

1 Write down step by step how you will make your toy.
2 What tools will you need?
3 What do you think may be a problem?
4 Say which things you enjoyed, did not enjoy, found difficult, which made you cross, and so on.
5 What problems did you meet and how were they overcome?

First I would get some wood and then get a pencil and draw the shapes on the wood so it would come out as shapes after sawing it. Then we will make a box for the shapes to go in. We will paint the box pink and then paint the shapes and then put the shapes together. We will need a saw, hammer, nails, paint, glue and paintbrush.

The first thing we did to make our slide was measure up the wood and then cut it. Then we had to nail and stick the legs, sides, the slide, and the steps together making sure it was safe for children to play on.

I enjoyed painting the shapes. We got quite cross when the shapes would not fit together, but we finally fitted them.

I enjoyed putting the barrow together but I found putting the screws in difficult as they were in an awkward angle. This made me cross. I overcame this by keeping my patience and doing my best with the help of my friends and a teacher.

One problem was we had to paint it three times.

Testing

1 How will you find out how well your toy works?
2 Describe how it was used and by whom.
3 Was your toy good or could it be made better if you had to do it again?
4 Describe how you would improve on your original design. Draw sketches of your new ideas.

We made sure it (the jigsaw puzzle) is the right shape and all the pieces fit where they are supposed to fit. It could be made better next time. Make it bigger and not so rough in the squares and round the edges. Put more shapes in it.

The hands of the clock could have been made safer and the numbers could have been better.

We let a child play with our toy. It was pushed along and bricks were put into the barrow. It was good, but the only trouble was that it was a bit high for the child to reach. It was soon rectified by cutting a bit of wood off. I would improve it by putting patterns on it.

I tested the sand-tray by filling it up with sand and letting children try it out. I could see it was very useful but it could be improved by putting it on a stand.

Case Study
Toys for Nursery Schools

Our school is a mixed school situated in a rural area. Three new nursery schools are under construction in the area, one within walking distance. It was this which provided the stimulus for our project. The interest being shown locally, and indeed nationally, in nurseries at this time offered us the opportunity to engage in what is proving to be a fascinating study of children's play equipment.

Why we undertook the project

From the outset we realized that it was not just a matter of making different pieces of equipment. The whole scheme has been geared to providing students with a range of educational experiences—the outcome being toys suitable for young children.

Throughout, students have been encouraged to investigate, identify problems and suggest solutions. By adopting this approach we have often required them to make decisions that formerly we as teachers had often made for them. At the same time they became aware of some of the requirements of a section of society that is nearly always in need of some form of help.

We were also able to maintain the standard of craftsmanship which we at this school are proud of. Even where new techniques were applied the calibre of work was at least up to the high standards that we normally demand.

Getting started

Much of the initial planning necessarily fell on the shoulders of the participating teachers. Initially, it was decided to familiarize our principal, staff and management with the work going on at Keele and the way in which our project would relate to that work. I felt it was important to create and maintain an awareness of the changes taking place in our workshops and to try to get others to participate meaningfully in this enterprise. In order to do this the following paper was prepared and distributed to all members of staff.

We, as teachers of subjects diverse in outlook and seemingly remote from each other in interest, rightly pride ourselves on being specialists in our particular fields. While publicly bemoaning the lack of inter-departmental co-operation we privately guard our sacred patch on the school quilt. The allocation of time for examinations, and indeed the general timetable structure, encourages isolation and aloofness. Too often, co-operation means nothing more than borrowing beakers or lending screwdrivers, 'letting off' a class for a film or a football match, having visual aids made or 'minding' a class during a colleague's absence. There is a lack of awareness of what one's fellow specialist is doing or what difficulties he or she is facing that seems to permeate all schools and all levels of education.

It is against this background that we in the craft department are about to engage on perhaps the most demanding, and indeed exciting, enterprise we have yet undertaken. We are about to embark on a two-year craft development study (I hesitate to use the word 'project') which will necessitate the involvement, rather than the mere co-operation, of other departments. There are spheres which can only be developed to their true potential if we are offered help in specialized fields. This transfer of ideas and assistance will of course benefit both sides and I would hope that teachers outside our department would see us as a useful source of help which they can tap to equal advantage.

Our area of study is one which I might loosely entitle 'furniture and play equipment for children'. The main factor influencing this choice was the fact that a new nursery school is nearing completion locally and offers an ideal testing ground for our ideas. It could be, and must be, a fascinating venture. We would hope too that some of the ideas evolved will find some form of practical expression in the nature of simple equipment which may be used in the new school. However, I must make it clear that our objectives are centred around our own school and our own students and any benefit derived elsewhere will be incidental and not really a major part of our aim.

All this may perhaps seem of little consequence to teachers 'outside' the craft department but I can say emphatically that, eager as we are, we cannot operate successfully unaided. Scarcely had we begun to discuss the project when we needed guidance. We will be designing and making chutes (carrying out friction tests to find out when the posterior begins to sizzle) ; making drums, xylophones, recorders (we haven't a note between us) ; making simple stools and tables (measuring and working out proportions) ; making dolls furniture and perhaps other items designed specifically for girls (we don't know much about them over here) ; making sand and Plasticene trays (art and its allied media play an essential role). So as you can see we already plan some infiltration into other areas.

It is stating the obvious to say that all help will be required on a voluntary basis. We do not expect an overwhelming surge of interest in what is, let's face it, something essentially connected with our department. We will keep those interested informed of our progress (remember it is a two-year undertaking). We will undoubtedly be seeking their professional knowledge and expertise during the coming months.

In the preliminary background work help was also sought from the school management, the Ministry Inspector in charge of nurseries, nursery school teachers and our local Education Committee (who offered generous financial backing). The local Health Authorities later gave us some very useful guidance regarding safety and health requirements.

Ultimately, the members of staff participating decided upon a 'three-pronged attack'. Five classes would be involved, representing a cross-section of academic and craft ability, guided by teachers from three departments. The woodwork department was to be concerned with wheeled, rocking and educational toys. The domestic science department would deal with play clothes and soft toys. Tapestry-work and advice on colour schemes were to be undertaken by the art and craft department. We decided that the work would normally be done during the periods allotted for craft on the timetable.

Collecting information

Visits by the students to both long established and new nurseries in Belfast proved immensely valuable in capturing interest and stimulating constructive debate. Teachers in these schools made many critical comments concerning the quality of available equipment and the safety aspect of many items, particularly rocking equipment. But what was perhaps most valuable was the closer awareness we received of the problems of size and scale which our project involved. Our students looked clumsy and overgrown in this world of tiny tots. But they enjoyed the experience. They filled in questionnaires, examined play articles, chatted with the children (and how they responded!) and collected a mass of information to be used later.

The basis on which the students collected information was directed by questionnaires that were prepared beforehand. The following items selected from them will give some ideas of the tasks they set the students.

1 What was the average age of the children observed?
2 What was their average height?
3 What was their average weight?
4 What size was the playroom? Name every piece of equipment you can remember seeing.
5 Did the children move around much? Were many sitting down?
6 Was any child alone? If so, what was he doing?
7 Were any children outside during our visit? What activities were they engaged in?
8 The following articles may be in use: a sand table, a work-bench, an easel, a music trolley, a nature table. Examine the way in which they have been constructed and note the essential overall dimensions.
9 Is there any piece of play equipment that you would enjoy making— perhaps to a slightly different design?
10 Many young children in our parish do not go to a nursery school. If you were speaking to them what would you say they were missing?

Planning and designing

In the woodwork department the students began to plan the toys that we hoped would be ready for the opening of the new school. The fact that no established nursery existed anywhere near us proved to be a serious problem at an early stage. The choice of suitable dimensions for the toys was difficult as there were no small children available to help test our ideas. Some of the things we wanted to find out were: What would be a safe height for a rocker or see-saw? How much seating space would be required for the many trucks being made? What is the safe angle for a child's chute? How high should a child's blackboard be?

These questions were answered by inviting local children of nursery age (many of them children of the staff) to the school and simulating as closely as possible a typical nursery environment. Our students could now collect essential data for use in the workshops. A strange miscellany of objects were used to find out measurements and the children had to be coaxed and gently manœuvered into all sorts of positions in order to carry these out. While one group busied themselves drawing lines around children sitting or kneeling on sheets of plywood, others experimented with blocks and planks to find out the safe height for rocking equipment.

Tests were recorded in visual form; sheets were prepared illustrating in clear and simple lines the activities being carried out. These were later pinned on to the craft department notice boards where a close eye could be kept on the optimum measurements.

6.7 Communication of ideas on 'rocking
devices' via sketching and model making.

Safety was obviously to be an overriding consideration in all our planning. British Standard regulations are stringent and uncompromising in this respect. One student designed a tip-up lorry and was posed with quite a problem on reading:

> Folding mechanisms, brackets, arms and bracings shall embody a safety stop or afford protection for the fingers against crushing in the event of sudden movement.

The toys had to be modified constantly. In many cases extra equipment had to be made to test the article under construction. Take for example the problem this extract presents in relation to work with soft toys:

> Soft toys' and dolls' eyes shall be attached in such a manner that they cannot be gripped by human finger-nails or teeth, or, if they can be so gripped, the method of securing them to the toy should be such as to withstand removal by a weight of 30 lb.

Such limits often taxed the students' ingenuity in planning. The relevant parts of the regulations were kept constantly in view and added interest and challenge to their work in many ways. Even the intensity of noise emitted by toys must be controlled and, although no instance of this problem has yet arisen, it would lead to an interesting side study in the case of some musical instruments for example.

The domestic science department's contribution to the project has helped to balance what might appear to be a heavy craft bias. Naturally, the boys tend to assume that the nurseries will be male dominated and fall shy of becoming involved with girls' toys. However, the girls have helped to counteract their failings by designing dressing-up clothes, wall-furnishings, dolls' clothes, etc. As we are working within the normal timetable there has been little opportunity to overlap, although the girls have helped much in the painting and finishing.

Recording and reviewing

We decided that it would be important to keep progress records. Written reports were and are being made by individual students to record difficulties and successes. The teachers took photographs and are now planning to prepare tapes in conjunction with students. Slides, we found, are by far the best way to record the story of 'Our Nursery Project', but even they fail to convey the sense of communal involvement that such an exercise gives and the sense of gratification felt by the students on making something that works and receives general approval. Nevertheless, regularly taken slides can help to build up a good general outline of the work done which can be seen by future generations and hopefully will provide a seed from which other community projects will grow.

Concerning examinations, great emphasis is placed on the course work carried out by the student in the years prior to his examination. Evidence of planning and research is required and a large percentage of the total marks are allocated to this part of his work. The project therefore presented our GCE boys with a splendid opportunity to engage in a purposeful piece of work which would be acceptable for the final moderation. A particular article, such as a child's workbench, was chosen to be designed and made as it both fulfilled course requirements and contributed the best available skill to the project.

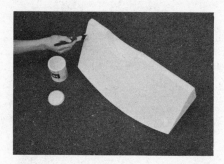

6.8 A coat of paint for a partially completed 'rocker'.

At the time of writing our work is approximately at the half-way stage. Wheeled and rocking toys have been made as have a miscellaneous collection of items by the domestic science department. It is the students involved who can honestly assess the success of our undertaking. I feel that the majority gave their time unselfishly and only on an odd occasion did I hear a dissenting voice. The following extracts from a taped conversation with one of the students are typical of the general reaction:

Before we started making the toys we visited several nursery schools. We found this very helpful and very interesting. We talked to the children and watched them using toys. At first they were a little shy, but as we got used to each other an atmosphere of trust developed. It was rather difficult trying to be as inconspicuous as possible in the process of making notes, but somehow we managed to get plenty of information as well as several photographs.

As we grew accustomed to watching the children playing with their toys it became clear that there were several dangers which at first weren't apparent. We found several pieces of rocking equipment which, although looking very attractive, proved to be rather dangerous in use, particularly when it came to rocking the toy violently as some of the children were doing. There was a danger that the toy would topple over. Apparently the designer had spent most of his time considering the shape and attractiveness of the toy and had missed out on these hidden dangers. Our fears were further reinforced by the teachers who agreed with us that several of the toys were badly constructed. Obviously this fault grew from a bad design. Our rocking toys incorporated a footboard; not for the child to stand on but to prevent the toy from rocking too far.

My main contribution to the project was in designing and making a chute. We started off by looking in magazines and books to find out more about chutes. At the nursery school we observed several chutes and took down dimensions, watched children playing on them and looked again for hidden faults.

We carried out experiments on a quarter-scale model to check measurements. We didn't run into any problems until it came to finding the gradient of the slide. We thought we could overcome it on the model but in fact we couldn't. We got some dead-weights in the same quarter-scale ratio to represent a small child and we let these roll down the slide to simulate a child sliding down the actual chute. But when one takes into consideration that this is literally a dead weight, the difference between it and a child is so great there is in fact no comparison.

The final experiments were carried out using actual children on the full-sized chute. Some of the teachers kindly brought their children to school. We set up the chute and several other toys and just let the children play with them as they wished. As well as being helpful in determining the gradient of the slide it was interesting to see how the children reacted to all the toys.

When we were first presented with the topic it was, to us, something new and original; it seemed a wonderful idea. It seemed an opportunity to spread our wings and to express ourselves through our work. Without exaggerating I would say that each boy's job has something of himself in it.

It certainly would have been easier if our teacher had given us drawings to follow, but from our point of view it would not have been a better approach. We wouldn't have experienced the same feeling towards the work as we did. I sense a greater feeling of 'inventiveness' in the craft department. The creative atmosphere really enables one to do one's best and thoroughly enjoy oneself.

It will be nice to look back at the end of the course and think that I really achieved something by taking part in this project. I can only speak for myself but I am sure that most, if not all, of the other boys taking part feel strongly the same way as I do.

Now we look forward to the final part of the project starting in September and to the time when our work is passed on to be used, perhaps abused, but most of all enjoyed by the local nursery children.

Case Study
Designing and Building an Adventure Playground

A more detailed account of concrete work appears in the teachers' book The Creative Use of Concrete.[13]

The whole thing came into focus after Mr G. Warren, HMI, visited our school in October 1968. His interest and vision in the scrutiny of plans for new schools left us with the challenge of designing and building an adventure playground for a local primary school that was under construction.

For some time several ideas had been toyed with for developing our handicraft curriculum, but no detailed plans had been formulated. This one, though, had scope! The subject had appeal for secondary school students—visions of young Tarzans flying around etc! Added to this, the very thought that they were considered to be mature enough to provide a real playground for the 'children' of the primary school, sold the idea anyway!

The headmaster accepted with alacrity, and it was decided to call a meeting of all members of the staff who were interested. About twelve attended, from whom a team of eight were finally involved. My role was that of liaison officer between members of staff, head, county architect's office, education office, and primary school; and general factotum to boot!

The team decided that the fourth year (school leavers) plus a number of volunteers from a CSE form, were the more suitable students. They· were old enough to cope with the work, and had sufficient time left in school to see the job through—or so we thought!

Finding out about adventure playgrounds

Now, if only someone knew what an adventure playground really was. We felt this was where best the children could start work. Their maths and English teacher took them through the painful chores of writing letters to all sorts of people and places (names and addresses of which were found in a number of leaflets and brochures supplied by the Director and Mr Warren). It was a delight to see the beaming face of a lad being ceremoniously handed his personal mail 'I. Sawicz, Esq, Form 4D . . .'.

One could not help being impressed by the courteous and helpful tone of the letters received. The students were receiving their first real impression of being treated as adults, and liked it!

The information piled up, and it soon emerged that the leading authority on the subject was Lady Allen of Hurtwood. Imagine our astonishment when a most charming and encouraging letter was delivered to one of the smallest boys in the group from Lady Allen herself.

Soon, the general idea of an adventure playground was visualized. To round off the exploratory stage, everyone visited the site to be used and were told that the playground was to be used by about 125 infants.

Play and equipment

The children were now asked to devise apparatus and equipment that may be suitable. The boys did this, whilst the girls, directed by the biology master, investigated the playing habits of infants—the type of games they played; the size of the groups; the amount of space used; and so on. All this was observed and noted. Infant children and their teachers were interviewed, in an attempt to get as much information as possible. At this stage other factors, such as safety, cleanliness, (clothes and dirt dangers), and freedom from interference from others, emerged as valid considerations. The art and crafts teachers were additional consultants on design details.

There was no shortage of ideas for equipment. The contribution of comic literature to their proposals was enormous! Many were quite ingenious, most were interesting if not always practical! Considerable guidance and patience was required here, and final choices were postponed until costs and space were considered further.

Many more letters were written, shops and merchants' yards visited, telephone calls made, and knowledgable parents 'pumped'. The handling of some items involved mechanical earth-moving equipment. Mounds of earth were to be built, hundreds of concrete slabs were to be used. Could boys do it all? Obviously not. So, as the practical consideration of the project gradually became apparent and dominant, many of the early ideas were now seen to be quite impossible.

Planning for construction

Eventually the general final plan was developed, final constructions decided, and action stations were established.

An interview with the Deputy County Architect settled the division of work between ourselves and outside contractors and the finances of the total project discussed.

The actual ordering of materials was undertaken by myself, although the metalwork teacher organized the purchase of a stainless steel slide. This was one of the few wholly manufactured items we incorporated into the playground—the others being some concrete pipes. Staff participation in this way was for purely administrative convenience but it is accepted that there is scope for student involvement here.

The need for a concrete mixer was very obvious. A remarkably active and generous local branch of the Round Table heard of our need and determined they could and would help. Presto—one mixer! They had contacted a plant-hire firm in Widnes who were delighted to give us one. A 'Barro-mix' was given most readily by a local newsagent, a load of sand came from another local man. The community was not only aware of our work, it was interested and helpful.

At this stage two of my colleagues took over the main responsibility. They led the boys over the problems of construction, materials, transport and general organization of the practical work.

The site was approximately one mile from school; the only way of getting there was by walking or in staff cars. The local Technical/Agricultural College was helpful in the provision of a tractor and low-loading trailer, so that many quite large items could be assembled and completed at school and then taken down to the site.

Starting work on site

The contractors bulldozed the mounds, laid drains and moved out.

Nevertheless, heavy rain had made a quagmire of the site, delaying our start for over two months.

We did not get on site until after the summer terminals. To make up for this, the last two-and-a-half weeks of term were given completely over to the project.

Hundreds of concrete blocks had been made in school and were carried down. Where possible sectional constructions had been used. All kinds of walls and floors were made. Houses, forts, look-out towers, conning towers, sand pits, balancing poles, a fireman's pole, bridges, scrambling frame, roof climbs, hop-skotch area, prehistoric monsters in concrete, seats, tables, gardens, shrubs; there seemed to be an endless list. The rural science teacher made his contribution with some landscape gardening, shaping the mounds to an angle of less than thirty-five degrees. This was so that grass roots would not be torn out by climbing feet.

The efforts of all were positively Herculean. Needless to say we did not do it all in the time left that term, so we continued during the first two weeks or so of the new term full time, and after that in handicraft periods for two more terms, when weather allowed.

Now the last touches are being added. Contractors have seeded the grass areas, perimeter trees and one or two scattered shrubs are all that remain to add.

Most of the original team of students left school before the end, but recruits were easily found. Estimates were roughly treated and harsh comments made by the professionals! Nevertheless, the finished work is well up to standard, and a source of undoubted satisfaction to most people concerned.

Outcomes

When attempting to assess the outcomes of the venture clearly students grew in many directions. Although involved with play equipment the problems were undoubtedly of 'man-sized' proportions. There was a tremendous atmosphere of team work both within the ranks of students themselves and between teachers and students. Some understanding of the nature of 'play' developed and, furthermore, the diverse way in which tools and materials can contribute towards this field emerged. In general, contact with people outside normal school routine added greatly to giving the project relevance in the eyes of the students.

Putting aside the rose-tinted spectacles, one feels that many opportunities were missed to give more responsibility to the children, both in design and constructional detail. Avenues of enquiry were opened but not fully developed because of the lack of time, certain difficulties of integration with other subjects, pressures from examination syllabuses

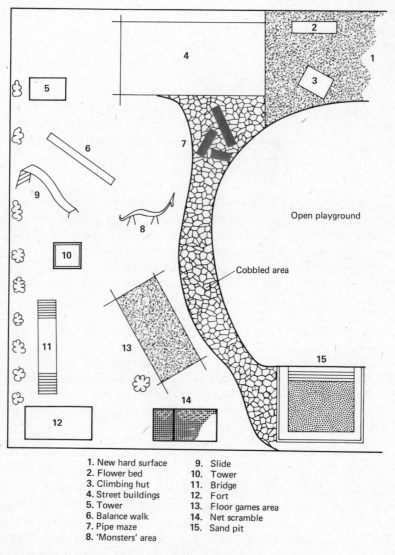

2
1
4
3
5
6
7
8
9
Open playground
Cobbled area
10
11
13
15
12
14

1. New hard surface
2. Flower bed
3. Climbing hut
4. Street buildings
5. Tower
6. Balance walk
7. Pipe maze
8. 'Monsters' area
9. Slide
10. Tower
11. Bridge
12. Fort
13. Floor games area
14. Net scramble
15. Sand pit

6.9 The layout of the adventure playground.

and changes in timetables from one year to another. The size of this project was enormous, but its potentialities were even greater.

The greatest problems from the educational point of view were those of integration, the time-factor, and examination pressure in certain parts of the work, preventing our developing the full potential of each situation. We are pleased with what has been done, we can see what could have been done if. . . . We can conclude that in spite of all the good things achieved, we are still only half-way there.

6.10 The concrete 'monsters' were a popular feature.

Case Study

The Paddington Playmobile

A rather unusual project undertaken by a school in the Paddington area of Liverpool was the purchase and conversion of an old Liverpool Corporation double-deck bus into a mobile play unit for a deprived area of the city. The theme of play, incidentally, continued to be used in the school after the construction of the 'Playmobile', as fourth-form students designed and made equipment for an adventure playground sited on a derelict plot of land in one of Liverpool's 'priority' areas.

6.11 An exterior view of the completed Playmobile.

In many areas of the country the lack of nursery accommodation is a severe problem. Liverpool 8 district knows this all too well as there are some six or seven infants to each available place.

It was this which led Dr Eric Midwinter, who is Director of Projects in the Educational Priority Areas of this city, to approach us with the tentative proposal that an ex-Liverpool Corporation double-deck bus be purchased and used in some way as a portable playing space. Our job turned out to be the complete conversion of the vehicle to produce a mobile nursery/play school (aptly named at its 'launching' as the 'Paddington Playmobile').

An essential qualification in all Community Service projects is that funds must be available. Fortunately, in this instance, this was the case.

A programme of work

Since our fourth-year extended course students were already committed on other aspects of work it was decided to introduce fourth-year non-examination boys to this problem and to call for volunteers for the project. These were readily forthcoming and a programme of work was drawn up thus:

1 Strip out all passenger seats except the rear inward facing pair which housed the batteries.

2 Remove all other fittings and fixtures not required.

3 Arrange meeting with prospective teacher/crew of the finished play unit to determine nature of fittings, toys, etc, required.

4 Allocate jobs to teams when final proposals were known.

As it turned out final specifications suggested the following division of tasks:

Mainly Woodwork

Design and fit toy steering wheels to front of lower deck.
Design, make and fit Wendy house at stair corner on upper deck.
Convert infant size desks to line side of upper deck.
Provide storage space.
Re-build entrance and design and fit fold-back door.
Design, make and fit gates at head and foot of stairs.
Design and make slide and ladder for lower deck.
Design, make and fit sand pit.

Mainly Metalwork

Design, make and fit pivots to toy steering wheels.
Make up oil drum for slide and ladder support.
Make various fittings as requested.

General Work

Dismantle seats and strip interior.
Lay chipboard floor and skirting on two decks.
Build up over wheel arches, etc.
Lay vinyl type floor covering.
Paint and decorate interior and exterior of vehicle.

Facts emerging from this project

1   Projects of this nature must find their origin in a real and obvious need in the community. This leads to staff having the enthusiasm so vital in first approaches to potential volunteers. (All workers should be volunteers and not 'pressed men'.)

2   Stimulation of thought and activity is best provided by allowing students to see for themselves the problem and the difficulties it can create. In this instance we were fortunate in that our own home management department has a nursery school so we did not have far to go to see what activities were attractive to pre-school children.

3   When the nature of the work is known after the drawing and work schedules are able to be completed, teams will often form naturally, e.g., some boys will feel happier at metalwork than woodwork, etc.

4   It would seem that such projects would be better timetabled rather than being dependent upon such time as staff and students can give.

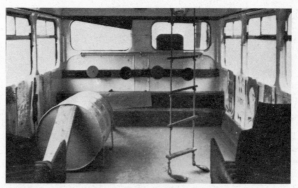

6.12 The lower deck play area.

This does create great difficulties both in staffing and in forming a special set of volunteers. It is, nevertheless, our intention to try to accomplish this on our next venture: the equipping of an adventure playground on a site close by. We may then be able to plan ahead with more certainty and the whole project should move ahead more rapidly.

5 The extent to which 'whole involvement' can be true depends largely upon the time factor. Should time be limited then certain facts may have to be presented to teams thus limiting the true potential of student investigation. Sometimes when undertaking community service projects it may be necessary to guide students, at a fairly rapid rate, to possible design solutions. This is by no means ideal as the students should start by coping with the problem themselves and subsequently the solving, costing and purchasing of materials.

6 One can see the possibility of this kind of community service project forming the basis for integrated courses between several departments

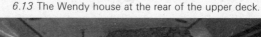

6.13 The Wendy house at the rear of the upper deck.

but great flexibility of timetable and staff movement would be one essential requirement. In our case we were able to work with the art department who provided the attractive nursery figures which adorn the exterior of the vehicle.

In view of these latter comments it is rather unfortunate that much of the work of real value, which is undertaken for the community, is usually dominated by the need for urgency. The usual request is that the job should be finished 'yesterday'!

We must be sure when undertaking these projects that the technical department is not being used only for the facilities it may offer, but that these projects are based on a sound educational, aesthetic and moral basis. In this way the department, the children in it and the community will gain and be the richer for it.

Conclusions

All work of an experimental nature must of necessity be viewed with a critical eye. It is possible that after all our work the scheme might have failed for some unforeseen reason.

In the case of the Paddington Playmobile we are happy to report that, during its short service to date, it is a great success. It is reported that the main difficulty encountered by staff is persuading the toddlers to leave when the session ends.

So much for the 'consumer'.

The evaluation of gain on the part of those students working on the project is far more difficult. So many older boys seem loath to show their deepest feelings. Nevertheless, we can say with certainty that most of the boys were extremely keen and proud of their individual contribution. Volunteers for after school sessions were readily forthcoming.

This kind of work gives boys far more scope in experiences of work not readily available in the workshop. They can see how the facilities of the workshops can be adapted to circumstances arising from problems in their own allotted task. Even a potential vandal's strange urges may find some outlet in removing the seats from a public service vehicle. (The difference between 'dismantling' and 'wrecking' was pointed out at the onset of Phase 2)

Surprisingly, in some instances, boys were able to suggest some basically sound and original solutions to design problems, e.g., the difficulty in siting the slide was overcome by two boys obtaining and modifying a large oil drum. This was subsequently also used to support the small climbing ladder. Most boys saw fairly promptly that the prospective clients would be very small people and that this had great importance in the design of all furniture and toys. Boys found themselves thinking outside their own part of the job since there was a great interdependence across the different design tasks. This kind of activity may bring an understanding of other people's work problems. This is an aspect which usually finds no real importance in the individual job.

It may be found that some aspects of the work by their nature must be handled by the staff involved. In our project such items as road tax, insurance, garage and maintenance, the finding of a suitable driver, etc, all came into this category. Nevertheless, there is scope here at least to make students aware of certain requirements and to show how they may be satisfied.

This project took many hours of patient planning and careful work but to see the vehicle attracting so much attention in the city streets and to know that it serves a real and valuable purpose is extremely rewarding to all who were involved.

Case Study

A Climbing Frame

This project, undertaken by a grammar school, began with a request from a local junior school for a piece of activity apparatus for the playground. Materials were to be purchased from the school fund.

Early investigations

A third-year class went to the school to discuss the project with a teacher. At an early stage the chief requirements of the apparatus were defined as climbing, swinging and sliding, and considerations of size, cost, positioning, materials, construction, safety, stability, fixing to the ground, and so on, were mentioned.

An early technical consideration was the type of materials to be used. Steel apparatus was looked at and the problems of rusting, even when painted, were noted. A coating of GRP on steel was proposed but later abandoned as it was thought to be a potentially hazardous idea—

wearing in places and endangering hands and fingers. The group realized that galvanizing was the best answer but no facilities existed for doing it. At this point the parent of a pupil at the junior school offered the group a quantity of scrap 60 mm dia. aluminium scaffolding tube, which was accepted.

Ideas and solutions

Early design ideas of functions and layout were visualized by sketching or model-making with polystyrene and metal rods. Once each student had organized his own ideas they were discussed by the whole group and about fourteen selected for further development.

At this point students worked in groups of three or four. The tubes were in a number of different lengths and in order to achieve the most economical use the models made at this step employed metal rods of similar scaled dimensions. Metal tubes also limited the type of construction envisaged and the idea of a slide or sliding sections was abandoned mainly because of the size of mould needed for a glass-fibre construction.

The models were painted and given the most realistic impression possible and were then taken to the junior school. There, one of the project's most interesting features occurred when the staff organized a school vote to select the most popular design. Most popular was the highest structure; the reason given was that it gave the 'best outlook'.

Construction and installation

The site for its installation was also a question of some debate among the children themselves. Finally a position overlooking the Cheshire Plain was selected. A pit was dug and the ground prepared for a concrete platform to be poured around the feet of the frame.

6.14 Climbing frame models.

H

As with the design work, the construction of the apparatus took place in normal time-table periods. Much discussion centred around alternative methods of construction—total assembly in school with the problem of transporting such a large assembly, construction at the junior school with the problems of transporting students and portable welding apparatus, the use of sockets rather than welded corners, and so on.

The decision was finally taken to construct it by welding the frame in two halves at school and complete assembly on site. The difficult task of welding the tube was undertaken largely by the boys of the class after several practice runs with some making-good by their teacher.

Filmstrip

Design and the Environment*

Teachers' notes

This filmstrip is intended to help introduce senior students in the secondary school to a study of their environment. The central point is that the quality of life frequently depends upon the material elements of the environment that are designed and made by man and are therefore within his control.

Control implies a freedom of choice, of judgment and the taking of decisions. This filmstrip raises some of the issues of modern society in which the material design of the environment is affected by the choice, judgment and decisions of ordinary people. Thus it seeks to introduce the idea that design education is concerned not only with the process of turning raw materials into small end-products but also with wider studies of the design of the environment.

Inevitably the process of designing and making produces waste elements. In addition, every end-product has a limited length of life and will itself eventually be discarded as waste. In this sense the entire process of industry may be seen as a mass garbage-producing enterprise that threatens large scale pollution of the environment.

Consequently the safe and effective disposal of waste is a major design problem. And where conflicting interests are concerned the problem may be of a humanitarian and a moral nature in which an individual person or a small group may need substantial intellectual skills to plead their case against powerful industrial opponents. The dispute over the site of the third London airport is a case in point and illustrates that pollution of an environment is not confined to waste material. Excessive noise can make life intolerable and is therefore a form of pollution.

This filmstrip is concerned with ways in which design affects the

*Design and Craft Education Filmstrip No. 12

quality of everyday life. An attempt is made to introduce young people to those areas of responsibility for the environment that affect the individual, the designer and the industrial producer. The central issues concern the desolation of the countryside through industrial processes, air pollution, water pollution, the design of living accommodation, the design of cities including problems of high density living, transport problems, the recycling of waste products and noise pollution.

In each of these aspects of design a number of conflicting interests may be found. The manufacturer competing in world markets is compelled to sell as cheaply as possible. He will therefore be tempted to dispose of waste at a minimum cost. His methods may not be in the best interests of preserving a clean environment but they may be in the best interests of maintaining employment for large numbers of people.

High-rise blocks of flats may not offer ideal living conditions in which to rear small children, but for a given amount of money they may offer accommodation to more families than would be the case if houses were built. They are also far more economic in the use of ground—an important factor in large cities.

The route of a motorway through a city is bound to affect the quality of life for a large number of people, many of whom may have to be rehoused. But the rapid increase in the numbers of motor vehicles, especially heavy lorries, is vital to the industrial life of the city and the country as a whole.

It must therefore be recognized that there can never be a perfect solution to such problems. Decisions will always be a compromise between conflicting interests. The problem of cost will usually figure largely in discussions. The manufacturer, the architect, the road builder are all limited in what they can do by the amount of money available. And at the end of the line the money they use comes from the general public either in the prices paid for goods or in rates and taxes from which government provides social amenities.

It is naive to suppose that problems of pollution can be solved simply by making new laws, or that in redesigning our roads and cities everyone will benefit immediately. Progress for one section of the community may be possible only at the expense of others. It is therefore necessary to consider all the factors involved before deciding where the best course of action may lie.

These slides show a number of factors in broad relationship to each other as starting points for discussion of local conditions. It is intended that students will select aspects of their own environment for detailed study.

A course of studies in design may lead to a CSE assessment. An example of such a course is given in *Education Through Design and Craft*[11] Chapter 4. One part of this course is a broad study of the problems that arise in man's attempts to design the environment in which he lives. The student is required to undertake a detailed study of a topic of his own choosing within his own locality and to present a written project for assessment. This type of study may be seen as an extension of design and craft education in the senior school. It is a positive contribution to the student's awareness of social problems and an attempt to alert him to his own capacity and responsibility for the decision making processes of society.

Teachers interested in developing such courses may find the following extract of value:

The course will be based on a study of the interplay between man, the design of his material environment and the quality of life.

Part 1

A study of man's primary needs in:

  1 shelter—the home, the community;

  2 food—production, distribution, preparation;

  3 clothing—function, aesthetics, fashion and personal expression.

Part II

A study of changes in the natural environment that improve or pollute the quality of life:

  4 problems and benefits of industrialization;

  5 tools, machines, and production processes;

  6 pollution and conservation, social responsibilities of the individual, of the designer and of industry;

  7 automation and the changing pattern of employment;

  8 buildings and cities;

  9 transport;

  10 communication;

  11 advertising and consumer discrimination.[19]

This filmstrip is intended to offer a starting point for such studies. In the local situation teaching material can be obtained from a variety of sources—newspaper articles, photographs, visits, students' own experiences, visiting speakers, and so on.

The choice of visiting speakers merits particular attention. A doctor or nurse may have much to contribute about the problems of hospital provision, a social worker may give detailed first-hand information about the problems of elderly people living in old accommodation, an architect may be invited to speak about town and city planning, high-rise flats and high-density living, an engineering executive may be able to offer young people valuable information about industrial production and the disposal of waste or about problems of reduced employment arising from the development of automated processes, and a housewife with infant children may well be the best person to talk about the problems of rearing young children in the limited accommodation offered by a high-rise flat.

In the fifth year the student's individual study should take him into real social situations that involve face to face contact with real people and the design problems that affect their lives.

Commentary

Many areas of our lives depend upon things that have been designed and made by man. We are therefore able to improve the quality of our lives by improving the quality of things that we use. Stonehenge is one of the earliest buildings designed by man for a specific purpose. When it was built it was a great feat of engineering.

Only a few thousand years have elapsed since Stonehenge was built. During that time man has gained most of his knowledge. From primitive beginnings he can now design and build rockets that will take him to the moon and explore outer space. Earth satellite tracking stations, such as this one at Goonhilly Down in Cornwall, now exist in many parts of the world. What do you suppose the men who built Stonehenge would think of flying to the moon?

Primitive man developed into space explorer because he has always looked for better ways of doing things. When something new was designed the old became waste. New processes cause machinery to become out-dated and old buildings give way to new. You can see this process taking place in almost every town or city in the world.

New houses such as these offer better living accommodation than the old terraced houses we have just seen. But to build anything new raw materials are required.

One of the main raw materials used in building is clay processed into bricks. Bricks, of course, cost money. But there is another kind of price we pay.

The process of turning clay into bricks involves heat treatment. If the heat is provided by burning coal this is the sort of damage that we can do to the atmosphere we breathe. In some industrial areas people still live and work in atmospheres like this. In recent years clean air laws have done much to reduce this problem but it is worth remembering that no law yet exists to prevent motor vehicles discharging poisonous exhaust gases into the air you breathe. How much exhaust gas do you think they discharge into the air every day?

Sometimes pollution is not easy to see. This picture shows the chimney of a central heating boiler. The fumes that come from it are colourless. Before the boiler was installed the trees on the right were all sound and healthy. Two years later the one in the middle was dead and parts of the others were no longer able to produce leaves.

217

This picture shows what a clear atmosphere can be like. This is Loch Dery in central Ireland and the hills in the far distance are several miles away.

This desolate stretch of countryside in central England is part of a clay works. The water in the pool is stagnant and lifeless, the ground is barren.

Desolation of this kind can make people careless of their surroundings. This old pram was thrown away by someone who thought that it didn't matter. That person helped pollute the world we live in.

Pollution of our world often occurs because people take the easy and cheap way out. The waterways of our country offer a cheap and easy means of waste disposal. This waterway has already become an open sewer with empty tins and other rubbish being dumped in it.

The waterways are especially attractive to those who wish to dispose of chemical waste. This waterway in an industrial town discharges into a major river. This picture may give you a clue as to why dead fish are often seen floating in our rivers. One solution may be that manufacturers should be responsible for the safe disposal of all waste. But this would result in higher prices that would be passed on to the customer.

This river flows through a large park in the heart of an industrial city. Thanks to laws recently introduced to prevent the dumping of industrial waste, the river now supports wild life and offers a pleasant amenity to the people.

Unfortunately some of the people do not appreciate a clean river. This picture was taken from the same position as the previous one. This is not industrial waste, it is rubbish thrown into the river by ordinary individuals.

One of the most important parts of our life is the home we live in. These flats are part of a new housing scheme that is replacing the old property we saw earlier. Notice that the architect has provided a car park but no play area for small children. They still have to play in the street.

In many towns and cities high-rise blocks of flats provide living accommodation for large numbers of people. In many ways they are better than the old accommodation they replaced. But they present some new problems in family life. For example, what are the problems of rearing small children when you live on the fifteenth floor? For them play is one of the most important activities through which learning takes place. But where can young children run and jump and make a noise, and be curious about their world when they are confined to four rooms and the corridor outside? Local councils obviously have a difficult problem. With limited money and land they often have to provide living accommodation for large numbers of people. Are high-rise flats the best solution to this design problem?

Not only housing but entire cities are in the process of being re-designed. In many shopping areas large numbers of people compete with large numbers of vehicles. Here we see a street that has been closed to traffic in order to make a safe shopping concourse.

In many cities large shopping precincts are designed specially for the pedestrian. In these precincts the shopper can buy almost everything he wants. But they are often built some distance away from the areas where people live.

Thus the provision of transport may be viewed as part of the problem when a city is being redesigned. If people are compelled to live some distance from the shops what are the arguments for a free transport service? Or should a transport service have to make a profit in order to survive?

The development of new roads presents society with major problems. People and goods have to move about quickly and efficiently if industry is to work smoothly. And people want to use motor vehicles for leisure purposes. But new roads cut across people's homes and take up valuable farm land. If you live near a motorway the noise can become a major nuisance. When new roads are being planned, how can the people who will be most affected have their views considered?

One result of better motorways is that ever increasing numbers of people drive into city centres instead of travelling by rail. In some American cities this problem now presents a major health hazard from vehicle exhaust fumes. Ways of reducing this danger are known but would cost more and result in lower engine performance. Do you think motorists would willingly pay more for lower performance to achieve a cleaner atmosphere? If not should the law demand cleaner exhaust systems?

Not only do cars take up road space, they also take up parking space. Large areas of ground are now required for this purpose. Multi-storeyed car parks are now found in every city. Some are not very attractive buildings. Could they be made more attractive or even be put underground out of sight?

Today the car may be taking the family on an outing. But some day it will go to the breaker's yard. Like everything else it will become waste. Fortunately much of the material on an old car can be melted down and used again. But what about plastic waste, dangerous chemical waste, and nuclear waste? Do you know what types of waste are produced by factories in your area? And more important, do you know how they dispose of it?

Noise is a form of pollution. It can make living conditions unbearable if it is uncontrolled. Heavy traffic on narrow roads passing through older towns causes this problem. Airports are another source of trouble. We know that aircraft and lorries are essential. The problem is to decide where the balance lies in allowing a level of noise that does not destroy the quality of life of the people who have to live with it.

For example, can you as a future citizen demand of your local authority or of your government that ring roads be provided to divert heavy traffic from your town or village? How can you join in the decision-making processes that affect the quality of your life and the environment in which you live? If your voice is to be heard your arguments must be based upon a sound knowledge of design. What are the important questions that need to be asked about the future development of your town or village? And more important still—will you know how to ask those questions?

Examples of study topics

1 Design problems in bed-sitter accommodation.
2 The ergonomics of kitchen equipment and layout.
3 House design for the small family.
4 The design and provision of social/recreational amenities for young people on housing estates.
5 Play equipment for small children.
6 Problems of providing play facilities for small children in 'skyscraper' blocks that house large numbers of people.

222

7 The design of new methods of food production on small farms.
8 The design of food processing methods in factories.
9 The design of labour saving equipment in the home.
10 Trends in the use of plastics in the home.
11 The importance of fashion to the clothing industry.
12 The increasing use of computers, automation and techniques of mass production and their effect on the employment of young people during the next ten years.
13 Mechanized processes that enable one man to do work that formerly required several workers using hand processes.
14 Noise as a form of pollution.
15 Problems of conservation.
16 Benefits and problems of the motor car.
17 Road design and related social problems.
18 The future of the railway as a means of transport.
19 Transport systems of the future.
20 Consumer choice. The testing of branded goods such as washing powders against the claims of the maker.
21 The technique of advertising.

Filmstrip

Helping Out*

Teachers' notes

The purpose of this filmstrip is to help teachers introduce the subject of school and community service to senior students in secondary schools. It is intended that the examples given shall be used as starting points for discussion and the identification of problems within a local situation. In some instances needs similar to those illustrated may be encountered locally, but it is stressed that the examples given should not be copied. The educational value of the approach lies in the problem-solving activities with which students become involved. To copy

*Design and Craft Education Filmstrip No. 13

existing solutions to problems would therefore substantially reduce the value of the work.

Before students view the filmstrip it is helpful if the teacher discusses with them the broad idea of school and community service, suggesting that they may know people who could be helped by the designing and making of simple equipment. The teacher should also try to arrange visits to nearby institutions such as geriatric hospitals, schools for the disabled and infants' schools in order that students have the opportunity to identify problems for themselves. Such visits are not often fruitful if they are limited to a quick conducted tour; students need to spend at least half a day, and longer if possible, working with, playing with and generally living the lives of the people they are visiting. A discussion following the viewing of the filmstrip may serve as a briefing session for such visits.

When arranging a visit it is probable that the teacher will receive many suggestions from the resident staff concerning problems the students could tackle; most institutions will have needs for repairs to be carried out, shelving to be fitted, and so on. In such a situation the teacher is faced with the delicate problem of explaining to the institution staff that his students must be allowed to identify design problems for themselves. He should point out that, although the students will probably look to the staff for considerable help, direct requests for specific jobs to be done should be avoided if the work is to benefit both parties.

It may also be extremely helpful if someone who works in or has close connections with the institution—such as a doctor, nurse, social worker or headmistress—could give an introductory talk to the students.

Commentary

All the slides you are about to see illustrate work that has been carried out by senior students in secondary schools. The important thing to notice is that all the work was undertaken to solve problems either within the school or for other people outside the school. You may know of similar problems.

While you are watching these slides think of the people you know for whom a special piece of equipment may be of great help. Perhaps you know an elderly person or someone with a disability who requires help of a practical kind. Or perhaps there is an infants' school or a hospital close by where you could find many design problems. Perhaps the easiest place in which to start looking for design problems is within your own school, so let us take this as a starting point.

Most schools possess articles of furniture that have been made by members of staff helped by senior students. This table, in the entrance hall of a school, was made in this way, but it is interesting to see that concrete has been used in a decorative fashion in its construction.

Canoe camping is now a popular activity in many schools. In this particular school students built a fleet of ten canoes. This, of course, presented a problem of transport. How would you tackle the problem of transporting ten canoes with camping equipment to the waterside?

The students explored a number of ideas. They made sketches and models to try out the ideas and finally produced a design for a trailer which would meet their needs.

The box trailer houses the camping equipment and the canoes are fastened on racks. The whole thing can be towed by a small car.

These girls are making tea for some of their friends in what they call their school flat. Originally, the room was a classroom but they divided it into the living areas one would normally find in a flat. Then they designed and made the furniture and decorated the flat themselves.

The layout of the kitchen for ease of working and the testing and selection of kitchen equipment involved the home economics department in a great deal of work. The ceramic wall tiles were designed and made by pupils in the pottery department.

Smaller items provided many opportunities for design work. Here we can see work in wood, metal, fabrics, beaten metalwork, pottery and an attractive piece of sculpture made of milk straws.

The flat is now a meeting place for senior students where they can relax over a cup of tea with their friends. Few schools are fortunate enough to have a classroom to spare for such work. Although there may be an old building which can be renovated.

The old building you see here housed toilet facilities, but the students of the school knocked out the partition walls and redesigned the interior. The building now contains a vehicle maintenance workshop at the front and fifth-form centre at the rear.

These boys had no ready-made accommodation. They wanted a fifth-form centre so they designed and built one. They prepared the site and worked with concrete, brick, timber, plaster, polystyrene and every other material used in building structures. They now have a large centre that includes a common room, shop, office, and other facilities.

This old cottage was bought by a school to be used as a field study centre. Not only did the students undertake the repair and interior decoration of the building, they also designed and made all the equipment necessary to enable groups of students to live in the building for periods of several days.

This is the dining room. A new floor has been fitted and furniture designed and made by students in the school has been installed. The cottage was seventy miles away from the school so the transport of bulky furniture in small vehicles was a problem. A solution was found by transporting the furniture in pieces and assembling it at the cottage.

This is another school project which was designed and built by students. Although the building is not complete, because the ends have still to be fitted, it is already in use as a base for community service. It is full of old timber which is converted by students into firewood and distributed to old age pensioners.

There are endless opportunities for students to help other people. The first step is to find out who needs help. For example, this old lady is a widow. A few years ago her only son died in rather tragic circumstances and she is now completely alone in the world.

Her needs were discovered by a local secondary school. Great care was needed in approaching her with an offer of help because old people often do not like to accept help from strangers and they are sometimes frightened of vigorous teenagers. Nevertheless, the students gained her confidence and were able to redecorate her bungalow completely.

They even took some school equipment to the bungalow. This girl is working in the lounge on a school sewing machine making new curtains.

Elderly people often develop infirmities that make even simple actions like climbing or descending stairs very difficult. This sort of problem can be worse after a period of illness. If they are confined to their beds for any length of time elderly patients rapidly lose their muscle tone and need carefully supervised exercise to regain fitness.

This boy found such a problem on a visit to a geriatric ward, that is, a hospital ward for elderly patients. The only equipment available to help elderly patients learn to walk again was the walking frame you see here. There was nothing to help them learn to climb stairs.

This boy is holding a model of a unit designed and made by a group of students to meet this need. It consists of a central platform with handrails, at one end are two fairly high steps and at the other, three shallower steps. This unit has been built full size and is now in use in that hospital ward.

The needs of small children also offer many opportunities for community service projects. The seat on which these infant children are sitting was designed and made by boys in a neighbouring secondary school.

Having identified the need for seats of this kind in the infant school playground the secondary school students then became involved in a number of design problems. For example, the height of the seat was established by measuring the knee height of a number of children and finding the average.

The ends of the seats were made of moulded concrete. Since the students were unfamiliar with the working properties of this material some experiments had to be carried out to discover the best mixtures and reinforcing techniques.

Infant and junior school children find great pleasure in keeping pets at school. There are many good reasons why this should be encouraged but unfortunately the right sort of facilities do not always exist. Again, senior students can help by making the right sort of equipment to fit the needs of the school.

A study of the play habits of children can be fascinating. Why do they play? How do they play? When we look at these questions in relation to the design problems that they raise it is obvious that the school workshop has much to offer.

Look carefully at this picture. What is wrong with the horse? If you were designing a rocking horse for this child how high would you make it?

This little girl attends a special school for educationally sub-normal children. Complicated toys would be beyond the abilities of children like this. Here, simplicity is essential and this box of bricks, of different sizes, shapes and colours, is a good example of the sort of thing a senior school can make to help these children.

The problems facing disabled people, regardless of their age, can be very great. Disabled people usually have their own individual problems because no one else has a disability quite like theirs. Consequently, each case presents unique design problems which may not be suitable for tackling on a commercial scale. This is where the school workshop can help.

The child you see here is suffering from spina bifida. His particular need was for a piece of equipment that would enable him to exercise his legs and would also allow him to move about. Equipment such as this could often be designed and made by students in a secondary school.

Most of us enjoy working with tools and materials. I think you will agree that when this work can be turned to the advantage of others less fortunate than ourselves it becomes very much more worthwhile.

Filmstrip

Playthings*

Teachers' notes

It is well known that play activities are vital to the learning process, helping the child to progress from infancy to adult status. But play activities involve many facets and stages of learning and may, therefore, be studied in several ways and to different levels. The child psychologist, the parent, the toy designer each have a different view of play and make a different contribution to the child's development.

The purpose of this filmstrip is to introduce the subject to senior students in secondary schools to help them undertake design-based activities related to the needs of children. It draws attention to various stages of child development and the way play equipment assists the child's progress in certain directions. A number of design considerations are mentioned but only to alert the student to factors that must be taken into account. The filmstrip should, therefore, be used as an introductory statement to prepare students for visits to primary schools, playgrounds or other places where children may be observed at play.

A number of factors should be stressed:
1 Play is a learning experience.
2 Play experiences are a vital part of a continuous process of development.
3 Play usually involves equipment of some sort, whether it be a purpose-designed toy or an object found and used in some way.
4 Play is a complex activity usually involving more than one element

*Design and Craft Education Filmstrip No. 14

of child development. It is often not easy to separate the various strands or stages of development.

5 Although a single toy may serve more than one purpose it is important to try to specify its purposes before trying to design it. Vaguely defined problems can be confusing; for example the briefs 'design a toy for a nursery' or 'design a wheeled vehicle' will not help the secondary school student focus on any particular facet of child development.

6 The student will not be equipped to focus on any particular aspect until he has observed children at play and gained an understanding of their needs. Before undertaking observation visits it may be useful for students to compile a set of questions so that they are constantly reminded of the things they should be observing.

Commentary

Play is an important activity for many kinds of young animals. Not only does it offer valuable physical development but also enables other forms of learning to take place.

The process of learning begins from the moment of birth. Throughout childhood play is an important means of learning. This baby, playing with a rattle, is learning about his own senses of touch and hearing.

As the baby grows further exploration of materials takes place. He chews, pulls, throws, tears, and so on, all the time learning more about the materials that surround him.

From these activities he learns that some things are related to other things; that things can be fitted together. Play such as this helps him learn to control his own movements.

These bricks demand the same degree of precision to fit together as those in the last picture. But their sheer size means that the *scale* of the construction becomes an important element.

The developing ability to move about with safety means that the environment of a house can be explored and all sorts of tools and inventions discovered. 'Where does the water come from?' His mother may say that he is getting into mischief; actually he is trying to learn more of the world about him.

Children are able to shape materials to suit their own needs from quite an early age. Consequently it is important that they should have access to easily-worked materials such as paper, card, Plasticine and powder paint. What they make at this stage doesn't really matter; it's what they learn about themselves and about the materials that is important.

This sort of play enables the child to act out his own fantasies and imagination. From a few blocks of different sizes this boy has made a railway engine. Can you identify the cab, and the boiler and the funnel?

This child has not used ready-made materials at all. He has collected an assortment of things and assembled them quickly using simple tools. Is this, perhaps, a space vehicle in which he is playing the part of some television hero?

Once again the scale of the toy has become important. Even though these boys are using only small blocks they have assembled them into a large railway engine which they are now driving.

Some forms of play stay with us right into adult years. This man too is playing at trains. To build this engine required very high levels of skill and knowledge. As we grow older play becomes more skilful.

At some stage in a child's development it begins to copy the behaviour of the parents. Using a real hammer and nails is great fun, but perhaps more important is an understanding of the weight and movement of the tool and the sensation of hammering.

The urge behind other forms of play may be to imitate more general roles. This little girl with her doll and pram may be imitating the role of a mother.

Similarly this little boy playing with his garage and vehicles is exploring the world of the motor car.

The desire to explore the world and the life of adults can be seen in the urge of young children to dress up. This is another form of play acting in which children try out different roles. Care must be taken, however, to prevent the use of dangerous materials. For example, the use of a plastic bag to represent a space helmet could easily cause suffocation.

Learning to communicate is a very important skill developed through play. First we learn to speak, then to write. Toys that encourage young children to speak are very useful. Because of its telephone shape this simple wooden toy helps the child imitate grown-up behaviour and encourages him to practice his speech skills too.

The ability to calculate is also very important. Playing shops can be a great help in learning the simple skills related to numbers. The equipment here is very simple; all the children can buy in this shop are conkers and acorns. The senior girls here improved this equipment in several ways which offered these children greater opportunity to develop their number skills. Can you think of ways in which the equipment could be improved?

A toy such as a wendy house may be the focus for several kinds of play. This one can also be used as a shop. An important aspect of toys like this is that they enable children to play as a group. In co-operating with one another they are learning some necessary social skills.

The physical side of a child's development is also very important. Activities such as rolling, tumbling, climbing and wrestling help develop confidence in many physical skills.

In this way climbing is particularly important. Young children will climb most things—gates, trees, and so on. Given the right units they will even build their own mountain. These units offer wide opportunity for imaginative physical play but they could perhaps be made safer if some means of locking them together were provided. Do you think you could design and make such a locking unit?

This apparatus is professionally made and it, too, enables children to climb. But there are many ways in which apparatus like this can be enlarged to help children extend themselves in other physical ways. How many ways can you think of?

When you observe children at play you will probably notice how much they love to hide inside things. These infants are playing with a ready-made toy on which they can stand, or put things in, or hide in. It must be remembered, however, that some play situations are potentially dangerous. The 'hiding' type of activity has resulted in many serious accidents resulting from small children hiding in old refrigerators, workmen's tool chests, and so on.

These children, older and stronger, need something more durable. This wooden box, which has clearly been played with a good deal, serves the same purpose as did the cardboard box.

Many toys offer a child opportunity to explore and develop ideas by using some form of construction. Such toys range in difficulty from simple wooden building blocks to complex units and may be used by children over a wide age range. This nine-year-old boy is now developing the ability to organize his ideas in a very orderly way. Toys of this type may be very helpful here.

These boys are constructing a model aircraft and most people, perhaps, would describe what they are doing as 'play' or 'a leisure activity'. In fact, what they are doing is very serious; it must be done properly and accurately if they are to achieve the best results. If this is play then it is very serious play and involves a great deal of learning. At the beginning we said that play is an important means of learning. At this stage play is becoming very controlled indeed and gradually as these boys grow older their learning through play will become learning through work.

When you go to a nursery school or observe children at play you may, perhaps, understand a little about the sorts of things they learn from their toys and apparatus. But sometimes the equipment young children have to use makes difficulties. These toddlers have a problem—their sand tray is too high and seems to be causing them some annoyance. It is certainly causing them some difficulty and restricting their ability to play. What might you do in a situation like this?

This boy found an answer of his own. He has brought together two previously unrelated things—the chair and the tray. In this way he has acted very much as a designer in resolving the problem.

Later he found a still better answer. He has now achieved a natural state of affairs in which he can play in the sand as he would on the seashore.

Climbing equipment as we saw earlier is often provided in infant and junior schools. This secondary school boy observing these children at play decided that he could build a better climbing frame than this. What kinds of improvements would you suggest?

Students in one secondary school designed and built a complete adventure playground. They worked with timber, plastics and concrete to provide a wide range of play opportunities. But before they could begin they had to learn about the way in which play activities help us all to learn and to develop. You, too, will find that in order to design and construct satisfactory play equipment you will have to study the needs of your customers—the children at play.

Section 3
Materials and Leisure

7
Designing for Leisure

Patterns of work related to leisure activities

Few would deny the desirability of increased leisure; few also would deny the importance of the constructive, even creative, use of leisure time. The opportunities for gaining knowledge, experience and pleasure outside one's immediate surroundings are expanding rapidly; even those who live in crowded city centres are able to participate in such pursuits as sailing or gliding. At the same time modern travel has made it possible to reach other countries where climate conditions are more suitable to a particular pursuit —skiing is a good example.

But the field of leisure covers more than just the physical sports. For some it may mean work in the garden, improving one's home, 'customizing' a motor car, designing a stage set for a local dramatics society production or devoting one's energies to the relief of hardship in the community—in fact any activity that takes place outside of the work situation. All such activities should be taken into account when providing opportunities for students to become involved in leisure pursuits.

Possible activities

Work springing from school workshops can help young people to come to grips with a range of activities and to realize that what is work for some can be pleasure to others. Whether a pastime is drawn from a field where physical effort is important or where less strenuous approaches are appropriate, school workshops may be able to make a contribution by bringing about a more expert understanding of many aspects of the subject.

One example of such a contribution is in model-making. This is a vast field that calls for relatively little strenuous physical effort, yet much of the work that it generates is synonymous with activities in school workshops.

The increasingly popular hobby of making model trains requires know-

243

J

ledge, skill and the ability to seek out information if replica models are to be successfully produced and operated. A range of tools and materials may be required for the fashioning of various parts and, in addition, the student may call on a range of school subjects in his pursuits. The same could be said of many other model-making themes such as air-craft, boat, cars and soldiers.*

The production of equipment for a range of sports such as archery, boating, canoeing and karting has long been considered a legitimate part of craft education. Indeed, there are many aspects of craft education that can be viewed, ultimately, as a contribution to leisure. Motor vehicle work, for example, is both a study in its own right and the beginning of a responsible and competent enjoyment of motoring in later life.

Because of the necessary safety factors and the rigid design limits imposed on equipment used for some sports, particularly where a system of competition classification operates, the opportunity for students to undertake original design work may be limited in such activities as yachting and canoeing. In this situation there may be no alternative to the use of ready-made designs, at least as a starting point for the students' own design work.

Opportunities offered

Together with other subjects in the curriculum, design and craft offers opportunities to stimulate latent interests, promote existing interests, increase competence and develop enduring enthusiasms.

Expertise within a particular field may require skill in using and maintaining manufactured equipment, yet demand a different set of skills in producing the equipment itself. Although the two may be connected, it is in the area of the production of equipment that much of the work related to leisure may be developed in school workshops. The values of such work lie, of course, not only in the manipulative practices involved but also in problem-solving and the wider satisfaction that results from the application of equipment. At the same time, school workshops may be a necessary stage, even a spring-board, in the development of interests in which the actual production of apparatus plays no direct part.

A planned development

Some work may arise quite spontaneously from the present interests of students. Nevertheless, on a long-term basis it is wise to plan for additional opportunities to be made available.

*'War game' enthusiasts often go to considerable lengths to ensure the authenticity of the soldiers they make. There is scope here for the involvement of mathematics and technical drawing in the scaling of men and equipment, and history in checking the accuracy of costume, equipment and battle strategy.

Leisure may influence the work of the secondary school at any stage, although it is likely that greater emphasis, both of time and magnitude of undertakings, may be found in later years. Not all students will take up all available possibilities; a flexible approach is therefore necessary. As with so many other curricular activities there is a blurring between work based in school and that based outside the school. Indeed, one of the values of leisure activities is that the school may be linked with local and national organizations functioning outside the school.

A problem-solving approach to leisure activities

Structured developments within the school usually begin with the recognition that the production of leisure equipment may be as educationally beneficial as any other kind of activity and, that being so, that much of the work can lend itself quite naturally to a problem-solving approach.

There is considerable scope for investigating and establishing the boundaries of a problem and for determining the individual aspects of the function, form and construction of a piece of equipment. The nature of the work also permits an exhaustive evaluation period from which further knowledge can be gained.

A possible danger is that, motivated by a strong leisure interest, students may attempt to tackle problems that are beyond their capabilities.

Only the most able may be in a position to undertake the full design of a musical instrument, for example, beginning with an examination of how sound is produced and amplified, or the design of a full-size boat hull taking into account the necessary safety considerations.

In cases of this sort the majority will be forced to seek some expert help. But in many other instances, where the constraints are either less complex or less critical, the entire problem-solving approach can be successfully adopted.

Extending the scope of an activity

An examination of the problem-solving potential of an activity may often reveal ways in which it might be extended to include additional elements. An activity like photography, for example, is commonly tackled in terms of the production of photographic equipment—developing trays, tripods, and so on.

While this is valid in design and craft terms the practice of photography itself leads to a much wider field of activity, including not only its theory and application but also photo-journalistic and advertising techniques in which visual stories and ideas are put together, and the design of filmstrips or slide sequences to tell a story or convey information.

This might lead to the design and production of films or sophisticated 'photoplays' in which slides are used in a two- (or even multi-) projector system synchronized with a tape-recorded sound track.

Links with other subject areas may become essential if adequate investigation and evaluation are to be included. For example, it would probably be in conjunction with teachers arranging outdoor pursuits that camping gear would be assessed. Historical elements would be important where a thorough understanding of, say, the development of steam engines were required. A study of flight would necessitate the appreciation of relevant scientific principles.

All these extended activities will be affected both by the availability of resources within the school and the commitment of the students. One object in including such activities as part of design and craft would be to illustrate that there are many possible levels of involvement within a particular field. Some people are willing to spend all their spare time developing a single interest, others may pursue several, while some may be spasmodic in their approach devoting short periods of effort at irregular intervals.

Activities outside the school

It may sometimes be necessary to undertake practical work away from the school itself. This may take the form of surveys, since for many the idea of leisure means not only participation in an activity but also the planning, organizing and preparation that precedes participation.

One school, for example, is involved in the restoration of a thickly overgrown canal bank area to provide picnic and recreation areas, information points at which local *flora* and *fauna* are identified, seating, rubbish bins, and so on. An important aspect of this scheme is that the students are contributing to something that is not necessarily of direct benefit to themselves but offers opportunities for the increased enjoyment of leisure by other members of the community.

Another project linking community service and leisure is described in 'Case Study: A Place for Drama'. Here the students designed and produced a number of portable, standard platform and screen units for use in local village halls and community centres which, it had been discovered, had very limited facilities for mounting any kind of theatrical production.

The students' contribution was, again, not so much to the enrichment of their own but other people's use of leisure.

The value of leisure-based work

Some further indications of the range and depth of work possible will be found in the supplementary teachers' book *Design and Karting*[12] and in the case studies in this chapter. The conclusions of the experiences described in these publications are that work in this field is valuable because it:

1 springs unequivocally from students' interests;
2 establishes co-operation between schools and outside organizations;
3 enhances the students' vision of possible leisure time pursuits;
4 enables students to become more discerning purchasers, both of leisure equipment and of goods for general use;
5 often makes a pursuit economically viable, especially where equipment can be manufactured;
6 offers opportunities for students to form their own clubs and societies;
7 enables students to gain experience of working as individuals and as members of a team;
8 gives scope for those who wish to compete to do so.

This list is probably as good an indication as any of the potential of education for leisure through the use of materials.

Case Study

A Place for Drama

In the following report a craft teacher explains how his school, situated in a rural area of Wales, attempted to deal with some of the social and leisure needs of its students and the local community. In this project aspects of community development were at least as important as those of leisure.

One of our main problems is to compensate for the lack of certain social and cultural experiences readily available to students in a more highly populated district. Not only do we see our role as providers of opportunities in, say, music, art and drama, but also that we leave our students able to develop and extend their particular talents in their own locality.

We were happy to join the Keele project since it has given us the chance to rationalize approaches which encourage our students to become aware of and involved in a range of activities associated with stage productions in this area. Furthermore, we feel that our ongoing activities are achieving something more than the 'know-how' of stage productions and their role in this rural area. Our students have developed their ability to undertake and analyse surveys, to identify problems of a practical nature and, what is even more important, to solve some of these problems.

The background of our project

In the main our students have concentrated on developing equipment which could fulfil a number of needs in the surrounding villages. It would seem that with the rich tradition of home-spun entertainment within the villages we have a central part to play in designing and making portable stage equipment.

However, it did not turn out to be as easy as we first anticipated. Except for the rare visit to one of the seaside towns during the holiday season students at this school have not in the past had much opportunity of seeing professional stage shows of any standard. This in itself need not be a drawback since there is often a certain honesty about the sort of 'peasant culture' (if one dare mention the term) associated with home-made entertainment. This is often easier to tolerate than the veneer of professionalism associated with some professional shows.

The visits of 'The Welsh Theatre Company' to rural areas are gradually changing this situation, and we now get the opportunity of seeing two or three very professional performances of new, modern Welsh plays each year. These are always very well presented and have served to make people aware of what can be achieved with limited resources.

Musical shows of a very high professional standard have also been held recently in centres within the school's catchment area. Such shows performed on their own school or village hall stage prove to the children that the magic and mystique of the professional theatre or opera do not demand purpose-built accommodation before becoming realities.

One factor that is rather disappointing is that the new community centres that are springing up in a number of villages are sadly lacking in the basic necessities of staging a show of any sort. This perhaps underlines the fact that the Welsh are still rather suspicious of those who smear themselves with grease paint and are in any way responsible for a bit of make-believe.

An incident comes to mind of a well known local drama company arriving at a small village hall to perform a play which called for luxurious settings. They themselves provided all the scenery except for the furniture which the local committee had promised to provide. The producer was presented with an old, heavily carved bardic chair, a sofa which had lost most of its stuffing and a broken-down piano. When, it was explained that something more elaborate was required the ready reply was 'People have bought tickets to see a play, not a furniture exhibition!' This is the background against which we have begun to develop in our students a deeper appreciation of the role of the stage in their leisure time.

The boys working on this project are from the fourth year and have chosen not to take external examinations. These students are likely to remain behind in these rural areas and therefore the maintaining and furtherance of village life will rest on their shoulders.

An initial survey

In order to convince ourselves that we were becoming involved with a relevant problem and to provide information that would be of assistance later, we drew up questionnaires. These set out to establish the attitudes of local people towards different forms of stage productions, the likely support that could be expected for possible future ventures and to assess the standard of accommodation available in the area. Analysis of the questionnaires confirmed that there is still considerable activity and a great deal of interest in shows performed at local level.

In compiling and analysing the results of the questionnaires fourth-form students were supported by students from the fifth and lower sixth forms although these have not been concerned with the designing and making side of the project.

7.1 Finding out the attitudes and needs of local people.

Actually, much of the work of evaluating the results was carried out by the fourth-year group. They appeared to find real purpose in calculating such things as percentages and averages when dealing with the nature of the locality, distribution of houses, location of buildings, nature of construction, and so on. By the time sufficient information had been gathered to make drawings and then scale models of possible solutions to problems that had been identified, enthusiasm had risen to quite a pitch.

Identifying the basic problems

Since our survey showed that concerts appeared to be the most popular entertainment (with plays a close second) we decided to concentrate our efforts in this general direction. Nevertheless, we were still confronted with rather a wide scope, so it was decided to select one or two basic problems.

Different stage levels with suitable backgrounds presented themselves as the first necessities. Different elevations are versatile in that individual or large groups of people can use them. (Effective lighting will obviously play an important part in later development.) Elaborate productions calling for large numbers of scene changes can also be attempted with these basic pieces of scenery. (The use of curtains and their introduction into the scheme were also discussed at this stage.)

The boys by this time had identified and confronted themselves with a real design problem—that of designing light, portable platforms that could be folded easily when not in use. The model of the stage which represents typical accommodation in the locality proved quite invaluable in the investigation work.

Experiments showed that platforms measuring approximately 2×1 m and 2×0.6 m and on three different levels of 150, 300 and 450 mm would prove ideal. But when the proposed materials were weighed it was found that each unit would be too heavy for one person to handle, especially in a situation which called for a quick scene change. The platforms for this reason were reduced to 1×1 m and 1×0.6 m.

The back sets for these platforms did not present such a difficult problem for the students. It was clear to them that a vertical surface was required and that it could consist of a lightweight material. Suitable supporting frames were designed and at present the screens are undergoing trials. With these boys we find that wherever possible it is beneficial to isolate individual or groups of problems. Thus we still have to decide on a final method of fixing the screens together (at the moment loose pin hinges are being used) and another system for keeping them upright will have to be developed.

7.2 Loading the platforms before taking them to a village hall.

We are confident that during the trials now being undertaken—already the platforms and screens have proved successful for a variety of scenes in three recent school performances—the students will devise worthwhile practical solutions. The solutions may not always be original but they will spring from experience, the ability to discriminate between alternatives and a desire to help improve facilities for local stage productions.

New insights and interests

Although the work is far from complete signs are that the boys involved have acquired a new insight and interest. The work has already given a direct link between their community and school—they have talked to locals about, what is for them, a new and exciting venture. There is little chance that many of them will make a name for themselves as singers or actors. Nevertheless, they will be able and interested enough to give practical assistance in staging a show in their own village.

As well as suggesting new ways of spending one's leisure hours, the project should prove valuable in furthering the excellent teamwork and community spirit always found when people are involved in this type of work.

Case Study

Constructing a Swimming Pool

Like the preceding case study, this has a large element of school and community development. Not only did it result in the acquisition of additional leisure facilities, but it provided an opportunity for students (and teachers) to work together on a 'man-sized' job. Naturally, in a project of this type the problem-solving approach must be applied with an awareness of the technical problems involved and the need to bring in expert assistance when necessary. Nevertheless, there is considerable educational potential in this type of work, as the following report indicates.

The erection and construction of a heated outdoor swimming pool for the school was suggested to the members of staff in September 1969, quite a bomb-shell at the beginning of term. The intention of the Principal was that the project should not only give educational value in its construction but also provide long-term recreational enjoyment.

The idea was accepted and, after giving the matter serious thought, suggestions were offered as to how some of the money might be raised. Target amounts and approximate dates were discussed. Such was the enthusiasm of the staff—who had worked as a team on previous ventures such as parents' evenings, pantomimes, concerts and sales of work—that the Principal was encouraged to face the challenge.

Raising the money

Things got off to a flying start and the children were soon involved in the financial aspect of the project. Our first effort was an 'Earn-a-Pool Week' along the lines of the familiar Scout Job Week. During this week—the third week in September—the students raised £320. This was a good beginning and they soon found themselves preparing for a sale of work the following month. As well as producing items for sale the budding retailers were responsible for calculating suitable prices and displaying and selling their wares. As a result of their good salesmanship the very rewarding sum of £480 was realized.

Money-raising activities continued throughout the project. A second sale of work produced over £500. By these and other activities— including selling Christmas cards and arranging concerts and dances— we raised a sum in excess of £3000, enough to pay for our pool.

Starting the practical work

After the plans had been accepted by the local authority the craft department was able to start the practical work in the spring of 1970. The site was pegged out and boundary sods were dug to mark the area to be excavated. The mathematics department gave valuable assistance at this stage and many of the boys were interested to discover at first-hand the practical applications of their arithmetic and geometry.

The students calculated the volume of earth which would have to be removed, taking into account the variation in depth between the deep end and the shallow end, and then worked out how much water the pool would contain. They were amazed to discover that it would hold 120 thousand litres !

An excavator was employed to handle the main digging work although, in the interests of greater accuracy, it was necessary to finish off with picks and spades supplied by the rural science department. In this and all other stages in the construction the interest and enthusiasm of the students was maintained. On many occasions were such questions asked as, 'Are we going out to the pool today ?' or 'What's the next stage ?'

The next stage involved laying a sub-floor of a weak mix of concrete and then placing the reinforcing bars. The use of concrete is surely something that every boy should experience and understand—how it is mixed, how a uniform depth is laid, consolidated and spread to a required level or fall. Although most of the concrete was delivered in large quantities by a 'pre-mix' lorry it was necessary to mix smaller amounts with a shovel so students were able to experience most aspects of the use of concrete. With the knowledge and experience gained they should certainly have no trouble laying a garden path !

The amount of planning that went into organizing the biggest 'fill' —nearly 30 cubic metres on the main floor—resulted in a satisfactory day's work. The laborious task of building up the walls of the pool was considerably eased by professional help from a few parents. Soon the cavity wall of patent blocks containing a cage of reinforcing rods was ready to receive the concrete.

The age of the students involved ranged mainly from twelve to fourteen years. Working side by side with their teachers in gum-boots they saw them from a different angle. The students were capable of carrying out all the various tasks; some worked in groups, others were employed on individual jobs, such as measuring and spacing reinforcing, wiring and tying metal bars with pliers, or levelling with the spirit-level to ensure that the hand-rail was correctly positioned with respect to the proposed water level. Some of the less accurate boys in the group proved their endurance and willingness to see the job through, surely a useful attribute in their future lives.

We think that the way the work was arranged was realistic. Clearly our students could not be expected to make all the major decisions concerning the design and construction of the pool. On the other hand it would have been wrong for us to view the students as nothing more than cheap labour. Consequently we endeavoured to engage students in problems as they arose and they were constantly encouraged to think out their own work plans for tackling specific tasks. We learnt that there can be value in accepting ready-made solutions to some problems—a new problem situation then arises of how best to undertake the work with the available resources. This is an organizational and planning problem that we found students were happy to accept.

The team spirit of the male members of staff when extra manpower was required should be mentioned here. This was a reflection of the working spirit in the school and the excellent relationship between the departments.

Final stages

Professional workmen were called in to plaster the walls and floor and to place tiles at hand-rail level. This operation was not without its educational value as the students were able to see a skilled job being done which kept their interest going and, who knows, perhaps helped them to make a decision concerning their future employment.

Teams were organized in relays to paint the floor of the pool blue and the lower portion of the walls white. Our original idea of terrazzo was rejected in favour of paint on cost grounds. Old shoes and clothing were again the order of the day at this stage.

One of the other jobs was the construction of the heating store. The roof members, door and window were fitted by the woodwork department. Skilled craftsmen among the parents were called in again to give expert help with the heating and plumbing. The heating store contains a diatomaceous earth filter, which keeps the water clear and sparkling, and an oil-fired burner capable of raising the water temperature to 24°C.

The calculation of oil consumption together with chlorination and filtration expenses involved the mathematics department. The cost of heating the pool worked out at the surprisingly low amount of 11p per hour. The science department is responsible for keeping regular checks on chlorination and the pH value of the water. These daily records hold the interest of all.

A dream realized

Although the original cost was estimated at £2000 the actual final cost worked out at just over £3000. This total sum was raised in just one-and-a-half years from the conception of the dream. The work that went into planning, raising money, construction, and so on, proved of value to all the students and involved practical links with other subject areas such as mathematics, science, English and rural science. The pool was opened for use amid great excitement on 6 May 1971. It is proving a tremendous asset both to our own students and to those of contributory primary schools. It is, for all of us, the realization of a dream.

Case Study

Designing Land Yachts

During the past three years our craft department has been trying to adapt its teaching methods to cope with the needs of the older non-examination students in the school.

We chose to tackle a project in the 'Materials and Leisure' area and wished to involve wheeled vehicles in some way. Land yachting was finally decided upon for three reasons:

1 running costs are low;
2 the local RAF station had a land yacht club and wished to improve communication with the local populace;
3 the design and manufacture of a land yacht was well within the ability of the students concerned.

Preparing the ground

Having decided on a topic we began to make the necessary plans. The students to be involved were the non-Certificate fourth-year boys and girls. Some difficulties arose over timetables and workshop space which we overcame by making the woodwork and metalwork rooms available one afternoon per week.

The project lent itself very well to team-teaching. After gaining the interest and enthusiasm of various members of staff it was agreed that land yachting should be the central theme in the workshops and should involve other subjects when the occasion arose. We felt that co-operation across a range of subjects would help to identify and solve the wide range of problems that we anticipated.

At this stage we were encouraged because things were going so well. But we were now faced with the big problem of interesting the students in something far from the conventional idea of a craft project which meant a student completing an article to take home. The idea of working together on one job was novel; its success or failure would depend entirely on the reactions of the students themselves.

Another problem we met was our inability to find any information or visual aids of any kind to provide an inspiring introduction. We overcame this problem by shelving the idea of building a land yacht and getting the students to design and build a vehicle with which they were familiar and which they readily accepted as being within their scope—a trolley.

From trolleys to land yachts

When the trolleys had been constructed they were taken into the playground and tested for manoeuvrability, speed, ability to carry passengers, and so on. After much pushing up and down enthusiasm waned as energy ran out and the students decided that engines ought to be fitted. There followed a lively discussion on how to motivate the trolleys other than by manpower. Although the obvious answer seemed to be an engine the initial expense, installation problems and running costs soon discouraged this line of thought.

At this point some enterprising youth suggested a sail and unwittingly launched the project. Sails were soon fitted to the trolleys to see if the idea was feasible and they proved reasonably successful. It was now a simple task to sell the idea of building a land yacht and our project proper was at last under way.

Designing and making

At this stage the students were temporarily divided into two groups. The girls were in the woodwork room constructing model land yachts for

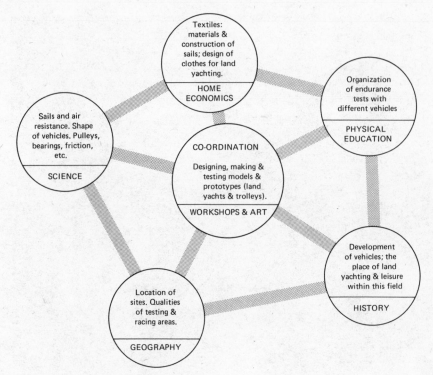

7.4 Possible contribution of subject areas.

experimental purposes, while the boys worked in the metalwork room planning the size, shape and constructional details. Some of these problems were solved by using the models and soon there was a brisk interchange of ideas and information between the two groups. The models were tested in an improvised wind tunnel made by the girls. For a time the corridor between the two rooms was frequently used as a test area.

As the boys had to work out a design appropriate to the materials available there developed a brisk trade with a plumbing contractor who was fitting new boilers in the school. The end result was two $5\frac{1}{2}$ m lengths of 50 mm diameter steel tubing! With this valuable prize enthusiasm burst forth in a series of new designs, one of which was selected and work commenced. I must point out here that we did not produce working drawings, but rather simple sketches with approximate sizes.

As work progressed the students soon organized themselves into work teams—welding, fitting, machine-work—each team having an expert in charge of the rest of the workers.

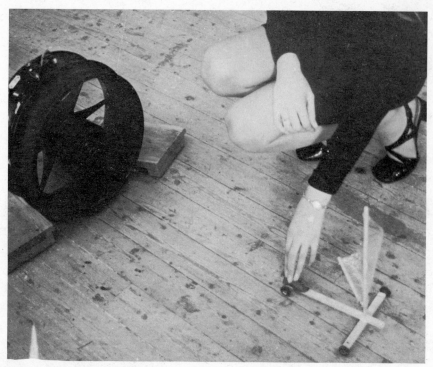

7.5 Testing model land yachts.

Meanwhile, in conjunction with the PE department, a Mirror Dinghy kit had been purchased for the girls to build in the woodwork room. It soon became apparent that some of the girls wished to work on the land yacht and some boys on the dinghy. We did not object to this and soon we had girls welding, fitting and turning, likewise the boys were advising and helping in the woodwork room—a most rewarding sight.

Throughout the project problems were dealt with as they arose and many stimulating discussions were centred on some odd-looking pieces of metal. Many were the looks of amazement from the members of staff as they passed the workshops and glimpsed an apparent shambles of tubes, wheels and valuable scrap. There were questions in the staffroom: 'What time did you finish last night?'—'You were here early this morning!'—'Do you ever close the workshop?' Such questions are an indication of the students' enthusiasm.

Final stages of manufacture

Slowly a shape emerged and the day came when the frame was assembled. In the workshop it seemed enormous; the students stood back and looked on in amazement. This first fitting together boosted their egos and they were ready to tackle the problems of wheels and steering. A few days later a pair of alloy wheels appeared. These were a gift from a parent, one of many who were becoming as interested as their sons and daughters.

At this stage work centred on land yachts started in many other departments in school. The comments of other teachers about the work the students were doing in their subject areas were most rewarding.

At last the wheels and the steering were completed and only the seats, mast and sail were required. Two old tractor seats from a local scrap-yard appeared (a free gift) and were duly fitted to the frame.

This left the mast and sail. These had been a problem from the very beginning. However, a trip to the National Boat Show in London had proved most useful in this respect. While there the students had enquired of various firms specializing in the manufacture of masts and sails and had some idea of what was needed. But, as time was running out, the mast and sail of the Mirror Dinghy were commissioned as a temporary measure.

After some discussion the 'experts' fixed the position of the mast. One week later, resplendent in a coat of paint, the land yacht was assembled in the school playground ready for her first test run.

'Going like the clappers'

There was no shortage of volunteer 'test pilots', complete with crash helmets, and soon two of them were aboard. A brisk breeze was blowing as we eased them out onto the school playing field . . . but the results were most unsatisfactory. She trickled along at a snail's pace taking no advantage of the breeze which had increased quite measurably by now. There were glum faces as they returned and much discussion followed as to why she had failed to meet expectations.

It was finally realized that the mast was too far forward. Work began on the spot to move it to the rear. Never has so much been done in so little time ! Soon she was ready for her second trial, proudly showing the scars of her amputated mast socket.

The results were amazing. She started with a leap and began to accelerate at an alarming rate, manned by two 'pilots' who had never sailed before. As she sped away I began to have visions of trying to explain to parents, governors and all the powers-that-be what had gone wrong.

But my fears were unfounded. With a graceful sweep she turned and headed into the wind and, much to our amazement, was sailed back to her starting point by the owners of two beaming faces whose comments were : 'Fantastic, great, goes like the clappers, you should try her sir.'

Evaluations

Since its trial the land yacht has been used extensively by the students and has been inspected by many interested parties. It aroused much interest at an exhibition of work done in West Riding Schools.

I feel that the students and staff gained much from this project. The staff found that they were no longer teachers but advisers and helpers. As well as being able to use the skills learned in earlier years the students gained many new ones that they would not have encountered had they followed a normal fourth-year course. This enabled individual students to develop skills to a much more advanced level. These skills were soon utilized by the other students and group leaders emerged who were the experts in their own field.

The students were usually able to anticipate problems before they arose and always displayed an eagerness to solve them. It was often the spontaneous solution of unforeseen difficulties that impressed us. In all this one important feature was that for the first time students realized that there was a need even in practical work for maths, science and English. This was certainly the result of these subjects being related to the work in the workshops.

It was on the social side, however, that we noticed the biggest changes. We found that boys and girls would accept each other when working as a team and that they would also accept the natural leadership of individuals. The barrier between teacher and student soon disappeared and we found ourselves treated as one of them. As a result, many of us now believe that it is only when this barrier is removed that we can fully understand the needs of our students. In addition, the gulf between the classroom and the adult world was partly crossed in that the project took the children beyond the classroom; they had to communicate with the 'outside world' many times when seeking help and information.

Project work of this kind is most beneficial and has an important place in the school curriculum, not only for the non-certificate students but as part of the curricular activities of all students. In a narrow sense this project did provide the answer to the problem of meeting the needs of the fourth-year non-certificate student. It was so successful that even before its completion we were doing the vital work of planning for our next project. We hope that it too will 'go like the clappers'.

Section 4
Materials and Work

8
Introducing the World of Work

When considering the world of work the difficulty lies not only in defining the precise role of the school but also in determining the nature of the relevant curricular activity. Dangers arise in that schools may present an image of work that is exaggerated and too removed from the real situation, with the result that young workers quickly become disillusioned. Alternatively, young people in school may become so committed to a purely local occupational role that they may effectively be prevented from seeking or even looking to wider horizons. Schemes must, therefore, be realistic and open ended.

At one level it can be said that schools should provide opportunities for students to find out about work. At another level there is the case for attempting to foster certain attitudes towards work. In practice it is difficult to achieve either one without overlapping with the other. It is difficult to discuss mass production, automation, retraining, unemployment, strikes, and so on, in their social and economic contexts without some idea of commercial and industrial organization and the division of labour that goes with them.

The influence of industry and commerce on the curriculum is broad and does not fall into any particular subject area. It is clear that studies of unemployment, for example, can be a springboard for investigating the economics and politics of and attitudes towards the situation. Similarly, the sciences may adopt a technological phenomenon in order to demonstrate its social and economic impact. The whole field of electronics is a case in point. This area of work, as many schools have shown, can be an extremely fruitful source of design studies for school workshops.

Clearly, there is scope for co-ordination when careers guidance becomes part of the curriculum. Within this there are workshop-based areas of study that may form, not a hybrid, but a contribution with its own particular qualities. Starting with the practical approach may, for many students, be the only means of engaging them upon investigatory and opinion-forming activities related to social and economic factors; activities that are the core of many present-day curricular developments.

The materials subjects and the world of work

If a practical approach is to be included it becomes apparent that the role of the materials subjects needs defining. Themes based on 'work' may be so diverse that school workshops will find it impossible to become directly involved with everything. The scope should be considered in broad terms with workshops making contributions at general and specific levels.

Teachers promoting such work will need to determine their own aims after considering the needs of their students. These are likely to include: making decisions; forming and expressing opinions; exercising responsibility; being aware of their own abilities and limitations; understanding their own role in relation to others; gaining insight into the economic and social organization of the country; buying and using goods and services effectively.

In school workshops there has been a trend to concentrate on 'industry'. This is partly a result of the previous industrial experience of some teachers, and the apparent similarity that sometimes exists between work in school workshops and work in a factory. This has led to activities that present students with opportunities to understand industrial procedure and gain insight into industrial organization. An important addition to this work has been the opportunity for students to apply the design process.

By adopting the outline of work described here and devising a range of suitable activities students may begin to understand:

—employee/employer relationships;
—possible conditions of employment;
—human relations on the job;
—the roles of different personnel and departments;
—the kinds of machinery used in industry;
—the range of processes used in certain industries;
—the influence of new materials on production methods;
—the pressures of advertising and marketing;
—the relevance of school work and further education.

Activities that can have a direct link with school workshops include schemes of work experience, link projects and courses with colleges of further education, and periods of simulated experience when students design and operate a school-based production unit. These areas of work are discussed in this chapter and Chapter 9.

Works visits

In many schools the works visit may be the only occasion when a joint

264

enterprise is planned by school and industry. Such visits may be of little value if they are arranged as isolated activities at the end of term or after examinations. To be of real value visits need to be coupled with the work in school, and the students should be fully involved.

Too often a visit is confined to one aspect of industrial procedure, leaving students with an imprecise and unbalanced impression of how a business enterprise is organized. Appropriate preparation by teachers and students is essential before the visit in order that it may be used to best advantage. Afterwards it is useful to analyse and discuss observations so that the knowledge and experience gained may be consolidated and used effectively in current school work.

Before a visit takes place its precise purpose should be clear. It may often be linked in some way with a theme being conducted across several subjects. At a modest level a visit may be arranged merely to *inform* students that a particular enterprise exists in their locality; that it employs a certain number of people; that it exports a certain proportion of its products; and so on.

At a less superficial level, however, a visit may form part of an experience that enables students to become aware of some of the social and economic effects of industry. Actually seeing an operative carrying out a repetitive routine on a production line may serve as a basis for subsequent discussion or may give insight into the organizational pattern necessary when planning a simulated experience in the school workshop.

Work experience

The essence of work experience is the placing of students in the actual work environment where they may gain first-hand insight into:

—the routine of an occupation;
—the people who work at a particular job;
—the tools, equipment and materials used in a job;
—the abilities required to undertake a particular job;
—the relevance of school subjects.

8.1 Students entering factory.

The potential and the problems

For a number of years, and a variety of reasons, countries such as Sweden, USA and USSR have operated schemes designed to provide students with limited experience of various kinds of employment. Often these schemes have a direct connection with careers guidance, and to some extent the same can be said of provisions made in this country. The Newsom Report[23] indicated the possible general nature of work experience (paragraphs 222–295) and in *Work Experience in British Secondary Schools*[24] the Institute of Careers Officers concludes that 'on balance this activity seems best regarded as social education rather than job sampling'.

How, then, can work experience contribute to design and craft education? For one important reason the contribution is likely to be minimal. The opportunity for placing students in factories will be rare if it exists at all in many parts of the country.

It was estimated that in 1969 less than 25% of a sample of 15-year olds participated in schemes of work experience. It is unlikely that this percentage will show any significant increase.

Nevertheless, for some students on some occasions in some areas valuable links with local industries may be established. (See 'Case Study: A Work Experience Scheme'.)

Links with industry at other levels

Foremost of these links is probably that which arises when work in a school reaches a stage at which the advice and help of industrialists becomes desirable. This may result from the need for expert advice of a technical nature or where special equipment or machinery is necessary to undertake a particular operation.

Examples of such links—which may range from the preparation and reproduction of working drawings and blueprints to highly specialized machining operations—are given in 'Case Study: Restoration at the Studley Royal Estate' and 'Case Study: A Geriatric Project'.

The scope for links with local industry may be illustrated by the following quotation from a report on the design and construction of a piece of play-sculpture undertaken by the Ellesmere Port County Grammar School for Boys which appeared in the Spring 1971 issue of *Education in Cheshire*[25]:

> The firms of Fibreglass Ltd., Re-inforcements Division of Birkenhead, and Freeman's Chemicals Ltd, of Ellesmere Port, were consulted about the use of glass fibre and polyester resin as a weatherproof, hard-wearing 'skin' on the skeleton of steel tubing. Both firms expressed great interest and provided not only the materials, but also most generously supplied free of charge the glass fibre and resin required . . . when a snag arose

in that the school bending-machine could not cope with the size of the tubing required for the 'hoops', Shell Thornton Research Centre very kindly offered their workshop facilities and a group of boys went to Thornton to assist in the task of bending the circles of steel. (The welding was undertaken in the factory and on the site.)

It is possible, therefore, for students to attend factory drawing offices and machine shops either to undertake work themselves or work alongside factory personnel who may be willing to help out.

There are always problems in engaging factory floor workers in the educational aspects of the work, especially where they may be working on a bonus system of payment.

Greater potential exists where factories have apprentice training schools and where regulations of employment and supervision may be more flexible. Although training schools tend to be fully committed they should often offer a flexibility that would enable students to work factory hours, meet apprentices under realistic working conditions, undertake practical work using industrial machines, and use the training school facilities as a genuine extension of those available in the school.

This form of co-operation between school and industry must be of an occasional nature and involve only small numbers of students, but the skilful teacher may introduce such possibilities for consideration at an appropriate point in a project.

The legal position

Setting up schemes of work experience can prove extremely difficult. In the first instance it must be remembered that there are a number of legal conditions which affect this situation. In essence, the law prohibits the employment of children and young people below the statutory school-leaving age as defined by Section 9 of the Education Act of 1962.

The term 'employment' covers activities of any kind in a normal place of employment, whether or not they are carried out for reward or as part of training. It should also be remembered that the law prohibits the employment of young people below the statutory school-leaving age in other kinds of activities except for those prescribed by the Children and Young Persons Act of 1933 (Section 18 and bye-laws).

In addition to these legal difficulties, problems of insurance inevitably arise. Arrangements may vary from LEA to LEA but the possible requirement for extra cover to allow for travelling to and from a factory should be borne in mind.

Safety is obviously extremely important; steps should be taken to ensure that rules are known and followed. Advice should be given regarding dress and behaviour to avoid accidents.

TUC policy

Official Trades Union policy, while supporting the notion that insight into the world of work is desirable, does not favour work experience. Nevertheless, schools which have successfully arranged forms of work experience have usually found little opposition from local TUC member unions.

LEAs and Factory Inspectors

Sources of help and advice are the Local Education Authority and the District Inspector of Factories. The Department of Education and Science has issued at least two memoranda (22/67 and 12/69) on work experience, and local authorities are aware of these. It is the responsibility of LEAs to ensure that proposed schemes do not involve students below the statutory school-leaving age, unless there is evidence to show that the activities do not contravene the law.

Even where students are over the compulsory school age, the LEA and Factory Inspectorate should be consulted. There are legal provisions relating to students between the statutory school-leaving age and eighteen years of age with which schools must comply.

Finally, it should be noted that with the raising of the school-leaving age there may be an increasing demand by schools for access to factories. It is vital that helpful employers be regarded as scarce resources to be conserved, and that local co-ordination be arranged to ensure this.

Case Study
A Work Experience Scheme

In and around our catchment area on the northern outskirts of the city of Leicester there are a wide range of opportunities, both in employment and in further education ; and as a large comprehensive school for the fourteen- to eighteen-year age range, we find that rather over one third of our students leave us each year.

Given this situation, obviously learning about adult working life ought to constitute one of the two or three most important things we do, and this fact has been recognized in a number of practical ways, of which our work experience scheme is one.

It has long been acknowledged, in the country as a whole, that the abrupt change from school to work can be a very worrying and even a frightening time. Too often school leavers go into jobs knowing nothing about them. While still at school they ought to find out about the conditions of work, training, pay, prospects, and other aspects of a wide variety of careers.

Many boys and girls are still in a stage of fantasy about certain careers : they need to realize that even 'glamorous' jobs have a dull, routine side to them. Moreover, it is educationally desirable that young people should have as wide as possible an understanding of all occupations, and not merely of those they may seriously consider taking up themselves. It is for these reasons that we believe work experience to be valuable ; and we are always conscious that it is only through the generous co-operation, support and enthusiasm of our friends outside the school that such a scheme is possible.

Principles of our scheme

In 1964 we arranged a couple of meetings at school with representatives of a number of local firms and organizations in order to discuss with them how we could give our students, while still at school, a greater appreciation and more first-hand knowledge of the world of work, and a better preparation for adult working life. It was as a result of those meetings that we were first able to launch our scheme. The following principles were agreed at the outset and still apply :

1 The school was not to see the scheme simply as a means of placing students, nor employers simply as a means of recruitment.

2 Although work experience could be valuable in itself even without preparation or follow-up, whenever possible it should follow on naturally from what was done in class and should be followed up at school.

3 Employers should give the school a general idea of what work experience they could offer and should then hammer out details with representatives of the teaching staff. Teachers of relevant subjects should be able to visit the firms to see how work experience could be related to lessons.

4 Although one taste of work experience, for the individual student, would be far preferable to none at all, a better aim would be to give a student experience of two or three fields of employment, or if his

269

vocation bent was already particularly strong, then two or three kinds of experience within his particular field.

5 A middle path should be found between offering 'experience' of sweeping floors, brewing tea or licking stamps, and presenting an occupation which has its routine side as something permanently exciting.

6 While large concerns, such as factories having their own training centres, were acknowledged to have an advantage in the facilities they could offer, goodwill and ingenuity would enable smaller firms, offices, etc, to provide work experience which would be equally worthwhile in its way.

How the scheme works

The scheme is chiefly aimed at the fifteen- to sixteen-year group, as these students have reached the legally required age, and the majority who opt for at least one period of work experience (it is not compulsory) are fifth formers.

They are, in fact, invited to make up to three choices. In some years, as circumstances allow, we are able to send fourth formers during the Summer term if they have reached their fifteenth birthday before 1 February. Some sixth formers also take advantage of the scheme. The length of time varies from a visit of only one day to a visit of a whole week, most visits being two or three days. During the school year 1969/70 a typical week involved sending out the following:

—three boys, each for three days, to an engineering firm;
—two boys, each for two days, to do foundry work;
—two girls, each for one day, to a hospital;
—twelve students, each for three days, to different retail stores;
—four students, each for five days, to the catering department of the local university;
—two students, each for two days, to do library work;
—two girls, each for two days, to do clerical work;
—four girls, each for four mornings, to a local play group.

There is some fluctuation from year to year; for instance, in the previous year we were able to send an unusually large number to do clerical work. In addition, sixth formers applying or considering applying to train as teachers at colleges of education are sent to junior and infant schools, or in a few cases to one or other of our associated high schools, for half a day per week for half a term or longer, to observe and help in any way possible.

In all, during 1969/70, approximately 280 students had one or two spells of work experience, each spell averaging a total of approximately three school days. It should be emphasized that the scheme has never been restricted to intending leavers; the fifth formers going out to work experience constitute a complete cross-section of the ability range, including non-examinees at one end and future university candidates (in their 'O-level year'!) at the other.

Each week, prior to a visit, the students concerned are briefed by members of staff. Engineering and foundry work are handled by the technical department, catering and child care by the home economics department, clerical and office work by the commerce department, and so on. Nursing is handled by a teacher who herself had a week's secondment to the Hospital Service. Preparation for other miscellaneous forms of work experience is still handled by the Careers Co-ordinator, who also gives a general briefing to all students.

Follow-up of work experience takes several forms. Sometimes questionnaires are used. Engineering and catering are integrated with the normal school course wherever possible. Tape-recordings of students' impressions were made, initially, for use at a parents' evening. They have proved to be very useful, not least to the organizers in the outside establishments which help us.

The role of the materials subjects

A few special words are called for about the school's technical department, which is particularly well placed for making positive and meaningful contacts with industry and for the preparation and follow-up of work experience courses. Technical subjects are popular options among boys at all levels, some boys spending over one-third of their school time within this department, although one-quarter is a more normal allocation. Girls are welcome to choose these subjects also, and a few of them do, but never as many as we should like.

Close contact is maintained, on the one hand with the art and home economics departments (the three departments constituting the recently integrated design team), and with the mathematics and science departments on the other. Although the general aim is not to train students for industry, the staff are all agreed on the necessity of preparing them for the world of work. This is achieved in the following ways:

1 Staff with industrial experience provide first-hand background knowledge; and between them, all the staff can offer specialist knowledge of and interest in various specific areas of industry.

2 The workshops, etc, provide a suitable environment in which direct

questions about going to work can most naturally arise and be dealt with.

3 Students are involved in 'team production' and introduced to industrial methods.

4 Work done at school level is related to direct industrial application, especially in engineering drawing and in technical work, e.g., welding and non-ferrous casting. In engineering science students are able to carry out experimental work at an industrial level, e.g., in the field of plastics. The teaching of design can be related closely to industrial design procedures, e.g., as regards costing.

5 Students are encouraged to select their optional subjects in such a way as to form subject groups appropriate to the requirements of further education, to which many of them will proceed.

The head of department has listed the following observable results of work experience courses as far as this department is concerned:

1 The students more readily accept workshop discipline and come to terms with the need to get a piece of work done within a reasonable time limit.

2 They realize that the craftsman is still required by society and that the accuracy of his work is essential in the industry in question.

3 They discuss and reach a better understanding of:
   (a) The economics of industry; the necessity of planning; the importance of the customer.
   (b) The 'hierarchy'; staff relationships; the colour problem.
   (c) Trades Unions.
   (d) The need to budget for meals and travelling.
   (e) 'Prospects'; where further education fits in; academic requirements.

4 Sometimes a student, after work experience, will reject that particular type of job, and search (often indignantly) for something better. This reaction involves further consultation with staff and fuller use of the careers room. The enhanced realization of the desirability of academic qualifications generally acts as a spur to prospective or potential candidates.

Observations

Much of all that has been said about the technical department in connection with preparation for adult working life and with our work experience scheme could apply equally, *mutatis mutandis,* to our school's home economics department. Domestic subjects are popular options among girls at all levels; boys are welcome to choose these subjects also, and the number of boys choosing domestic subjects is larger than the number of girls choosing technical subjects.

The curriculum in this department naturally draws attention to the problems of transition from school to after-school, including employment and eventually marriage and parenthood. The same is certainly true, in varying degrees, of other departments of the school.

It is implicit in all that I have written that the work experience scheme could not properly function, and cannot be considered, in isolation. It must be a natural feature of a school system geared to active preparation for a more or less imminent after-school life. An extensive and extremely busy careers department, a counselling service led by three trained school counsellors (two of whom are the deputy heads), and a programme of steady curricular reform, all involving close links with the outside world, are three other such features.

In the six years during which we have operated our work experience scheme so far, there has been, to the best of my belief, no Trades Union opposition and no insoluble insurance problem. It is to be devoutly hoped that when the school-leaving age is raised work experience for fifth formers will still be legal.

* * * * *

Link courses

For many secondary school students institutions of further and higher education may seem remote. This stems partly from the notion current among many students that the end of compulsory schooling means the end of any further studies of a vocational, technical or academic nature.

It also stems from the fact that in this country there is no real link between secondary schools and colleges of further education. This gap is, however, narrowing, mainly as a result of careers guidance within the secondary schools and the establishment of a range of link courses.

Aims and advantages

The intention of some link courses has been to provide opportunities for students to gain experience of skills required in a range of occupations. The pattern is often based upon students spending planned periods in college workshops and laboratories under the supervision of college staff. The facilities of most colleges enable them to create the industrial atmosphere discussed in the preceding notes on work experience, and at the same time to provide a realistic impression of the necessity and nature of further education as part of job training and the obtaining of additional qualifications.

Where such courses are planned it is important to appreciate that, in addition to the vocational implications, there exist opportunities for general education. Although students are participating in, say, a brick-laying course, there need be no commitment to a career in this field.

There may be value in arranging for students to experience a skill or skills required in occupations which they had not considered; at the same time, students who are keen on a particular career may be better able to decide, as a result of their experience, whether the job would or would not suit them.

W. G. Skinner, discussing the contributions that link courses can make to this aspect of secondary education, states that the main aims of link courses are:

1 To bridge a gulf between school and work giving students a more realistic atmosphere for their studies of the 'real man's world'. The 'outward-looking' emphasis stressed in Newsom can be developed in school workshops.

2 To give students knowledge of employment conditions with particular reference to their environment. Consequently, they should be better able to assess their own employment potential by assimilating the various means of self-assessment that practice in college workshops makes possible.

3 To make students familiar with the variety of further education courses available, to which many will subsequently enrol on either a full-time or part-time basis. They also come to realize the various 'second chances' that exist in further education for those who thought they would have to change their career aims because they had failed their 'O' or 'A' levels or CSE.

4 To introduce students to the diagnostic and problem-solving situations that occur increasingly in the changing industrial and commercial environment.

The same report lists six other advantages offered by link courses, although it is important to set these alongside educational goals:

1 A more economic use of accommodation, e.g., if there is space available in a college it could act as temporary accommodation for students and reduce the need for building extensions to a school.

2 Advantage can be taken of specialist staff that a school would not feel justified in appointing.

3 A college often possesses a wider, more expensive and up-to-date range of machinery and equipment.

4 Most college staff have had industrial or commercial experience and can more closely reproduce attitudes or atmospheres students will meet when they start work.

5 A college may be able to replace its equipment at a faster rate because of its more intensive use.

6 The staff of school and college will gain a better understanding of each other's work and points of view.

Links through design projects

Colleges of further education are largely geared to run specialized training courses that have only a minor influence on the curriculum of secondary education. Some teachers are prepared to develop this influence and such developments may benefit many young school leavers. At the same time there is an encouraging tendency for colleges to engage upon 'two-way' schemes which contribute to some of the fundamental intellectual and social aims of secondary education.

Take, for example, the problem-solving approaches of a secondary school project described in 'Case Study: Designing and Building an Adventure Playground'. Students were expected to explore the potential of a range of materials in constructing a range of possible solutions.

The use of brickwork, concrete and plastics may be very much enhanced if a school has access to the technical know-how and equipment found in a technical college. The same could be said for any one of a wide range of projects currently being operated in secondary schools.

Although major building and construction projects tend to lend themselves to links of this kind there is also scope for co-operation in other, smaller-scale projects. The selection of materials for, say, load-bearing purposes on the axles of a kart could involve the use of materials testing equipment readily available in colleges.

Co-operation and organization

The essence of co-operation at these levels is not spontaneity so much as flexibility within the timetables of both school and college to accommodate such work. This is not easily established, especially as the link may not be continuous throughout the year yet may, on some occasions, demand a high degree of involvement.

Much can be done at an informal level. But where possible it is often better to formalize the liaison. In order to facilitate developments it is desirable that joint meetings be held between college principal and school head. At the same time, meetings between members of staff likely to be involved in schemes could explore possible commitments on both sides.

The future for link courses seems bright. Provided that courses are seen as an extension to general education, and applicable to all students in the fifteen to eighteen age range, there is every possibility that link courses will develop and help provide a better understanding of industry and commerce.

It is important that such courses are seen as joint ventures to which both school and college can make their own special contribution to the ultimate benefit of the students concerned.

Case Study

A Link Course (1)

Within the participating schools of the Inner London Education Authority, 'materials and work' is, numerically, the smallest contribution being made to the research programme. There is, however, between Langdon Park School, Poplar, and the Hackney Technical College, a strengthening link being forged in the shape of a building course for fourth-form boys who are pursuing a CSE course. The project originated as a school service project, taking the form of a much needed motor vehicle maintenance department, designed with an eye to some of the requirements of senior non-examination students.

Initial contacts

In order to stimulate interest, develop motivation, encourage a high standard of craftsmanship and to link the work with industrial practice, the school team discussed the possibility of linking with the Hackney Technical College on the project work.

The initial contacts with the college were made after consultation with the headmaster of the school, and this step was quickly followed by a joint meeting between the staff of Langdon Park and that of Hackney Technical College with a view to discussing the broad philosophy of the link, the aims, curricula and the complex problems of timetabling, travelling, discipline, co-ordination and review procedures.

What happens

As a result of the preliminary developments, a thriving link course now operates, involving twenty fourth-year boys who, back at school, are building the motor vehicle shop, while pursuing a course at the Hackney Technical College in brickwork, carpentry and joinery, plumbing and painting and decorating. The course extends over one whole year, approximately nine weeks being spent on each of the four crafts. They share the same lectures and accommodation as the young apprentices from industrial organizations in the area. This, in itself, appears to engender a 'grown-up', responsible attitude. They are surrounded on all sides by advanced examples of the crafts they are studying in a way that could not possibly be parallelled in school . . . this is inspiring. They meet new faces in a fresh environment and—a major factor—they are working away from school in an 'adult' world.

There is reciprocity in the scheme in that the college lecturers meet the boys back at Langdon Park on occasions regularly arranged on site to discuss practical problems that arise on the job. The teacher involved accompanies the boys to college each week so that a close and continuing liaison is maintained between the school and college staffs.

Requirements of a link course

In the light of current experience, arising out of progress made so far, a number of essential requirements for a successful link course emerge:

1 There must be careful pre-planning between the school and the college staffs on such matters as:
   —curriculum requirements (this may well involve academic staff);
   —syllabuses;
   —ultimate responsibility for discipline;
   —provision of note-books, materials, etc;
   —provision of necessary protective clothing;
   —timetabling.

2 When the boys (or girls) are at the college, there should be a member of the school staff with them. This, in experiment at Langdon Park, proved to be of great assistance to the college staff. It was particularly

helpful on the question of guidance to the college staff in the handling of difficult, backward or deprived students. It helps forge a permanent link between the two sources of education and encourages a 'carry-over' between them. It can also help with disciplinary problems and may prevent a major 'blow-up' that could spell ruin to the whole concept of a link course. The teacher provides a contact between the college and his own colleagues back at school through which worthwhile revision of approach in subjects other than technical studies may take place. This can lead to a natural and desirable integration of subjects.

3 Transport should be provided where numbers make this a viable proposition; there are a number of legitimate complaints from the college that students, from some schools that do not provide communal transport, often arrive in 'dribs and drabs', making a prompt start impossible. This militates against the true reconstruction of workshop conditions and creates an atmosphere of disruption that could, where excessive, lead to disciplinary troubles.

4 College lecturers should spend a proportion of the year with the boys or girls back at school, thus emphasizing the true nature of the link. This situation is most naturally created where a practical project is in hand back at the school.

5 Headmasters or heads of departments should not use the college as a means of relieving strain at the school by sending only the poorest 'sets' or classes or a selection of the 'problem children' to the college. They should not use the college staff as relief teachers but rather arrange for the school staff to accompany the children to the college. This is good for both staff and students. The system will break down in disarray if the college lecturers feel that they are being used.

6 It is essential for the college lecturers to see their contribution as basically and broadly educational—certainly not as a preliminary year in the process of apprentice training.

7 Link courses have a great deal to offer at fifth- and sixth-form level. There is a viable link for 'O' level Land Surveying, for example.

8 At the moment, much of the detailed organization and development is at the head of department or even enthusiastic teacher/lecturer level. However, when schemes are being discussed in the initial stages, the head of the school and the principal of the college must be involved and they should also be present at review meetings. In this way a broad and natural development and integration covering all relevant subject areas essential to a completely successful link course could be evolved.

In this example staff of the school and the college would like to see the link course extended to the fifth-form CSE streams, consolidating and developing the work started in the fourth year. They feel that the opportunities implicit in the idea of link courses would reach their full potential if extended to sixth formers when the basic elements of surveying and civil engineering could be tackled—this element providing a stimulating and practical scheme for non-examination students.

It is hoped to include maths and English in the future schemes and exploratory talks are now being pursued. The inclusion of these vital subjects will be welcomed by the staffs of the college and school alike who see benefits both in the planning and execution of practical work on the link course and in the stimulation of interests that may be pursued in normal English and maths lessons at school.

It is an encouraging feature of these developments in the ILEA that an increasing number of schools are participating in link courses of the type described and the next academic year should see existing courses being further developed and new ones created. Whatever plans exist for increasing accommodation and for the provision of additional teachers, it is certain that colleges of education will play an important part in providing a realistic further 'finishing' school year for the increasing numbers of senior non-examination students.

Case Study

A Link Course ②

Since 1969 link courses have operated between several schools in the Kesteven (Licolnshire) area and its two colleges of further education. These courses were either examination courses in subjects not undertaken by the schools, or 'careers appreciation' courses for the non-examination early leavers.

The raising of the school-leaving age caused more schools to consider the careers appreciation course. So in 1971 the Kesteven authority, through its adviser in technical and craft studies, initiated discussions between six secondary schools in the Grantham area and the building department of the local further education college, to see if a unified course with broader educational objectives could be set up.

Planning

The social element of the course was seen to be the most important. It would provide an opportunity for senior school children to mix with the college's students in a more adult environment and to experience a different student/lecturer relationship.

It was also felt that the secondary school students should become more aware of the world of work and the local community generally. A proposal was made that some form of community service project might provide the central core of the course, pulling together the various elements.

A further outcome of the initial discussions was the decision to arrange an interchange of staff between school and college. It was hoped that this would increase the effectiveness of the link, reduce any feeling of isolation the children might have, and avoid any suggestion that the schools were shedding their responsibility for the education of these students.

Further discussions and visits to the schools took place over a three-week period. At the beginning of July, 1971, the final form of the course was agreed at a meeting between the head teachers of the schools concerned, the college principal and the head of the college building department.

Induction course

Later that month a residential induction course was held. This had five aims:

1 to bring together all those taking part in the link courses;

2 to establish a good working relationship between the students, teachers and lecturers;

3 to create an interest in the community development theme of play and to encourage students to believe that they were capable of designing and making equipment that would meet the play needs of primary school children;

4 to help students identify needs by observation during visits to several primary schools;

5 to acquaint teachers and lecturers with the course and to discuss their role and the teaching methods to be used.

The theme of the course was introduced to the students using a series of slides on community development and play.* Subsequent sessions were devoted to a discussion of the design process and a students' design work-book was introduced and distributed. (See *Education Through Design and Craft*,[11] Appendix 6.)

8.2 Introductory talk.

8.3 Observing primary school children at play.

*These trial slide sequences formed the basis for Design and Craft Education Filmstrips *Helping Out*[5] and *Playthings*.[7]

8.4 Observing primary school children at play.

8.5 Each student team elected a spokesman to report the findings of their visits to primary schools.

Although it would be fair to say that initially there was a certain amount of resistance from some of the teaching staff to the idea of students being able to find and solve their own problems, the induction course did go a long way towards overcoming this. It was felt that this introduction was a major contributory factor to the success of the link course. An enthusiasm was generated in students, and some teachers and lecturers were surprised at the originality of the ideas gained from the observation visits.

The enthusiasm of some of the girls was such that they visited their teacher during her summer holidays to ask for her help in carrying out further investigations and to discuss their ideas.

8.6 After making their reports students discussed their observations and ideas with teachers.

Course organization

The link course itself started the following September. Each of the six secondary schools involved sent twelve students to the college each Wednesday during the academic year 1971–72. Six students attended from an ESN boarding school.

A three-and-a-half-hour morning session was devoted to a study and practical experience of plumbing and building services, painting and decorating, timber trades and trowel trades. The electrical section of the department of engineering ran a course on electrical appreciation. A further course on building construction was provided to show how the various sections of the building industry are co-ordinated.

This part of the course was made up of six six-week sessions, one in each of the above departments. The students worked in groups of twelve, each group consisting of children from several schools.

The afternoon session of two-and-a-half hours was spent on the 'play' project. For these sessions the students rejoined their original school groups. They were introduced to the design process and, after observation visits to primary schools and similar establishments, they set about identifying a need for some form of play equipment.

The morning sessions were conducted by the college staff. In the afternoons the students worked under a college tutor and their own craft teacher. The teacher's attendance at the college helped to under-line that this was truly a linked course.

Design work

A difficulty noted during the induction course was that on some observation visits the students were virtually given a list of the items the primary schools required. Although such a list undoubtedly reflects needs felt by the staff some value is lost to the students if they are denied the opportunity to identify such needs for themselves. Clearly, it is important to 'brief' the staff of an establishment the children are to visit if this problem is to be avoided.

When the link course began in September, this problem and the lack of experience of the teaching staff in handling design project work resulted in the formation of set ideas which, once triggered, can block any opportunity for original and creative work.

Students, and some of the teaching staff, found it difficult to differentiate between a problem and a solution to a problem. For example, one group of students, encouraged by their teacher and the headmistress of a local primary school who wanted a climbing frame, decided without reference to any observation visits to build such a frame.

This, of course, was the primary school's way of meeting the children's need to climb, swing and jump. It is, again, extremely difficult for students to make an original contribution once they have been offered these image-forming solutions.

The organizers of the link course saw the difference between identifying a problem and accepting someone else's solution as a crucial one in design education. Difficulties arising from this are fairly common ; some ways of avoiding or overcoming them are discussed in *Materials and Design: A Fresh Approach.*[2]

An interesting technique was developed during this course in an attempt to overcome preconceptions and to stimulate creative thinking through the association of ideas.

During a collective 'brain storming' session the students were asked to list activities which children like to undertake, for example, running, jumping, skipping and crawling. They then made a second list of role-playing games such as soldiers, firemen, sailors, cops and robbers, and cowboys and Indians.

The group continued by trying to link a game to an activity—firemen, say, to climbing and running—and think of a piece of equipment that would combine these aspects of play. They were provided with polystyrene packing, wire, Plasticine and balsa wood to help them communicate their ideas. The intention was not to make scale working models, but simply to enable the students to express their ideas in three dimensions.

284

This work resulted in some interesting ideas which were investigated in detail and then, if satisfactory, developed to completion.

One such idea which emerged was an original design for a fort-*cum*-submarine constructed in brick and reinforced concrete, providing facilities for hiding, sitting in a small room, climbing through the conning tower, jumping, and crawling through a plastic tunnel with an intersection. The finished item measured 5 metres by 1 metre by 1·5 metres high.

8.7 Working on the fort/submarine.

8.8 The finished unit proved to be a popular addition to the play facilities.

The adventure playground described below also incorporated ideas developed during an 'association-of-ideas' session.

Two other projects were conceived as a direct result of visits to primary schools without recourse to the kind of session described above.

One group designed and made two original and interesting play shops for two primary schools. Another made a small mammal house which doubled as a constructional toy. The development of this dual use is worth recording. Coming from a rural secondary school, the students were amazed to find no animals in this town primary school. The reason given by the headmaster was that they had no cages. When the students offered to make some he found some other reason for not keeping animals! The group then had the idea of making a constructional toy which could also serve as a cage for small mammals in order to encourage the headmaster to have some in his school.

8.9 Constructional toy/mammal house.

8.9, 8.10 Models in 'soft' materials proved a valuable aid to design work.

8.10. Ideas for play shops.

Adventure playground

A group of girls decided that what was needed was an adventure playground which would give scope for a wide range of activities and games. So many good ideas were developed that they refused to select just one item; they wanted to pursue them all.

When told that neither space nor cash were available to do this they became most despondent and approached their headmistress to ask permission to raise money to construct all the items. These problems were overcome, however, through the headmistress's association with the Hospital League of Friends who agreed to finance the venture at the local hospital.

One of the detailed design problems was that the girls had no idea of scale and were unable to represent their ideas in generally acceptable ways. This was overcome to some extent by constructing full-size models from cardboard boxes and plywood sheet. These were photographed and used to convince the hospital matron of the value of the equipment.

It was agreed with the hospital authorities to make just one item until the hospital management committee gave their blessing to the whole scheme. This was given in principle, but work could not proceed until the scheme was approved in detail by several of the hospital's sub-committees.

Finally, after nearly five months had elapsed, the scheme was approved. Unfortunately, the girls had left school by this time.

Climbing frame

As expected, it proved impossible to redirect those students who had decided to make a climbing frame at the suggestion of a primary school headmistress during the induction course, although they were able to express some splendid alternatives.

While making a quarter-scale model the students learnt the necessary welding techniques. Consideration was given to the need for safety in such a construction. After the scale model had been made it was discovered that there was a British Standard for the safety of such equipment and it had to be redesigned. Because of the stringent safety requirements the college staff were responsible for the calculations and final specifications of the frame.

As the frame incorporated a large number of similar parts a production line technique was used for its construction. Students also had the opportunity to use pipe-threading machinery and learnt something about site work and reinforced concrete foundations.

They also became aware of the process of obtaining permission to build such a structure. Application had first to be made to the school managers, who supplied the £70 needed to buy materials, then to the local education authority who, in consultation with its physical education adviser and the county architect, approved the construction and the siting of the climbing frame.

Experience with this and the adventure playground project showed the importance of allowing sufficient time to obtain the necessary approval. Those involved also learnt that when providing fixed equipment in a playground it is advisable to consult the local physical education advisers at an early stage.

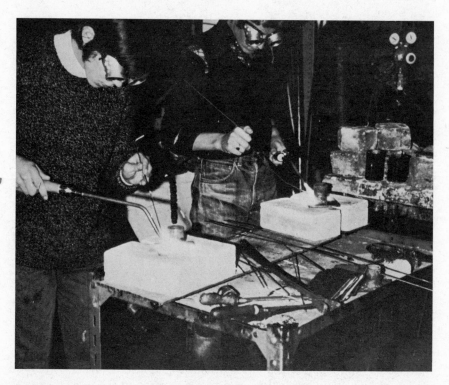

8.11 Part of the climbing frame production line.

Course assessment

In assessing the course three head teachers had this to say:
> The real benefits to the boys involved were, I feel, in those aspects of development so difficult to assess accurately, i.e., maturity, social conduct and general attitude to school, work and to the community.

In the more specific area of craft education the opportunity to work on a larger scale and to use materials not available in the school situation proved most stimulating and the results last year gave the boys a genuine sense of personal achievement.

Gave the girls greater maturity, widened their horizons. Gained in poise and confidence, increased social awareness.

Benefits to student: added experience *outside school's own environment*—greater sense of freedom and independence through a more 'adult' approach—greater maturity in meeting and dealing with a wider community—a developing sense of self-reliance and self-control—important 'social' mixing with students from other schools—greater variety of staffing, of methods, materials and equipment—attendance at the college leads naturally on to further education in a 'known' situation—wider 'sampling' is vocationally important—wiser choices are made through knowledge of opportunities available.

Benefits to staff: tremendous value in broadening outlook, in spreading alternative views, in co-operation, in knowledge of further education (of which many schools are ignorant), in forcing teachers and lecturers to see that education is a continuing process, in creating greater integration in the colleges themselves as well as in schools in promoting 'community' education and 'community' welfare'.

The majority of the teachers involved were in no doubt that these young people were more fitted than their contemporaries to face the adult world on leaving school.

One teacher complained that her girls 'asked questions' and no longer accepted things because she said they were so!

A number of students decided to stay at school an extra year. Others undertook full-time education at the college. Difficulties were created at some schools as the students were too late to slot into an examination course.

Further developments

When considering the content of a two-year link course to accommodate the 'extra year', this change in some students' attitude to education was taken into consideration. It was also felt that the work undertaken would be worthy of assessment in a CSE Mode 3 context.

The course was modified so that students who showed appropriate ability during the first year would be entered for a Studies in Design examination along the lines of the CSE Mode 3 course developed by the Design and Craft Education Project in conjunction with the North

Western Secondary Schools Examination Board. (See *Education Through Design and Craft,*[11] Appendix 5.)

It was decided to introduce a structure to the project teaching sessions as it was felt that some time had been wasted by 'playing it by ear'. To this end the management chart illustrated in figure 8.12 was drawn up. The course structure is shown in figure 8.13.

DESIGN PROJECT MANAGEMENT CHART

Week	1	Introduce community service theme.
Week	2	Design method — first stage — preparation for visits
Week	3	Observation visits
Week	4	Brief in behavioural terms (area of need).
Week	5	Ideas for apparatus
Week	6	Brief related to selected problem.
Week	7	Observation visit — to check brief.
Week	8	Ideas for apparatus related to brief.
Week	9	Specifications. (And teachers meet to decide materials required for each project.)
Week	10	Discuss and draw up final specification with group tutor.

At this stage tutors will be asked to prepare, within two weeks, plans on tracing paper, materials list, cost analysis and details of any special tools or transport arrangements required — for submission to appropriate authorities.

Weeks	11—13	Re-group in material-based groups for work projects to gain experience with predominant material.

·················· END OF AUTUMN TERM ························

Week	14	Students discuss drawings and cost analysis — opportunity given for ideas to be developed for selling product to client.
Weeks	15—16	Selling, package or motor skill work projects.
Weeks	17—18	Work organization flow charts.
Week	19	Start projects.
Weeks	20—26	Project practical work

··················· END OF SPRING TERM ························

Weeks	26—36	Project practical work all day.

8.12 Design project management chart.

TWO—YEAR LINK COURSE STRUCTURE

First year held at the college

	Term 1	Term 2	Term 3
a.m.	SKILLS IN VARIOUS BUILDING TRADES	SKILLS IN VARIOUS BUILDING TRADES	GROUP STUDIES IN DESIGN (House design for the small family)
p.m.	GROUP COMMUNITY PROJECT Teacher present	GROUP COMMUNITY PROJECT Teacher present	PERSONAL CSE PROJECT (Design work) Teacher present

Second year held at school and college

	Term 4	Term 5
a.m.	INDIVIDUAL CSE DESIGN STUDIES AT THE SCHOOL Lecturer present	INDIVIDUAL CSE DESIGN STUDIES AT THE SCHOOL Lecturer present
p.m.	PERSONAL CSE PROJECT (Practical) At the college	PERSONAL CSE PROJECT (Practical) At the college

8.13 Two-year link course structure.

In the new two-year link course students spend one day per week at the college during the first year and half a day during the second year. Another half a day per week is spent working on individual design studies at the school during the second year.

In the first two terms morning sessions are spent on practical work in carpentry and joinery, brickwork, plumbing and building services, painting and decorating, and building construction. This practical experience is supplemented by discussions of the effect of buildings on the quality of life.

In the third term school groups undertake directed studies in the design of the material environment in relation to man's primary needs and the quality of his life. The various building trade lecturers deal with such topics as:

—*painting and decorating:* effect of shop display and fascia boards on the environment, psychology of advertising, effect of colour in the home, factory, etc;

—*brickwork:* study of 'shelter', looking at the materials man has used for that purpose;

—*carpentry and joinery:* study of roof trusses and their visual effect in building design;

—*plumbing and building services:* effect of central heating, air conditioning and drains (public health) on the standard of life;

—*building construction:* study of the way buildings are constructed to suit particular needs, e.g., old people's bungalows, nursery schools, hospitals, factories, garages, offices, and how construction techniques affect the design.

This group study is to a large extent a 'trial run' for both lecturers and students. It is hoped that students will gain experience in recording information using cameras, tape recorders, questionnaires and scrapbook methods, and will also become interested in a topic for their personal study in the second year.

In the afternoon sessions during the first two terms students work in school groups at the college with a teacher and a lecturer. A community service project is undertaken so that they are able to become familiar with and use a design process as required by their syllabus. A standardized students' design worksheet and a teachers' guide have been drawn up for use at this stage.

In the third term students start their personal design project which will be offered for assessment in term five. By the end of this term they are expected to have completed early design work and to have started to generate solutions.

Detailed design work, making, testing and evaluation take place in the fourth and fifth terms.

Also in these final two terms, during the morning sessions at the schools, students tackle a personal design study, preferably arising

292

from their work in term three. This study will be offered for assessment. The following are examples of the type of topic which might be undertaken.

—design problems in bed-sitter accommodation;
—the ergonomics of kitchen equipment and layout;
—house design for the small family;
—the design and provision of social and recreational amenities for young people on housing estates;
—play equipment for small children;
—problems of play facilities for young children in high-rise, high density living accommodation;
—the design of labour-saving equipment for the home;
—mechanization and the hand processes it replaces;
—consumer choice: the validity of makers' claims;
—the techniques of advertising.

Discussions took place in May 1972 at the Kesteven Authority's other college of further education in Stamford with a view to replacing their existing link courses with one similar to the Grantham scheme described above. It was possible to make use of the Grantham experience to design a course with more precise objectives. An interesting feature of the course is that the engineering department and the business and general education departments make a joint contribution.

It was possible to make use of the Grantham experience to design a course with more precise objectives. The overall objectives were stated as follows:

1 to provide an adult environment in which senior schoolchildren can work together on a community service project to further their general education;

2 to provide opportunity for children to work with their contemporaries in other schools and with young adults attending the college;

3 to provide social education by creating a situation in which senior children come into contact with the various groups which make up a community;

4 to identify needs within a community and design equipment to help meet them;

5 to help school-leavers assess local career opportunities.

The course is organized in a similar way to the Grantham course: in the mornings mixed school groups gain experience of various aspects of electronics and plastics engineering, and light crafts, while the afternoons are devoted to project work.

The department of business studies and general education is able to make a useful contribution to the students' understanding of welfare needs and problems. The object is to introduce them to 'areas of need' or 'areas of distress' in modern society, e.g., handicapped children, children in care, the aged, those in hospital. This introduction is achieved in two ways:

1 by arranging visits to special establishments in the area, e.g., the Wilfred Pickles School for Spastics, the King's Mill Centre for Handicapped Children, Stamford Hospital;

2 by inviting speakers with specialized knowledge, e.g., a warden of a children's home, a social services worker.

It is hoped that this part of the course will help students to gain some awareness of welfare problems and be better able to identify areas of need in their project work.

Course objectives for the morning sessions are:

1 to enable the student to achieve certain motor skills and to experience work with particular materials and systems;

2 to enable the student to gain an awareness of welfare problems in modern society;

3 to provide skills and understanding necessary for the community service project.

A further five course objectives were drawn up for the afternoon sessions:

1 to develop the student's understanding of design factors in the interplay between man, the shaping of his environment, and the quality of his life;

2 to develop intellectual abilities and motor skills through the medium of design activities, i.e., decision making, problem solving and practical work related to community service;

3 to provide opportunity for students to work with materials and use acquired knowledge of systems to meet the needs of others such as the old, the sick, young children, schools and hospitals;

4 to enable teachers to gain experience in using the design process to meet educational objectives in the personal development of students;

5 to provide teachers with data that will help to establish if objectives can be used to plan and assess a student's development.

9
School-based Production Units

This is probably the growth point that lends itself most easily to the secondary school situation. There are likely to be few problems of insurance, legality of employment of youngsters or long and difficult arrangements to make with outside bodies. There is, however, scope—sometimes a necessity —to combine simulated experiences with work visits, work experience or linked projects with colleges of further education.

The essence of a simulated experience is that students should be able to accept the situation as real, or as near to reality as possible. This is helped by ensuring that they are identifying and solving real problems. It may not be possible to reproduce an industrial atmosphere for all aspects of the work but great involvement and enjoyment can be gained while attempting this.

The planning and preparation of a production unit adds a new dimension to workshop activities. A line production unit should use the available resources of the workshop in the most effective way. It may be based on the 'factory day' idea where students work as near as possible to the real situation, but this does not mean that the value is lost if industrial conditions are not precisely simulated. Indeed, this may be impossible. The basis of this work is that similar decisions need to be made, such as:

—how can we organize ourselves?
—which of our machinery will do what?
—from where do we get our materials?

Although many simulated experiences are labelled 'school-based production units' or 'factory days' there is more to the undertaking than operating a production line.

A full range of roles may be assumed by students of various abilities in the fourteen to eighteen age range. To some extent the whole cycle of industrial activity can be brought into school, either with different groups or the same group covering different aspects.

While it may not be possible to simulate with accuracy the kind of planning and control found in industry, the basic principles below may easily form 'compartments' for study:

1 identification of need;
2 review of resources;
3 simple planning;
4 production;
5 distribution.

Unless there is extensive co-operation throughout the curriculum it may prove impossible to emphasize all these aspects. Nevertheless, where one stage is highlighted students should have the opportunity to relate it to other aspects. For example, if the emphasis is on packaging and distribution, scope should be given for students to look at factors that may have played a part during market research, design and production.

Careers guidance

One important outcome of a greater understanding of the world of work is an increased awareness of the career possibilities in industry. A production line project should result in the student being better able to specify and assess the various roles played by both management and production staff in industry, and hence to form an opinion concerning the potential rewards and shortcomings of such a career.

The design process

The educational aims of a school-based production unit are not solely related to the world of work. Students will still need to investigate a selected problem and elements of the design process will be very much in evidence.

In fact one advantage of this type of work is that it involves both the design of an artefact and organizational design, and the outcome of the work will depend upon the successful combination of these two factors. Possible solutions will still have to be communicated via sketches, models, and so on, and then developed and assessed. At all stages special stress may have to be placed on methods of construction. In a 'batch production' situation these will almost certainly differ from the 'one-off' case.

These differences provide a fertile source of investigation in which the following factors may require consideration:

—number of parts;
—number of joints;
—complexity of shaping;

—ease of assembly;
—type and method of application of surface finish;
—time taken to produce the parts;
—time taken to assemble the parts.

The importance of planning

The planning involved in setting up a production unit is the most important aspect of the project. Although the production session will usually form the climax, the previous thought, planning and co-operation of the students will determine the final degree of success or failure. Production may be considered as a practical assessment of the planning that led to it; it is not merely 'cheap labour'.

One vital aim of the production planning must be to complete the work within the allotted time. In other words the students should work to a production time schedule. Efficiency must be the keynote.

From aims to objectives

After organizing and operating a production line students may be expected to review the various broad principles on which such work is based, for example:
1 how the product is identified;
2 the kinds of resources that will be required;
3 the range of production methods that can be used;
4 the techniques of marketing and distribution.

In reviewing these basic principles they will need to answer a number of questions, among them:

—who undertakes market research?
—who designs the product?
—who decides how it will be manufactured?
—who makes it?
—who costs it?
—who buys the materials?
—who sells it?
—who is responsible for interrelating these functions?
—who buys or receives the product?
—who checks that the product continues to function after distribution and installation?

The students may then, after examining these questions, be able to specify a basic framework for the production of a set number of items.

Objectives in social development

The objectives of a line production project may be other than intellectual. In addition to the benefits in social development that may be derived from working as a member of a team, it is also possible to link such work with

9.1 Linked aims and objectives.

INTELLECTUAL AIMS   **SOCIAL AIMS**

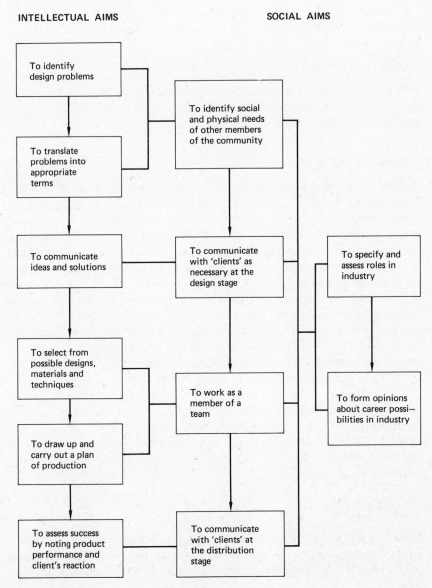

community service projects which often require the production of a quantity of items. 'Case Study: Batch Production for Disabled Children' describes the design and manufacture of equipment for handicapped children.

In the sphere of 'play' students may be able to identify several requirements of young children that could lead to the line production of toys. Experience of the production of a number of items of the same nature may lead students to discover factors in toy design that may not be apparent in a 'one-off' situation.

Examples of the kind of work that could be done in this field are given in the 'Materials and Community Development' section of this book.

Students and teachers

The wide potential of a school-based production unit project means that the range of students who could benefit from such work and the range of possible subject contributions are correspondingly wide.

Student age and ability

Depending upon the complexity of the work and the level of expected involvement, students between the ages of fourteen and eighteen find this form of activity attractive. Normal timetable arrangements usually mean single age groups but there is, however, tremendous scope for setting up teams of mixed ages and noting the roles adopted by different students.

Within a co-ordinated scheme it is possible to assign different aspects of the work to different groups of students. In more able groups, especially at the sixth-form level, students can take more executive roles, although the responses of fourth-form leavers have on several occasions exceeded expectations. Some forms could be responsible for market research and identification of the 'target population'; others could follow on by designing the article while some forms could confine themselves to designing and planning the production line and 'selling' the products.

Experience has shown that mixed ability groups lend themselves particularly to this form of team-work. Once the nature of the problem has been established students readily assume roles in keeping with their ability; although there will always be those who are content to 'ride' on the work of others. Where such teams have been set up there has been a remarkably low number of misfits.

A teaching team

Much of the work will fall outside the immediate scope of workshop activity, and in any case it would be unfair for the total burden to fall on one or two teachers. A team is required, with a co-ordinator. Some teachers may

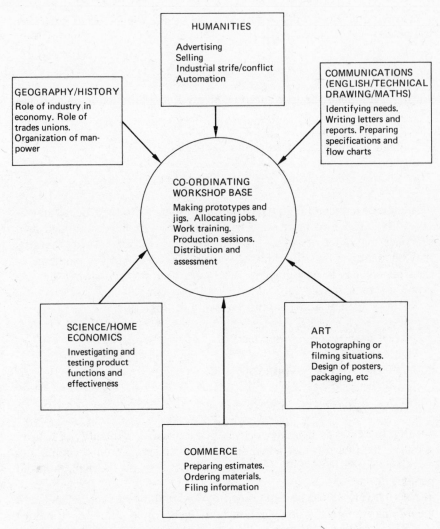

9.2 Subject contributions—a teaching team.

have an incidental role to play and one that may be covered quickly—perhaps in one or two lessons.

The kinds of contributions that different subjects can make will depend to a certain extent on the type of project. Figure 9.2 illustrates some of the subject contributions that will be common to the majority of projects.

Starting points for organization

Once a series of linked aims and objectives has been stated methods of approach must be considered. Careful planning by the teacher, or teachers, will be required since it is desirable that the students be involved right from the outset.

Motivation

Clearly, the students must want to be involved in a production unit project. This motivation may arise either from:

1 students identifying a need for a quantity of equipment
 or
2 a visit to a factory using line or batch production methods.

In either event careful guidance and prompting from the teacher may be necessary. These two motivating factors may be combined, although their sequence may alter according to circumstances. In other words the need may be identified first and a factory visit arranged to assist in planning, or the students may be encouraged, after such a visit, to discuss what they can do on a similar basis.

At this stage the students must be aware of three things:

1 the real purpose of the experience;
2 what can be made;
3 the market for the end-product.

Market research

Clearly, there has to be a means by which a need for a quantity of articles is established. As previously mentioned, this can spring from a community service project where items are required for, say, a play group or an old people's home.

Alternatively, it can be determined by undertaking market research and identifying a market in anticipation of a forthcoming school open day or fête. On occasions, the item to be manufactured may be established as a result of a whole class of students deciding that they all wish to produce the same item for themselves or their families.

Some form of market research is essential if students are to come to understand how industry works and what the role of the product is. Through research a company establishes who will buy the product, what the customer wants, why a product is bought (as in motivational research), and so on.

All this information helps in product design and deciding how a product is to be packaged, promoted and distributed.

Research may be done 'in the field' by observation, questioning, making tape recordings, photographs and films. A questionnaire may be distributed to prospective customers and others who are involved in the project, or manufacturers and distributors who may be able to provide useful information. 'Competitive products' and the associated promotional material may be collected to aid in market research. In the class room the information will need to be documented and presented in a convenient manner.

The organization of a project in which the emphasis is on marketing rather than production planning or product design is discussed in some detailed in Chapter 2.

Product design

Once a problem has been identified a number of solutions may be suggested. These may stem from a series of design briefs built around the problem. The whole group of students may be engaged in working out a satisfactory solution, either as individuals or as members of one or more design teams. A design strategy is essential; see *Materials and Design: A Fresh Approach*[2].

When a series of solutions has been established it becomes necessary to select the most suitable. For line production techniques to be effective the students should:

1 examine the effectiveness of the selected design in meeting the requirements of function, construction, use of materials, and so on;
2 determine whether the design lends itself to being broken down into a number of easily produced components. (This factor may have to be considered at the 'brief' stage of the design process.)

A sound balance should be made here, as the whole venture may become artificial if easily isolated components or sub-assemblies are introduced into the design solution merely to facilitate the setting up of a production line.

The importance of understanding in planning

A thorough understanding of the chosen solution is vital if the students are to take part successfully in the subsequent production planning. This may be achieved by the students actually being asked to vote on the proposed solutions and to give reasons for their choices. Class discussions may also help to give them insight into the criteria involved in choosing a particular solution for line production. The production of models is another useful aid to planning. There are two essential factors here:

1 students must understand the nature of the initial problem;
2 they must understand the framework of organization into which the chosen solution will fit.

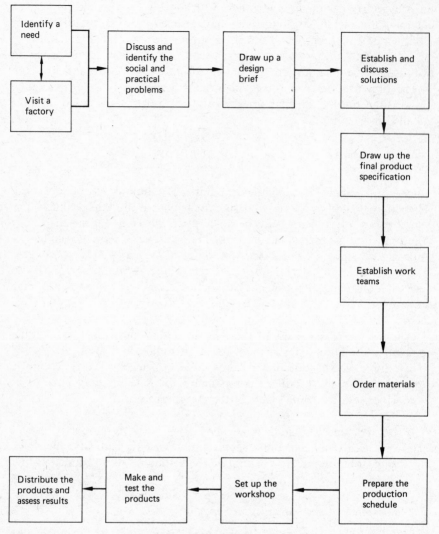

9.3 An approach to setting up a production line.

Organizing production

The establishment of design teams may be an early step in organizing the production unit, but it is after the solution is known that the different group activities really become apparent and can be introduced. For example, groups will be required to take charge of producing flow charts, designing and making jigs, estimating, ordering materials, and so on.

The final design specification

Some students will be required to analyse the chosen product solution, specify the final details of size, shape, and method of construction, and prepare a list of materials necessary.

This final design specification must be in a form that will be clearly understood by all students engaged on the project. The ways in which such ideas can be communicated—by the written or spoken word, by sketches, or by card or wire 'mock-ups'—is dealt with more fully in *Materials and Design: A Fresh Approach*[2].

However, a full-size prototype is probably a sound way to ensure that all students understand exactly what will be involved in producing the artefact.

Analysing the components of the product

The item to be manufactured will have to be analysed and broken down into its component parts. The students must discuss how each part is to be made. Once this has been done it should be possible to determine the number and types of operations that will have to be carried out on different machines or in different work areas.

Siting work stations and producing flow charts

Now the actual production line is beginning to take shape. Location of the work stations can lead to the drawing up of flow charts for each component. Bottlenecks can be avoided if the production operation is planned carefully. The layout of the workshop may need modification; some portable equipment will probably have to be re-sited or removed from the workshop. Some machines may be needed for work on more than one component. Careful cross-referencing is necessary between the component flow charts.

After preparing and checking flow charts for each component the students should be able to produce a workshop layout sheet showing the position of all work stations and points of assembly and finishing.

It should be noted that a self-contained production line where all the operations are carried out in the same room is usually easier to operate than one which necessitates the use of two or more workshops.

Preparing jigs

Production work often calls for the design and construction of jigs to ensure that components are manufactured to a consistent standard. This work is obviously best carried out before production starts. The design of jigs can be an important aspect of the project as it can provide scope for detailed design thinking. Jigs can often take some considerable time to produce, so ample allowance should be made for this to be done.

The bill of materials

It is essential that all materials required for the production session are available in good time. They may even have to be obtained some time beforehand if certain components need prior working. The costing and ordering is often a sizable part of the project, especially where an office procedure can be established.

There is scope here for links with the commerce department or with mathematics and English.

Allocating jobs

A breakdown of the production operations will suggest what man-power is required at each work station. The time at which various components are required and the actual time required to carry out some operation on them will have to be taken into account here. The flow of parts may be such that certain work stations are operating only intermittently.

To ensure the smooth running of the line parts of some components may have to be made before the actual production session. It may also be necessary to see that each member of the team has something to do right from the start of production. If operations at some work stations are short-lived certain students may have to work at a number of different stations—perhaps operating between two or more points as the batches flow.

In addition to the manufacturing jobs peculiar to the product being made there are other, less productive, roles that some students may have to take. A 'foreman' will be needed. It may also be necessary to appoint a 'store-keeper' to take charge of the materials, an 'inspector' to be responsible for quality control, a 'progress chaser' to check that production is proceeding according to the work schedule and perhaps to keep records of the number of man hours expended on the various operations.

If the products are to be packaged then packers will be needed. The packaging operation can often form a separate unit and the design and production of packaging material can become lengthy and involved. In such a situation it may be too much to expect the group engaged on making the actual end-product to handle packaging as well; an additional group of students could be made responsible for tackling this part of the programme.

Experience has indicated that students are capable of selecting their own jobs, although there may sometimes be competition for the more glamorous jobs like spraying or welding. But in the main their choices are realistic. The process of identifying and selecting jobs can often be aided by the students observing an actual production line in operation.

Work training

Certain operations may be outside the scope or experience of the students. If this is the case some work training will be necessary at the planning stage.

306

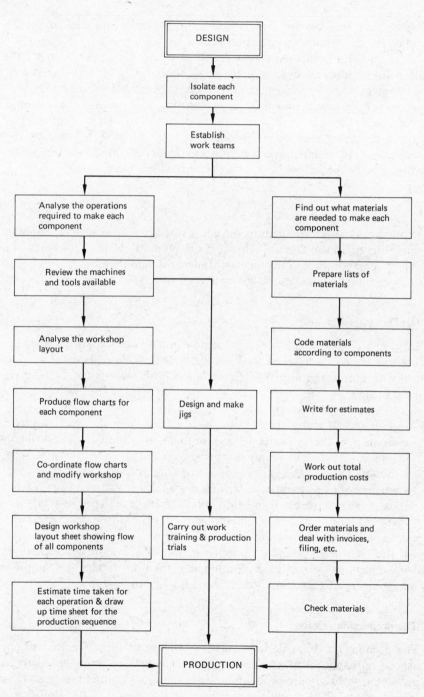

```
                    ┌─────────────────┐
                    │     DESIGN      │
                    └─────────────────┘
                             │
                    ┌─────────────────┐
                    │  Isolate each   │
                    │   component     │
                    └─────────────────┘
                             │
                    ┌─────────────────┐
                    │   Establish     │
                    │   work teams    │
                    └─────────────────┘
```

Analyse the operations required to make each component

Find out what materials are needed to make each component

Review the machines and tools available

Prepare lists of materials

Analyse the workshop layout

Code materials according to components

Produce flow charts for each component

Design and make jigs

Write for estimates

Co-ordinate flow charts and modify workshop

Work out total production costs

Design workshop layout sheet showing flow of all components

Carry out work training & production trials

Order materials and deal with invoices, filing, etc.

Estimate time taken for each operation & draw up time sheet for the production sequence

Check materials

PRODUCTION

9.4 A programme for production planning.

307

L

In any event, students may benefit from a trial set-up so that they can get the feel of the situation before the production session.

It should be remembered that absenteeism among key workers can greatly affect the production line, so precautions should be built into the system at this stage whereby some students are able to 'double up' if necessary.

In a school production line, as in industry, it is possible that certain operations—whether for reasons of lack of time, facilities or experience—cannot be undertaken by the production team. In such a situation the students will be required to consider the possibility of sub-contracting work, either outside the school or to other groups within the school.

Factory visits

Throughout the pre-production stage it is often beneficial to link planning with visits to a local factory. Although the situation in the school may not exactly represent that in the factory, students should thereby be better able to appreciate the elements of activity at each stage and in each area of work.

Dealing with problems

Snags are almost bound to occur during planning and experience suggests that this is best undertaken over several weeks to allow plenty of time to deal with unforeseen problems. Some of the problems that could arise are listed below:

—certain special materials may not be available from the usual sources;
—there may be delays in the delivery of materials (students should obtain details of delivery as well as price when costing and ordering materials, although quoted dates cannot always be guaranteed);
—students may be absent (the seriousness of this will depend upon what stage has been reached and how vital the absentee student's job is—there is a lot to be said for appointing assistants to those in key jobs who are able to take over in any such emergency); .
—if·the final design has to be approved or tested by outside experts or organizations—in the case of equipment for a hospital, for example—then plenty of time should be allowed for this to be done.

The production session

The product has been designed. The groups responsible for the various aspects of management, engineering and production planning have carried out all the necessary pre-production work. Flow charts and time sheets have been prepared. The materials, machines and tools are ready. Production is the next step.

308

The final briefing

A final briefing session is advisable before production starts. In this each student could outline his role so that points of uncertainty may be settled. If local industrialists have not been helping at the initiation or planning stages this may be a good time to invite a local factory manager, for example, to give a short talk on some aspect of industry relevant to the particular project.

Timetabling

In a 'factory day' project, where the idea is to create a reasonably close approximation to an industrial situation, the production session is best organized as a concentrated block of one to three days according to the complexities of the work and how many items are to be produced.

Where the work can be done in the equivalent of one day some schools have found that less able students respond better and keep their work rate up if the time is split into one afternoon session followed by a full morning on the next day. This arrangement does allow for some modification of the production line between sessions if necessary.

The length of the production period will clearly be related to that of the planning period. The time taken in planning will exceed that required for production. A ratio of 3:2 is common, although this should be taken only as a very rough guide as the proportion will vary according to the nature of the product and the ability of the students.

It has been found that the overall plan will usually consist of a 'part time' period of preparation spread over several weeks followed by a concentrated period of production. But this can vary according to circumstances and it may be necessary either to plan and produce within a concentrated period or to undertake the whole project as part of the normal timetable allocation.

If a concentrated period is available for either planning or production it is better to allocate it to production. This gives more meaning to a working day and enables the students to clock on and off or sign in and out. (It should be noted here that the recording of man hours takes several forms in modern industry. Students could be asked to investigate these.)

Meeting targets

To ensure that production targets are met it may be useful for the students to prepare a work schedule in the form of a large wall-chart. A progress chaser can be appointed to record the progress of the work team on the chart as production proceeds. If the team begins to fall short of the planned target then it will also be his responsibility to see that their attention is drawn to this fact!

Keeping records

If the production session is to be recorded by film or photographs experience has shown that this is better done 'live'. It is often difficult to set up certain operations especially for the camera, and even if this can be done the results are generally found to be inferior.

Where equipment is to be mass produced as part of a community service project it may be possible to invite a representative of the 'client' to observe, and possibly comment upon, part of the production run.

Packaging and preparing for distribution

Whether a production line project has been linked with school or community service or the products have been made to sell at the school garden party, distribution is important in helping the students to assess the success of the operation.

The comparison with the assessment of commercial objectives in industry is obvious. In addition, if the emphasis has been on the production of saleable items then the project could involve the design of attractive packaging, display material and advertisements.

The investigation of commercial promotional techniques is relevant to studies in consumer discrimination which, as is suggested in Chapter 2 of this book, could be a part of a design and craft education curriculum with considerable relevance to present-day society.

Depending on the scale of commitment, however, packaging may or may not be a major feature of the assignment. Where it is, work may run concurrently or follow on from the planning and operation of the production line. Not all the work will fall within the immediate boundaries of the school workshop, as the following pages indicate. Nevertheless, the production of packages or wrappings may offer scope for setting up an auxiliary production line.

The importance of graphics in pack design opens up possibilities for fruitful co-operation with the art department. By considering packaging in the context of a particular problem and in relation to a selected product and market, the student may be able to appreciate that graphics are important in order to attract the customer and convey all necessary information required to 'close' a sale. No detail or decoration should be added without justification. Photographs or drawings should be clear and relevant and wording should be kept to a minimum.

Aspects of post-production planning

In post-production planning there are four main aspects that will require consideration—the product, the package, the publicity and the selling:

310

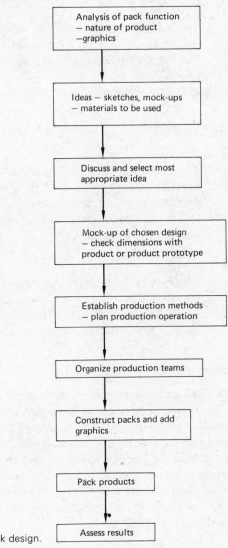

9.5 An approach to pack design.

Analysis of pack function
— nature of product
—graphics

Ideas — sketches, mock-ups
— materials to be used

Discuss and select most
appropriate idea

Mock-up of chosen design
— check dimensions with
product or product prototype

Establish production methods
— plan production operation

Organize production teams

Construct packs and add
graphics

Pack products

Assess results

1 *The product*
   a NATURE OF THE PRODUCT—its shape, structure, strength, etc;
   b OUTLET AND MARKET—place(s) of distribution and likely customers;
   c TRANSPORTATION—delivery by hand, car, rail, etc;
   d STORAGE—conditions and length of storage;
   e DISPLAY—when and how.

2 *The package*

a STRUCTURE—protection from crushing, scratching, etc; economical use of space and material; ease of assembly, storage, display and handling; whether it is to be re-used; visibility of commodity when packed;

b MATERIAL—selection on basis of qualities, requirements and cost;

c GRAPHICS—information to be conveyed; sequence of wording; type size and style; illustrations; colour.

3 *The publicity*

a THE PRODUCT—its advantages and attractive points.

b THE CUSTOMER—methods of approach;

c PRESENTATION—communication by word-of-mouth, the written word (brochures, press releases), photographs, films, posters, etc; use of newspapers, magazines, TV, etc.

4 *The selling*

a THE PRODUCT—display; delivery;

b THE SALESMEN—his role; knowledge, circumstances of sale;

c AFTER SALES—feedback of information; customers' criticisms; maintenance and servicing; consumer guarantees.

Meeting 'commercial' objectives

One important measure of the success of the project is the 'commercial' one. Were the production schedules met? How does the cost of the end-product compare with the original estimates? How well does the product perform the function it was designed to perform?

To help the students to make this kind of assessment they should be able to observe the products in use and consult 'clients'. They could be provided with a series of key questions relating both to commercial objectives and to those common to all applications of the design process and asked to prepare 'test market' reports.

Students' responses

In addition to judging the end-product students should also be given the opportunity to state their impressions of the project as a whole. Did they enjoy it? What value did they think it had? And so on. Individual responses and comments could usefully form a basis for class discussion. The basic information could be obtained by questionnaire or by a 'de-briefing session', or, as in the case study which follows this section, by a combination of both.

Whatever method is used careful planning will be required if the right kind of information is to be obtained.

As previously stated, the production session itself will act as a practical assessment of the organizational design work involved in production planning and of the factors in the design of the artefact which relate specifically to batch production techniques. But this must be supplemented by a more formal assessment involving the students if the full educational benefit is to be obtained from the project. The nature of this assessment will depend upon the aims and objectives set out at the start of the project.

Case Study
Batch Production
for Disabled Children

This is an account of a factory day project which was undertaken by a group of twenty-six fourth-form leavers at a secondary modern school in Crewe. Many of the boys taking part had a reputation for being 'low functioners' and the work took place during what was for the majority of them their last term at school. Following this case study the school's headmaster comments on the effects of the work on the students and on the school as a whole.

The intention was to combine production line work—a factory day— with a community service project. The main emphasis was on product design and the subsequent planning and operation of a production unit. It was felt that other related activities, such as the purchasing of materials, could be dealt with only at a superficial level in the circumstances.

Contact had been made with a consultant doctor responsible for the design of equipment for handicapped children. The doctor lent the school a range of slides which illustrated some of the problems encountered by handicapped children. Five of these problems were selected and the students were divided into five design teams. Their suggested solutions to two of the problems looked promising and within the scope of the school. These two ideas were chosen by the boys for further development. They were :

—a trolley for children with a spinal complaint (called, by the students, a 'boomerang chair') ;
—a 'walker' for children unable to walk unaided.

A team of teachers was formed from those who normally met the boys. Their subjects were woodwork, metalwork, technical drawing, English and mathematics. In addition, four students from a nearby college of education were invited to help with the project.

The aims
The project had four basic aims :

1 to help students to identify a range of needs and problems of disabled children ;
2 to help students to formulate proposals to meet these needs ;
3 to review resources for the effective line-production of selected solutions ;
4 to draw up proposals for a production line scheme.

Main organizational requirements

Before the project started it was decided that the main requirements of organization within the school included :

—a group of students to undertake the project ;
—time for the students to identify and solve problems ;
—time for the students to plan work stations, order materials, etc ;
—time for the students to undertake any job training that might be necessary ;
—a team of teachers to devote lesson time to planning ;
—accommodation for a one- or two-day production session.

A number of other basic requirements were met by the small team of four college of education students who provided :

—lines of communication between the students and the handicapped children's institution ;
—help at the school while students were working on the identification and solution of problems ;
—help with the production and testing of prototypes ;
—help in the planning and setting up of work stations ;
—help in the production of jigs for use during the production session ;
—help during the production session ;
—help with the distribution of the end-products.

Work on the project was to start and finish in the summer term. The teachers drew up a time schedule and it was decided that the project should be divided into fourteen steps.

1: Introducing the idea

The students were shown slides dealing in general terms with the idea of community service.* They discussed the slides, were interested and agreed to co-operate on a community service project.

2: Contacting the 'client'

Following the showing of the slides supplied by the consultant doctor, the students were able to isolate and discuss the following basic needs of handicapped children:
—walking;
—sitting;
—standing;
—feeding;
—working.

3: Isolating possible lines of development

Discussion of these needs enabled the students to draw up a simple design brief for each. They were then divided into five design teams each responsible for development work on one of the following:
—a walking device;
—a trolley for children with a spinal complaint;
—an adjustable support for a spastic child to help with arm control;
—equipment to help spastic children to feed themselves;
—a work-table which could be used by a child confined to a wheelchair.

4: Choosing what to make

The five solutions produced by the design teams were discussed by all the students after two lessons on design work. Each team elected a spokesman to present their ideas to the rest of the class. The final choice was made by voting.

5: Introducing the production line principle

A set of slides illustrating the various aspects of setting up a production line in a school was shown to the students and discussed.

6: Choosing the final solutions

The students now undertook further development work on the two

*Design and Craft Education Filmstrip *Helping Out.*[5]

chosen solutions. Consideration was given to the materials that could be used and the particular factors inherent in the use of batch production techniques. The final proposals were then discussed and adopted and the volume of production was set at eight walkers and six trolleys.

9.6 Working as a design team on one of the problems.

9.7 Design teams report back to their classmates.

7: Establishing production teams

At this point the class was divided into two teams—one to work on each topic. The following observations relate mainly to the team responsible for the walking-frame, although both teams followed similar procedures and achieved their aims successfully.

The walker consisted of two main 'U' frames of tubular steel. These were pivoted to support a rectangular frame from which a canvas seat was suspended. The seat frame clipped on to the main 'U' frames enabling the walker to be folded when not in use.

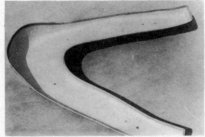

9.8, 9.9 Two ideas that came out of discussion and design work.

8: Planning the production sequence

While four students finalized the design of the walking-frame, material was prepared to make a prototype. At the same time three students measured up the metal workshop and produced plans showing the positions of fixed and movable equipment.

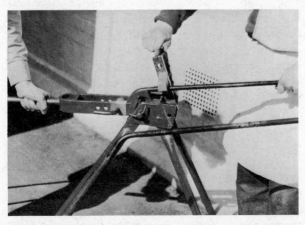

9.10 The production of prototypes also acted as a form of work training prior to the production session itself.

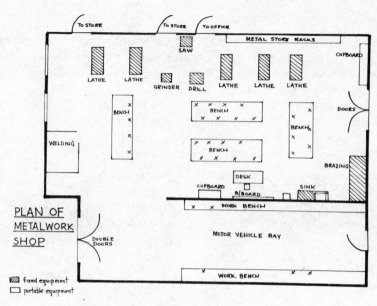

To STORE   To STORE   TO OFFICE

METAL STORE RACKS

CUPBOARD

SAW

LATHE   LATHE   GRINDER   DRILL   LATHE   LATHE   LATHE

DOORS

BENCH

BENCH
BENCH

WELDING

BENCH

BRAZING

DESK

CUPBOARD   B/BOARD   SINK

PLAN OF
METALWORK
SHOP

WORK BENCH

DOUBLE
DOORS

MOTOR VEHICLE BAY

▨ fixed equipment
▢ portable equipment

WORK BENCH

9.11 Drawings of workshops helped plan positions of work stations.

The remaining students worked on planning the flow of components and gave initial thought to the equipment that would be needed at the manufacturing stage. When the final design was ready four students prepared the production flow charts.

It was at this stage that the students decided on the allocation of jobs. This was straightforward and it was interesting to note how a sense of identification with a particular component was established. The fact that only eight walking-frames were being made did pose a problem since this meant that there was never a complete production line in operation at any one moment. In order to overcome this most students had to play more than one role. One boy was elected to act as foreman and also to help if necessary at any work station where output was falling behind schedule. The welding work station was manned by the group's metalwork teacher.

9: Ordering materials

The prediction that time would be getting short at this stage proved to be correct so it was unfortunately not possible for the students to be completely involved at all stages in the specifying, costing and ordering of materials. They did assist in drawing up lists of requirements but all materials were from stock or were ordered by the teachers.

FLOW CHART – MAIN 'U' FRAMES

WORK STATIONS

1. Cutting tube to length.
2. Bending main 'u' frames.
3. Size control and fixing of drilling jig.
4. Drilling for swivel and cross bar.
5. Bending feet.
6. Fitting bush for castors.
7. Brazing bushes to tube.
8. Cleaning frames.
9. Painting.
10. Assembly and check.

9.12 Planning the flow of components.

10: Making jigs

Students who needed to use the jigs took charge of making them. The following items were required:

—a jig to ensure the accurate drilling of holes in the main 'u' frames;
—a jig to ensure that all clips were the same size;
—a jig for bending the seat support frame.

It was found that the existing school workshop equipment was adequate for their purposes. The only additional equipment they had to obtain was a pipe-bender. If time had allowed even this could have been made as part of the preparation stage.

11: Job training

When setting up the workshop the students' attention was drawn to the range of skills and techniques that would be required. Each process was broken down into a series of relatively easy operations. To further ensure a smooth production run some students practised the work they would have to do. One such instance occurred in the making of nylon spacing washers on a lathe. Before production one student learnt how to set up the facing and parting-off tool. The assembly of the tailstock chuck and how to drill and centre-drill on the lathe was also part of this operation.

Seven weeks had now passed. A high proportion of the allocated workshop time had been devoted to the project. In addition, several

319

WALKING FRAME – Allocation of jobs

Form 4T/C

| OPERATIONS | MAIN 'U' FRAMES 8 outer | | | | | | 8 inner | | CASTOR BUSHES 32 | | | | SUPPORT FRAMES 8 | | | | | | | CLIPS 8 | | | SUPPORT FRAME BUSHES 16 | | | | W* 32 | | RODS 8 | | SEATS 8 | | | ASSEMBLY | | | |
PART / NO. REQUIRED	Cutting to length	Bending	Drilling	Bending feet	Cleaning	Spraying	Drilling	Turning	Fitting	Brazing	Cutting tube	Cutting bar	Bending bar	Welding frame to tube	Cleaning	Spraying	Bending	Brazing to support frame	Drilling	Cutting	Turning	Drilling	Fitting	Drilling	Turning	Cutting to length	Threading	Cutting out	Hemming	Fixing press studs	U frames	Main support	Castors	Seats
A. T	•	•	•		•				•	•																				•				
S. Q	•		•		•				•	•																				•				
M. B	•	•		•	•	•																												
D. K							•	•			•	•																		•	•		•	
A. K						•	•	•																							•			
A. T											•	•	•	•	•			•	•											•		•		
A. H											•	•	•	•	•			•	•							•	•					•		
R. J																	•	•	•															
P. H					•											•	•																	
R. B																				•	•	•		•	•					•				
N. B																							•											
G. O																												•	•	•	•			•
G. T																												•	•	•	•		•	•
Mr. R																																		
A. S																																		

W* - SPACING WASHERS

To control and record flow of all components. To help where necessary.

9.13 Students' job allocation table.

9.14 The design and production of jigs (in this case, for drilling tubular steel) was undertaken before the production session.

technical drawing lessons had been spent on design work, chart preparation, and so on. A number of students had also spent some of their own time working out ideas and collecting information. Altogether over thirty-five hours had been used, although not all students had been active all of the time.

12: The production session

Production was organized on factory day lines. The timetable was suspended for two full days. During that time the students worked from 8.30 a.m. to 5.00 p.m. They clocked on or signed in each morning and clocked off or signed out when the day's work was over. Special travel arrangements were made for students using school buses. Tea breaks were taken each morning and afternoon and a one-hour lunch break was allowed. Students who normally went home for lunch arranged to bring sandwiches or have school meals.

13: Distributing the goods

Where possible the students themselves delivered the goods to the handicapped children. This enabled them to see the reactions of the children and the parents and helped them to gain a better understanding of the social consequences of their work.

In some cases it was not possible for the student to have this final contact with the 'client' and this proved to be a weakness of the venture, as such contact can assist the students' evaluation of their work.

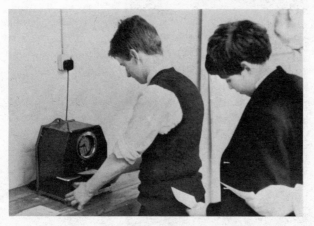

9.15 Students beginning a day's work on the production line they devised and set up.

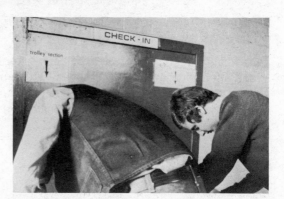

9.16 Not all students clocked in; some signed in.

9.17 Tea-breaks were enjoyed by all.

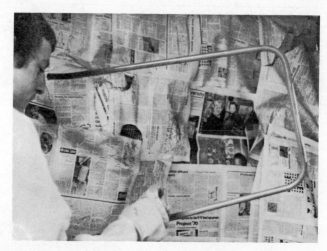

9.18 Painting was undertaken in a spraying booth set up by the team.

9.19 A full range of equipment, as well as materials, was used in the manufacture of the aids.

9.20 Components coming together on the assembly line.

M

9.21 Production schedules were almost met.

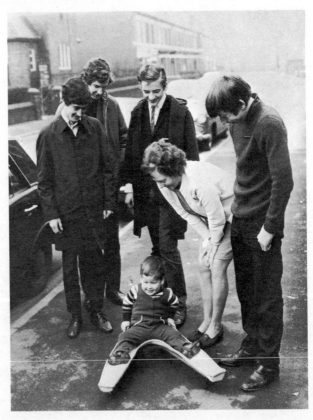

9.22 Delivering the goods.

14: Follow-up and feedback

After the production period a de-briefing session was arranged and a questionnaire was distributed and completed by the students. Some of the results of this are given at the end of this case study. In English lessons the students wrote about their experience and recorded their impressions. Ideally the teachers would have liked to have arranged a further follow-up a few months after production to see how the disabled children were using the articles made. Unfortunately, since it was the last term for most of the students, this was not possible.

Two examples of the students' essays follow:

Factory days by Mark T, 15

I chose to work on the trolleys which would be called boomerang chairs, made of a wooden support on castors, with a fibre-glass body rimmed in rubber for safety. We were also told what materials we would be working in and what job the trolley had to do. Mr Tucker, the woodwork teacher, told us what the children with spina bifida could and could not do. Planning and preparation took us five weeks.

At first some of the ideas were scrapped for practical reasons. For instance the screws holding the fibre-glass legs to the wooden base protruded and would have hurt the legs of the children in the 'boomerangs'. So we had to decide to countersink the screw holes and put a double thickness of fibre-glass under that part of the trolley. Our day was arranged and planned as a full-time 8.30 to 5.00 factory day. We were issued with a Work Card to clock on and off. The assembly line method was explained to us and we had to decide how to gear the production of each part so that we would not over-produce certain sections that could be made quickly.

One group was concerned with moulding the fibre-glass and another with trimming the edges and smoothing off. Simultaneously a group was employed in cutting and shaping a very thick plywood base which was sprayed to match the colour of the fibre-glass by yet another section of the assembly line.

When the paints were dry, castors were put on and we could begin to see the final product take shape as the various sections came together. Screw holes had to be drilled for fixing the base to the fibre-glass body and rubber rims and buffers were fitted around the edges for safety and to protect furniture which might otherwise get damaged.

The group concerned with the final assembly of the various parts had an interesting function and we were all agog to try out the first model on a volunteer from the lower school. The boomerang trolley proved extremely successful and easy to manipulate.

We were very pleased with our efforts and congratulated ourselves on producing something that was really worthwhile which would be so helpful to children less fortunate than us. We enjoyed working a factory day, particularly as we knew what the end-product would be and that some parents of spina bifida children in our locality had already been enquiring about our trolley.

Factory days by Michael B, 15.

We were having a woodwork lesson when the teachers were called to the staffroom, where they were talking for half an hour. After the discussion they came out and told us to pack away our tools and sit on our benches. After all the shuffling and noise died we walked in single file to the hall, and as we neared the doors an air of excitement rose. We went inside and sat down. I watched with awe as Mr Pemberton set up his slide projector. After the slide show he strode to the front and sat on the stage. There was a hush and he began to talk about boys and girls in America, and how they made different objects on an assembly line basis. He very carefully explained every slide clip he had shown us.

Mr Buckley, our technical drawing teacher, combined forces with Mr Tucker, the woodwork teacher, and with Mr Pemberton. They let us design trolleys and other different kinds of crazy inventions. Some were practical and some way out. We all forwarded our suggestions to the teachers and they picked out the ones which would be the best and most practical. There were all kinds of things that had to be taken into consideration—like the cost, quickness of making the components and the kind of materials we would use.

We first made a mould for the boomerang chair, which took some preparation. We sanded it to perfection and got it as smooth as we possibly could, and then waxed and polished it until it was silky smooth. We then fibre-glassed it and let it set and go hard.

Most of the boys who worked on this project enjoyed themselves, but needless to say there were the ones who were there just to get out of lessons and to fool around, but most of the boys worked very well and took a pride in what they were doing.

After we had made enough components to assemble one boomerang chair we put the different pieces together and made the chair. We got the smallest boy in the class to make a test run and it worked perfectly, so we made more on a larger scale.

The fact that the project was successful in achieving the four basic aims stated on page 314 is clear from the preceding pages. Further evaluation of the work is provided by the school's headmaster on page 329. The comments of students, teachers and college of education students were also of considerable assistance in evaluating the project and gaining further insight into the potential possibilities and problems that other schools may discover when setting up their own production line.

Students' answers to the questionnaire

Some of the students' spontaneous answers to the questionnaire distributed at the end of the last afternoon of the production session are given below.

1 At the beginning of the course I thought that:
—It would not work but it was a good idea.
—It would not get under way so fluently.
—It would be a squeeze to get up in time but I did get up in time.
—It was a daft idea because of the hours but I enjoyed it.
—It was stupid.
—It would be good but the first morning was boring but after that it was all right.
—It was a good idea to make the trolley but I thought the half-past eight to five bit was mad.
—It would have been a load of rubbish and that nobody would do anything.
—I was not going to like doing it.

2 As the course progressed the things that interested me most were:
—A free cup of tea at break.
—The arranging of the flow diagrams and the work procedure chart.

3 During the course the things I disagreed with most were:
—Being at school for 8.30 and going home at 5.00 pm.
—Coming early and going late.
—We did not have enough to do.
—The way it was planned. The way it was run. The clearing up of the material.
—Not long enough.
—Doing a horrible job.
—The design.

4 The thing that gave me most pleasure was:
—The tea break.
—Learning how to sew with a sewing machine.
—Going home after standing up all day.

5 I was unhappiest when:
—I had to do a job I didn't like.

6 To me the main value of the work was:
—Doing the work for someone else, and knowing it was going to a good cause.
—Experience in what it is like working in a factory and helping about 15 handicapped children.
—The organization and working together.
7 At the end of the course I thought that the work:
—Was dead good.
—On the whole it was good but my job was horrible because it made me itch.
8 If I were to undertake similar work in the future the changes I would like in the course are:
—To do the thing on a larger scale.
—Someone else doing my job.
9 As a result of this course I intend to:
—Do it again if I was asked.

Results of the de-briefing session

At a de-briefing session after the products had been distributed several interesting points were revealed that had not hitherto been apparent. For example, the teachers were more than a little surprised to discover that some students had given up paper rounds for the two production days. When the possibility was raised of the students receiving a small cash payment for their work they all agreed that they did not wish to be paid.

Some students revealed that they had not pulled their weight as team members and others said that they had become bored with their jobs after a while. Although at least one student was not really convinced of the idea until he had delivered the equipment to a handicapped child, there was unanimous agreement that it would be worth another try.

Other conclusions

Discussion between the teachers and the college of education students revealed a number of factors that would require attention in future projects of this type. Certain operations were not as well planned as they might have been, some required more time than had been allocated and some required less. Partly as a result of this, but also because of the inherent nature of the particular production operation, it was found to be difficult to keep all the students fully employed towards the end of the production period.

One minor point of costing would be worth bearing in mind on future projects. Because of the nature of the operation it was decided to use a quick-drying paint spray of the canned variety. Unfortunately the cans are somewhat expensive and costing revealed that a disproportionately high percentage of the total amount had been spent on the finishing operation.

Production schedules were almost met. (The seat of one of the walking frames had to be completed and fitted the following day.) It was interesting to see that the students became noticeably more proficient at their jobs as the work progressed. This increase in proficiency can have quite a considerable effect on the timing of operations, particularly if the work schedule is based solely on observations of pre-production trials.

Clocking on and off did not have the attraction teachers thought it would have, although this is not necessarily a valid reason for not using the system in future production line projects as the purpose of introducing it was to add an extra touch of reality. Timekeeping was generally good, although there was one absentee and one student late, both on the second morning.

*　*　*　*　*

'Young hooligans' and school projects

At the end of the project described in the previous case study the school's headmaster wrote the following report:

It is commonly held today that young folk are well and truly on the rampage against Authority. But also, apparently increasing numbers of public-spirited youngsters are revelling in doing jobs of service for the community. What is not quite so obvious is that often it is *the same young people* who are involved in disobedience and constructive usefulness at different times and in different circumstances.

Beginning to involve the students

Recently our relationship with the Keele Design and Craft Education Project resulted in a form of fifteen- and sixteen-year-old boys at my school becoming involved in a community service project.

A member of the central team introduced the idea to the boys when he explained that children suffering from a congenital defect—spina bifida children he called them—were often unable to walk. If they were able to stand at all they needed some support under them. Some of the children had their legs in plaster, and when sitting had to have their legs splayed out straight and horizontal. What a drag for a poor mother who might have to carry such an invalid child about with her all day!

Would my lads consider designing special equipment for these children to give them mobility, and an opportunity to work and play at a table? Perhaps some sort of trolley would give a spina bifida child independence from his hard-pressed mother, and a chance to enjoy a fuller life. 'What about it, boys?' Yes, immediately they were keen.

'Extra' involvement of students

But this project would entail considerable homework. Limbs of young children would have to be measured, and their contours moulded in plaster. Sketches would have to be made, and prototypes knocked up. This might not all be done between 9 am and 4 pm at school. A method of mass production would have to be thought out if a number of vehicles were to be produced in a given time.

Would the lads work 'factory hours', at least from 8.30 am to 5 pm on two consecutive days? Would they put in overtime to complete the work if necessary, all unpaid? No doubt about it, they certainly would.

Twenty-five boys volunteered for the scheme out of twenty-eight addressed. To be fair, the remaining three would have helped too but for pressing commitments at home. Many of the volunteers put their part-time jobs in jeopardy by volunteering. And part-time jobs are not easily come by in our town.

Making arrangements

For three weeks teachers conspired to make a difficult timetable flexible enough to allow the young designers and production planners opportunity to meet, discuss and decide upon the ideas to be accepted. Eventually, after much teamwork between students and teachers, the total manufacturing process for the two chosen designs was broken right down into individual or group operations, and our school's handicraft unit was prepared for the 'factory days'.

'Overtime'

The trolleys and walkers were completed only by boys and teachers working overtime on both 'factory days' and other days beyond them. The finished items were taken away to the university to help calculate the final cost of materials and evaluate the project. Later they were delivered to the local Medical Institute for trials and further evaluation. Two trolleys were presented to local spina bifida children and the rest of the equipment was delivered to an orthopaedic hospital.

Some reflections

I reported the project in the School Log and pondered over the list of the boys who had so promptly and willingly given their services.

330

As I read the names I realized that a number of the boys had appeared before juvenile courts recently. Two, for instance, had been involved, with others, one evening in smashing a sports shop window and making off with whatever they could grab quickly. They had no use for the articles they took but threw them away. Yet another three had stolen sheath knives during the school holidays and used them to threaten girls. Serious charges had been made, but the boys had claimed it was 'just a giggle'. Six other boys had been in trouble with the police over fighting at a Fourth Division football match. They also minimized the seriousness of their offence.

It dawned on me with surprise that at least half of the 'factory day' volunteers had been involved in acts of hooliganism about the town, and that I had written reports on them for juvenile courts.

There was substantial uniformity about the reports. I could not say that any one of them was openly aggressive or unpleasant in school. They were somehow 'unorganizable' though, forming a clearly distinguishable 'sub-group' within their year group. They were the boys who could never bother to bring swimming trunks for Baths mornings or PE kit for games days. The accepted (by most) appeal of organized games brought no response from them, although they often went swimming when they felt like it after school. An impromptu game of soccer in the playground—as rough as you like—would attract them. But not one on the timetable, to be followed by a shower. They often played truant, were sometimes 'barrack room lawyers' and were—not always obviously—the school's most difficult fringe.

Had they been consistently unco-operative, rebellious in class, aggressive, anti-social, they would have been a more clearly defined problem. But these were among the first to help the school with sponsored walks, fêtes and jobs at the weekend for an old people's home.

Students' responses

Now they had responded generously to the appeal to make vehicles for paralysed youngsters. Why had they done so? Their replies were predictable in the main:

It was something different to do.
He (the member of the Keele team) said none of these things had been made in our area.
He said we might be on TV.
We were going to organize the job ourselves.
We were allowed to think out our own designs.
My mate was going in it and I went with him.
After a bit I was glad I went on it.
I was sorry for the kids the way he told us about them.

Other replies were unusual:
> It was one job I wouldn't have to take home when it was done.
> This was a (genuine) project without house points.
> We are usually told they (the projects) will do us good. He didn't tell us this, we knew it was a serious job. Dead serious.

These were some of the revealing remarks that solved something that had been puzzling me for more than two years.

The diminishing influence of projects

About nine years ago my school began to interest itself in project work. At first the aim was to unite the school, and give it a real sense of purpose. The projects usually involved the whole school. They were well-planned by experienced teachers and seldom numbered more than one or two per year. Since the students had been used to a strictly formal and authoritarian regime a more relaxed and fresh approach worked well. Projects multiplied slowly, and eventually came on to the weekly timetable to provide a limited integration of subjects in real-life situations. This was well before Newsom!

For about six good years the school's life was enriched by its projects, which we thought induced security and responsibility, and offered the challenge of adventure. There was sailing, canoeing, camping, orienteering, rock-climbing, archery, home-making (a many-skilled project), and non-aligned community service. Students were first intrigued, then gradually and inevitably completely involved. Very few boys could resist the new approach. They were little trouble in school or outside. Our credit in the town was good. Older colleagues, who had known the school for a long time, said 'It was never like this!' and were grateful.

But inexplicably the 'light failed' about two years ago and somehow we lost our way. We had by then also lost some experienced staff, but this alone did not account for the change. Upsets inside and outside school developed. Furniture was spoiled, equipment 'became' smashed, decorations appeared defaced. More boys than usual trekked through the juvenile courts—some not to return to us. Projects disappointed and were abandoned for lack of support. We were following the general theme of juvenile disobedience in the country—but we had not expected to. What had happened?

A 'new' project

Not until the 'factory day' project has the depressing downward slide been arrested. Now we are thinking again, the word 'Projectitis' has been mentioned in the staffroom. This is suggested as another reason for our troubles.

The educationist who recently warned state schools about projects, was thinking of a surfeit of them taking valuable time from solid teaching of

332

basic subjects. This was the 'Projectitis' he felt might divert schools from important aims.

We feel that we may have 'Projectitis' of a quite different strain. We were presenting our projects in an unintelligent way, not really taking the sophistication and imagination of our students into account. What was fresh and novel nine years ago—against a background of formal classroom work—had gradually become uniform and ordinary. The projects which once arose naturally—from dire need sometimes—are now artificially contrived. 'Project' is on the timetable. Try as we may to disguise the aims and ends of some of them the students are not deceived about this subject. Their teachers are thinking up 'dodges' to keep the kids amused and busy.

The 'factory day' cut right through the normal timetable, and the disruption made the whole school, particularly the young staff, aware of the project. It caught the imagination of those boys most closely involved, and took them on a spiritual adventure such as comes infrequently to us in our lifetime. It was not something pushed to produce house points, but was, as the boys said 'dead serious'. There was no promise of reward. This project was offered as a yoke, in the same shape almost as the 'blood, toil, tears, and sweat' of Garibaldi and Churchill.

The 'young hooligans' accepted this yoke readily, and it was easily and naturally borne. Had it been presented in any other way it might have been mistaken for a fetter. And youth today is not inclined to wear chains—other than those it chooses for decoration.

Case Study
Batch Production and the
Craft Curriculum

Although our school has been developing materials for the Design and Craft Project under the heading of 'Materials and Work' it has become increasingly evident that there is more than a blurring between the topics being developed by the central team. We find that community service, leisure and design all very much overlap with our 'Materials and Work' experiments.

However, one salient factor inherent in 'Materials and Work' teaching materials centres around *organization.* If we can bring some semblance of effectiveness and relevance to the way in which we organize students and workshops, then we can impart to young school-leavers the notion that planning the mechanics of production is an important prerequisite of practical activities.

While the term 'factory day' may often overplay activities at Parkside we have attempted to get the students to analyse stages and operations in the production of a range of items. Inevitably, we have been drawn constantly towards group activities, but we do have examples of where one brain is better employed than several thus giving individual responsibility for an entire 'production line'.

For fear of giving the impression that our work has been geared purely to providing students with insight into the mere trappings of organization let it be clear at the outset that a diversity of objectives has always been kept in mind.

Some benefits of group activities

The Design and Craft Education Project started because teachers were beginning to question the basis on which handicraft had for so long been taught. The work of Morris and his concept of the artist/craftsman tended to predominate, thus catering for the needs of the individual often at the expense of groups, both within and outside the school community. We have attempted not to minimize the development of the individual but to place this inside the wider concept of communal needs.

When one considers the group as a working unit in handicraft then it shows that many more dimensions and activities become possible within the scope of the subject. One important value arises in that social relationships evolve, whereas in traditional handicraft we tend to work in rather a selfish manner with the boy working all the time for his own ends. Handicraft may have missed a great deal by continuing to use the artist/craftsman/individual concept.

Furthermore, we have persistently endeavoured to provide ample opportunities for students to reap intellectual benefits from working with tools and materials. It is not always easy to produce an Everest of intellectual qualities when working with less able students. Nevertheless, we at Parkside can justifiably claim that group activities have enhanced this aspect of our programme.

Group work and the development of skills

In our own case we arrived, over quite a long time, at the idea of using groups of students to undertake particular forms of work. It originally started in some of the second and third forms when we were having difficulties with machine work. At that time it seemed illogical tô put a new boy to work on a lathe every time. One must remember that a lathe is a somewhat sophisticated machine and it has something in common with a motor car; one would not give a learner driver one lesson and expect him to be competent to handle the machine. This suggested to us that in handicraft one should give the boy considerable time working on the more complicated items of workshop equipment until he becomes able to manage them with competence and confidence.

Where we found groups working on the production of similar items we began to divide skill assignments among the students. From time to time we changed the requirements thus ensuring a balanced approach so far as skill experience was concerned. By allowing a student to spend a full morning working on a lathe producing seven or eight components we usually found that quality and speed of operation rapidly improved.

We now regularly use this method of working, but from such modest beginnings we have developed to a stage where it has been discovered that teamwork has many advantages apart from smoothing out workshop bottlenecks and improving particular skills.

Design problems

One outcome has been that in our senior classes there is an expectation that activities will be based on group co-operation. For the past three years several of our senior classes have worked exclusively on some form of group project. Inherent in this expectation is the acceptance on the part of the students that the work will involve the identification of definite problems and the formation of design teams where corporate expression and acceptance of solutions will be evident.

Students have become aware that they may be required to help plan production sequences and decide how best to allocate different tasks. Jobs have different requirements in terms of thought and skill and there are cases where a competent student can be working alongside a less competent student, one helping the other.

In fact it has an almost built-in de-streaming effect. All these factors, stemming from the way in which we organize our factory days, are often linked to service projects, either for the school or some outside establishment. By fostering links with people outside the immediate school environment we find that added bonuses usually accrue.

Toys and furniture

We now operate a system of group working throughout the department with all fifteen-year old leavers during their final year at school. Last year, for example, we adopted a nursery school that was having some difficulty obtaining nursery furniture and toys. They provided a small sum of money for us to purchase some raw materials, and, using group organization, we designed and made for them a range of nursery furniture and toys. Incidentally, our students used to go over quite frequently to visit the nursery school and it was pleasing to see how some of them, and the students we are talking about here tend to be quite difficult, were very quickly on their hands and knees obviously enjoying playing with the three- and four-year olds—playing with a care that had never been apparent in school.

This year we have identified two particular needs in our own school. One of these, the design and construction of seating on a brick wall, cuts across a range of subjects and so involves a number of teachers. The need arose because students who came off the playing fields with muddy boots had nowhere to sit to remove their footwear before entering the school buildings. However, the scheme has been arranged so that seating will also be provided for use by students during break and lunch periods.

Mass producing music stands

We have a brass band of some seventy players and they use the traditional collapsible type of music stand and over several years of hard wear the stands had become completely collapsible!

We were at the stage when it was impossible to repair these items any longer so we decided it would be better to make a completely new set. (The purchase of them, of course, would have been out of the question.) Some of the boys involved in this project are players in the band.

Their need was discussed with teachers and two or three design studies were undertaken and lists of materials drawn up. A design which satisfied constructional possibility and economics was selected. However, an initial wooden prototype did not prove particularly satisfactory since it did not seem likely that the number required could be made quickly enough. This meant that we had to think afresh before a final solution emerged. Because of lack of storage space it was decided that the stands should be stackable. Here we found that students experienced difficulty in visualizing the design requirements of a stacking principle. We overcame this by getting them to engineer a half-size prototype. By the time they had built this up they had devised a method which was perfectly satisfactory.

Each of the eighteen stands that we produced is 1·3 m long, comfortably seating three players. They are made mainly from 25 mm square tube and 25 × 3 mm angle iron and 18 gauge sheet metal.

As in other production line experiments we found that it was necessary to arrange some job training prior to the actual production sessions. In this case six students were placed on a short gas welding course before they attempted work on an actual stand. When a satisfactory level of competence had been achieved it became clear that a series of jigs would be required if proper alignment of parts was to be ensured. The design of these provided a worthwhile exercise in itself.

No matter how well production sessions are planned a bottleneck inevitably occurs. Such problems can in themselves provide students with useful experience; in this case we found that the welding tended to slow up the flow of components. Without any pressure from staff the boys involved quickly sacrificed their lunch time in order to keep the line moving.

Planning a factory day

At this point it may be helpful to say a word about our internal organization which allows us to do this kind of work. The students concerned have one full day in the workshop. On one occasion we had production sessions running for a single day from nine o'clock in the morning until four in the afternoon. We found this too long a period for students of lower ability.

Present organization, which is very much more successful, still allows the equivalent of one day, but the boys come for an afternoon, starting their factory day at two o'clock and finish at four o'clock but, after tidying the workshop, leave work out and machines set up so that they may resume again the following morning and work through until midday. The break is useful to the technical assistant as well, because it does help him to take care of needs which may have been determined in the course of the afternoon's work. This has a flow promoting effect which would not be so apparent if the boys worked for one clear day.

Working on this basis it took twelve students almost a term to produce the eighteen music stands. This included the identification of the actual need, production of a suitable design, preparation of prototypes, work training for some of the operations and design and construction of a series of jigs. The whole venture cost approximately £15.

Students' reactions

Reactions of students during and at the end of the music stand project were similar to those recorded on other group efforts. Undoubtedly they feel that they are working in a worthwhile field producing equipment that is appreciated.

Almost all the students feel that our group activities enable them to tackle jobs of man-sized dimensions. As a consequence we have noted a definite improvement in the relationship between staff and students and the students' general attitude towards the school.

Looking back we find that with the less able students we used to have much more trouble when we followed a conventional kind of course. Never before did we find these students talking freely about their work; but then never before did we really give them the opportunity to stand up as more than boys.

Assessing the benefits

An analytical assessment has been made of our group programmes and always one significant factor emerges. It centres around the willingness and ability of the students to be objective about themselves and their contributions to the finished job. With the kind of jobs we have tackled students are aware that success is essential and that 'outsiders' are likely to pass opinions on the results. This appears to lead students to a situation where they are eager to defend the quality of their work. Frequently we find quite fierce arguments arising at the end of a project if one of the team is severely critical about the merits of a particular component. This is something that was usually lacking when our students followed a course on which they produced individual articles, where the home situation offered the only real opportunity for critical discussion.

It would appear that students of average and below average ability have a natural liking for working in a group. Sometimes this may be because they feel secure in numbers and are able to come forward at the point where they feel confident to make a valid contribution.

On the other hand the group may sometimes shelter individuals who are idle and wish to avoid using their talents in the best way. This is a factor which must be considered when groups are set up and a pointer which suggests that careful checks must be made on individual performances throughout a project.

Now, as we go on to develop and record the full implications of this kind of work, we find ourselves on yet another group project. This time we are designing and making a series of modules suitable for providing a diversity of elevations on the school stage.

To some extent the job itself is incidental. We are really concerned with how best to organize students and workshops in carrying out man-sized tasks that are now within the capacity of the school. We are intent that our workshop programmes shall consider the changing stature and needs of young people; we are willing to remodel our courses to meet these needs and the wider needs of society.

It does seem that a common factor in all our group work/materials and work activity is that there is always an element of the unknown, in the mind of the teacher as well as the boy, regarding the way in which a given project will develop in terms of design, materials and techniques.

We at Parkside sense that this has a drawing together effect and channels energies to the common objective. 'Sir', being fallible and human, becomes possible to work with, and all feel the same pride or deflation when the jobs go well or badly. A team, proud of the diverse skills that go to make up a complete team, not a foreman and a set of labourers, is the only basis on which to work.

Case Study
Bridging the Gap Between School and Work

One of the initial aims of the Project was to provide a new approach for the thirteen- to sixteen-year-old non-examination students. With this and the environment of Leeds as an engineering city in mind, and remembering that perhaps fifty per cent of our school leavers would be eventually employed in the engineering industry, a group of Leeds teachers decided to try to bridge the gap between school and work; between being a schoolboy and becoming a working youth. To do this we introduced the methods of industry into the school workshop, using:

1 industrial visits;
2 work experience;
3 'the factory day'.

Industrial visits by groups of boys had always taken place. This has now been increased by dividing the fourth year into three main groups according to the choice of the boys and their future employment. These groups were:

a engineering;
b building crafts;
c miscellaneous (clothing, shops, officework).

Each group's visits, although mainly limited to the industries of their choice, were interspersed with occasional visits to the industries of the other two groups.

Work experience was introduced twice a year. Easter leavers in February, and Summer leavers in late June or July, spent two weeks in places of employment according to their choice of occupation. These have ranged from a photographic studio (which resulted in a group of boys from school taking part in a George Best TV commercial) to the heavy engineering of earth scrapers; from helping in a mental hospital to working at a ready-mix concrete depot. Here we owe our grateful thanks to the many Leeds firms who gave us their help and advice.

School production lines

The splendid relationship between the school and local industry has been most helpful in the third of our ventures: the 'factory day', which is the main topic of this article. During the Project we have made several items in the school workshop by applying this method of operation. They include the following:

1 a router;
2 a sash cramp;
3 an adjustable spanner;
4 a coffee table;
5 a small stool;
6 an adjustable table-lamp;
7 a telephone table.

The results are quite amazing when one compares the quality and the average time taken to make something by the line production technique with the same job done in the usual 'one off' way.

Our main venture

More recently we attempted the final experiment in our contribution to the Project: the 'factory day' or more precisely the 'factory fortnight'. A group of boys were to spend two weeks full-time in the workshops while another group was taking part in work experience. The planning of the project was spread over the whole year and work in technical drawing lessons was also used for the experiment.

Industrial visits as a starting point

At a preliminary discussion we talked about a visit to a firm, the products they produced and the departments necessary for product marketing. A series of slides with taped commentary was shown. These dealt with a similar experiment conducted by an American high school.

It was soon discovered that the work carried out on the factory floor was only one cog in a giant wheel. In the initial stage the class was split up into four departments:
1 design and drawing;
2 production and planning;
3 costing and ordering;
4 sales and marketing.
    All the boys had to discard their white collar role for overalls when the time came for the actual production.

Designing the items for manufacture

Many items were suggested for manufacture but the choice was narrowed down during discussion until we finally decided to concentrate on two products:
1 a sledge (saleable to the boys of the school);
2 a plant trough (an article in demand for the home).
    Each boy worked on a design for the two articles and by discussion and modification two designs were chosen for production. It was decided to make a 'mock-up' of each and then a prototype using only a limited number of jigs. The prototypes were examined and tested and modifications were made as required. The four departments were now ready to go ahead.
    The design department made working drawings and designed jigs. The planning department drew up suggestions for the production flow-line; they timed the various operations with a stop-watch and organized how many boys would work in each section. The costing department worked out material costs and ordered the materials required from the figures supplied by the sales staff.

Finding a market

The sales staff arranged a display during a parents' open evening. On display were the two prototypes, some of the jigs, working drawings, preliminary sketches and information about the Design and Craft Project. The salesmen had their order books at the ready and the evening's activities resulted in firm orders for twenty-nine plant troughs and twenty sledges—a good start and most encouraging to the boys taking part.

The production session

Everything was soon ready for the great day and fifteen boys and one member of staff clocked in at the workshops to start a very hectic factory fortnight. We thought of working factory hours but decided against this for various reasons and contented ourselves with the hours of 9.15 to 12.30 and 1.50 to 4.15—the normal school hours minus registrations and assembly. Tea breaks were held during normal break times but our shop stewards must have been on a special bonus, as the boys decided to ignore these breaks and to work until the end of the sessions. I encouraged them to have a break and suggested that if they did not wish to go outside perhaps a chat for five minutes with the other production sections would be beneficial and of interest.

The first morning was fantastic; hacksaws, files and lathes became almost white-hot as lengths of wood and metal were cut to size, squared and machined.

'They will never last the morning never mind a fortnight.' 'Shall I buy a stock of salt tablets?' These were my thoughts during the first on-slaughts. However, commonsense quickly prevailed and the students settled to a steady and very productive rhythm.

Typical reactions

By Tuesday morning two plant troughs and one sledge had rolled off the production line ready for painting. This steady flow continued during the week. The boys' instant reactions were: 'What's the total now?' and 'How many today?'

My reactions were of pleasure in seeing the boys working so well and taking an interest in the accuracy of their work. I noticed their pride in a well-finished article and their smiles of joy when they saw another job leave the painting section. One outstanding pleasure was to see the social behaviour of the groups—how one would help another in his own group who had fallen a little behind schedule—how one group would go to the assistance of another group—how all the groups joined in towards the end to become part of the assembly section.

All this needed no prompting from me; the boys used their eyes, ears and common sense. They were a community united by a common bond.

The production planning department did an excellent job. Our target was achieved on Thursday of the second week. It would have been earlier but for a slip up in the organization. We ran out of acetylene. Whose fault? It was mine. Needless to say I lost my share of the production bonus!

A final summing up

—Would I attempt another similar experiment? Yes please!

—Was it a success? Most certainly.

—Were the jobs well done? We received many requests such as: 'Are you still making . . .?' 'Will you make me one?'

—Did the boys benefit in any way from the experiment? Ask them! Their comments were: 'Smashing!' ... 'Super!' ... 'Can we do something like this again?'
—Did the teachers benefit from the exercise? The answers are in this article.

References

[1] Schools Council. *Education Through the Use of Materials* (Working Paper 26). London, Evans/Methuen Educational, 1969.

[2] Schools Council. *Materials and Design: A Fresh Approach*. London, Edward Arnold, 1974.

[3] Schools Council. *Houses and Homes*. London, Edward Arnold, 1974.

[4] Schools Council. *Value for Money*. London, Edward Arnold, 1974.

[5] Schools Council. *Helping Out*. London, Edward Arnold, 1974.

[6] Schools Council. *Design and the Environment*. London, Edward Arnold, 1974.

[7] Schools Council. *Playthings*. London, Edward Arnold, 1974.

[8] Schools Council. *You Are a Designer*. London, Edward Arnold, 1974.

[9] Schools Council. *Connections and Constructions*. London, Edward Arnold, 1975.

[10] Schools Council. *Looking at Design*. London, Edward Arnold, 1974.

[11] Schools Council. *Education Through Design and Craft*. London, Edward Arnold, 1974.

[12] Schools Council. *Design and Karting*. London, Edward Arnold, 1975.

[13] Schools Council. *The Creative Use of Concrete*. London, Edward Arnold, 1975.

[14] Schools Council. *Designing with Plastics*. London, Edward Arnold, 1975.

[15] Schools Council. *Kart-Ways*. London, Edward Arnold, 1975.

[16] Schools Council. *Designing with Concrete*. London, Edward Arnold, 1975.

[17] Horrocks, A. 'Art Rooms', *Attitudes in Design Education* (Edited by Ken Barnes). Lund Humphries, 1969.

[18] Ministry of Transport. *Driver Training for Young People*. HMSO, 1969.

[19] Schools Council. *A Course of Studies in Design* (A pilot study undertaken in conjunction with the Design and Craft Education Project). North Western Secondary Schools Examination Board, 1971.

[20] Rudinger, E. and Kelly, V. *Break for Commercials*. London. Penguin Education, 1970.

[21] Brocklehurst, J. C. *The Geriatric Day Hospital*. King Edward's Hospital Fund for London, 1970.

[22] Statutory Instrument 890. *Standards for School Premises Regulations 1959*. HMSO.

[23] Central Advisory Council for Education (England). *Half Our Future*. (The Newsom Report). HMSO, 1963.

[24] The Institute of Careers Officers. *Work Experience in British Secondary Schools*. The Institute of Careers Officers, 1971.

[25] Thomas, J. 'An Experiment in Play-Sculpture and Design', *Education in Cheshire*, Spring, 1971.

Bibliography

The following books, magazines, films, etc, have been found by teachers and students to be useful sources of further information when developing the areas of work outlined in this book. We do not claim that this list is complete; students will be able to discover other, perhaps more relevant, sources during the course of their investigations of a specific topic.

Section I

Williams, P. H. M., *The Young Householder*. Mills and Boon, 1969
Ratcliffe, H., *Home Decorating: A Craftsman's Approach*. Mills and Boon, 1970
Wilson, F., *Architecture and Interior Environment*. Van Nostrand Reinhold, 1973
Household Science series, Heinemann
Learning Home Economics series, Heinemann
Do-it-Yourself magazine
Do-it-Yourself annual
Practical Householder magazine
Practical Motorist magazine
Custom Car magazine
Studies in Design Education and Craft magazine, Nufferton, Driffield, York, YO25 O3L.
Which? magazine and other Consumers' Association publications (Consumers' Association, 14 Buckingham Street, London, WC2N 6DS)
Design magazine and other publications of the Council of Industrial Design (including the Design Centre Publications series published by Macdonald in association with the CoID)
Many manufacturers of household equipment and supplies produce leaflets, wall-charts, films, etc, for use in schools. Details of these are readily available.
Smith, M. E. H., *A Guide to Housing*. The Housing Centre Trust, 1971
The Nationwide Building Society, *The Prospect for Housing*. 1971
Rodinger, E. and Kelly, V., *Break for Commercials* (Connexions series). Penguin Education, 1970
Barr, J. *Standards of Living* (Connexions series). Penguin Education, 1970
Department of the Environment. *The Highway Code*. HMSO
Department of the Environment. *Roadcraft: The Police Driver's Manual*. HMSO
Ministry of Transport. *Driver Training for Young People: Suggestions to Heads of Schools and Others*. HMSO
Department of the Environment. *Driving*. HMSO. (General roadcraft law and advice)
The Royal Society for the Prevention of Accidents (RoSPA). *Proceedings of the*

Conference on Vehicle Crash and Injury Prevention 1966. RoSPA. (Chapters on ergonomics, safety features, vehicle design)

RoSPA. *Safety Education.* RoSPA. (A quarterly magazine)

RoSPA. *Accidents: How They Happen.* RoSPA

RoSPA. *Turn to Better Driving.* RoSPA

RoSPA also publish a number of useful wallcharts. Details are available on request from The Royal Society for the Prevention of Accidents, 52 Grosvenor Gardens, London SW1

Sargent, K. and Colborne, H. V., *Pre-Driver and Driver Training in Secondary Schools* (RRL Report LR 263). Road Research Laboratory, 1969

Nathan, L. *Car Driving in Two Weeks.* Elliot Right Way Books, 1968

The Automobile Association. *Drive.* Drive Publications. (A quarterly magazine)

Leaflets giving facts and sdvice on road traffic law are available from India Tyres Ltd, Inchinnan, Renfrew, Scotland

The Camera Centre, Fleetwood, Lancashire, supplies sets of slides dealing with road signs, the Highway Code, accidents, driving instruction, road situations, quizzes, etc

Suitable films made by Vauxhall, Ford and other motor vehicle manufacturers can be obtained from Sound Services Film Library, 269 Kingston Road, London SW19

Wallcharts and films about two-wheeled vehicles are available from the Cycle and Motor Cycle Association Ltd, Starley House, Eaton Road, Coventry, Warwickshire

Details of the RAC Junior Drivers' Course and the RAC Training Scheme can be obtained from The Royal Automobile Club, 83-85 Pall Mall, London SW1

Shell Education Service. *The Motor Car.* Shell Mex & BP Ltd, Shell Centre, London SE1. (A series of free booklets)

Shell Education Service. *Shell Education News.* Shell Mex & BP. (One issue per term)

Shell Education Service. *Aids for Teachers.* Shell Mex & BP. (A full catalogue of Shell educational publications)

Castrol. *Car Care.* Castrol Ltd, Castrol House, Marylebone Road, London NW1, 1969

Castrol. *Two-Wheeler Care.* Castrol

Pirelli. *Car Tyre Care and Maintenance.* Pirelli House, 343–345 Euston Road, London

Department of Education and Science. *The Motor Mechanic* (Careers booklet No. 71) HMSO

Road Transport Industry Training Board. *Training Recommendations for Apprentice Motor Vehicle Mechanics.* Road Transport Industry Training Board, Capitol House, Empire Way, Wembley, Middlesex

Consumers' Association. *Consumers Car Glossary: A Consumers Publication.* Consumers' Association, 14 Buckingham Street, London WC2

Motor Manual. Odhams

Brooks, R. and Harrap, G. G., *Questions and Answers for Motor Vehicle Mechanics.* Harrap

Motor Magazine *The 'Motor' Manual.* Temple Press

Service Training Centre. *Fault Diagnosis.* Joseph Lucas (Sales and Service) Ltd, Birmingham 18

Rolt, L. T. C., *Motor Cars.* The Educational Supply Association

Mudd, S. C., *Technology for Motor Mechanics*, Books 1, 2 and 3. Edward Arnold, 1972

Burdett, W. J. and Ellis, J. G., *A Motor Mechanic's Course.* Cassell, 1971

Howell, F. and Willard, B., *Junior Motorist: The Driver's Apprentice.* Collins, 1969

Wynyard, J., *Roads and Pipe-Lines.* Wheaton, 1967

P

King, C., *Car Making*. Blackie, 1966

Singham, J. R., *Autocar Handbook*. Autocar Magazine

Section II

Students engaged on a community action project will usually need to have some form of contact with their local authority. The relevant bodies might include the following:

Department	Contact
Town Hall or Council Offices	Town Clerk
	Information Officer
Social Services	Social Care Officers
Health Dept.	Medical Officer of Health
Training Centres for the mentally handicapped	Mental Welfare Officer
Home Helps	Supervisor
Housing Dept.	Welfare Officer
	or Housing Manager
Probation	Probation Officer
Safety	Safety Officer
Residential Homes:	Social Care Officers
aged	
physically handicapped	
homeless families	
Youth Service	Youth Service Officer

There are also many voluntary organizations that may be able to provide useful information, or even suggest suitable project work for the students. These will include:

British Red Cross Society
Churches
Clubs for the blind, disabled, etc
NSPCC
Old People's Welfare Committee
Rotary Club
Round Table
St. John Ambulance Brigade
Salvation Army
Toc H
Women's Royal Voluntary Service

In addition, there are many voluntary organizations that go beyond local boundaries. A classified list of some of these together with details of books and films is given below.

Old People

National Old People's Welfare Council and National Council of Social Service, 26 Bedford Square, London, WC1

348

National Association for Workshops for the Blind, 105 Salisbury Road, London NW6

British Red Cross Society, 14 Grosvenor Crescent, London SW1

Workers' Educational Association, 27 Portman Square, London W1

Christian Education Movement, Annandale, North End Road, London NW11. (List available giving details of books, projects and 'probes' for this and other subjects)

Community Service Volunteers, Toynbee Hall, 28 Commercial Street, London E1

King George's Jubilee Trust, 166 Piccadilly, London W1

International Voluntary Service, 72 Oakley Square, London NW1

Central Council for the Disabled, 34 Eccleston Square, London SW1

Lifebelt Association, c/o Toc H, 42 Trinity Square, London EC3. (This association deals with emergency call schemes for the housebound)

National Association of Youth Clubs, 30 Devonshire Street, London W1. (List of films and books on voluntary service available)

Books

Youth in the Service of Age. National Old People's Welfare Council

Age is Opportunity. National Council of Social Service

Employment and Workshops for the Elderly. National Council of Social Service

Films

I Think They Call Him John. Contemporary Films

Community Responsibilities. Concord Films Council, Noreton, Ipswich, Suffolk

Suitable films may also be obtained from the British Film Institute, 81 Dean Street, London W1, and the Central Film Library, Government Buildings, Bromyard Avenue, London W3

Children

Save the Children Fund, 29 Queen Anne's Gate, London SW1

National Children's Home, 85 Highbury Park, London N5

Dr Barnardo's Homes, Stepney Causeway, London E1

Church of England Children's Society, Old Town Hall, Kennington, London SE11

Invalid Children's Aid Association, 4 Palace Gate, London W8

Films

A Place to Play and *The Adult in a Small Child's World.* Concord Films

Hospitals

The Hospital Centre (24 Nutford Place, W1H 6AN) have produced a series of slides and scripts. These can be obtained from Camera Talks Ltd, 31 North Row, London W1

Some hospitals appoint directors of voluntary service who may welcome approaches from schools

Mentally handicapped

National Society for Mentally Handicapped Children, 86 Newman Street, London W1P 4AR

National Association for Mental Health, 39 Queen Anne Street, London W1

Films

Stranger in His Own Country. National Society for Mentally Handicapped Children
Heaven Helps Those . . . . and *The Outstretched Hand.* Concord Films Council

Physically Handicapped

Spastics Society, 12 Park Crescent, London W1
National Deaf-Blind Helper League, Market Chambers, Cathedral Square, Peterborough, Northants
Central Council for the Disabled, 34 Eccleston Square, London SW1
National Polio Research Fund, Vincent House, Vincent Square, London SW1

Books

Department of Education and Science. *Special Schools for Handicapped Pupils.* HMSO
Index of Equipment for the Disabled. National Polio Research Fund
RIBA. *Building Design for the Disabled.* RIBA Technical Information Service (66 Portland Place, London W1)

Films

The Long Way Back. Concord Films Council

Immigrants

'Myrante Services' Division, Jamaican Embassy, London
Embassies of other commonwealth countries might be prepared to help.
The Christian Education Movement, Annandale, North End Road, London NW11

Conservation

National Trust, 42 Queen Anne's Gate, London SW1
Conservation Corps, 41 Queen's Gate, London SW7
Civic Trust, 79 Buckingham Palace Road, London SW1. (This organization will supply their directory of publications and visual aids to interested schools)

Play

National Playing Fields Association, Playfield House, 57b Catherine Place, London SW1. (List of publications available)

Books

Yardley, A., *The Teacher of Young Children.* Evans, 1971
Yardley, A., *Reaching Out.* Evans, 1970
Yardley, A., *Discovering the Physical World.* Evans, 1970
Yardley, A., *Sense and Sensitivity.* Evans, 1970
The Institute of Education, University of London. *First Years in School.* Evans, 1963
Lady Allen of Hurtwood, *Design for Play.* The Housing Centre Trust, 1965

The Nursery School Association. *Infant School Playgrounds.* The Nursery School Association of Great Britain and Northern Ireland, 1964
The Nursery School Association. *The New Nursery School.* The Nursery School Association of Great Britain and Northern Ireland, 1962
The Nursery School Association. *Nursery and Playground Facilities for Young Children.* The Nursery School Association of Great Britain and Northern Ireland, 1967
Lady Allen of Hurtwood, *New Playgrounds.* The Housing Centre Trust, 1966
May, D. E., *Suggestions for Play Activities for Young Children.* The Save the Children Fund, 1968
Scottish Education Department. *Our Young Children.* HMSO, 1969
ILEA Media Resources Centre. *Child's Play* (work-cards, slides and tape). ILEA, 1973

Housing

Shelter Youth Education Programme, 86 Strand, London, WC2R 5EQ. (Shelter produce a regularly updated range of folders, posters, etc, that include a useful list of relevant films and publications)

Books

Rose, H., *The Housing Problem.* Heinemann, 1968
Lindley, K. *Landscape and Buildings.* Pergamon, 1972
Fraser Reekie, R., *Design in the Built Environment.* Edward Arnold, 1973

General publications on community service

North West Regional Curriculum Development Project. *Social Education Kits.* Macmillan Education, 1972-73
Schools Council. *Community Service and the Curriculum* (Working Paper 17). HMSO, 1968
Department of Education and Science. *Youth and Community Work in the 70s.* HMSO, 1969
A Consumer's Guide to the British Social Service. Penguin
Hobman, D., *A Guide to Voluntary Service.* HMSO
Focus on Service. Christian Education Movement
Ball, C. and M., *Education for a Change: Community Action and the School.* Penguin Education, 1973

Section III

Specialized publications on all types of leisure activities—from sport to model-making —are readily available and no useful purpose would be served by listing them. Some teachers have found the following useful as a good general introduction to the growing importance of leisure in society:
Parker, S., *The Future of Work and Leisure.* MacGibbon & Kee, 1971; Paladin, 1972
Entwistle, H., *Education, Work and Leisure.* Routledge and Kegan Paul, 1970
Publications related to karting activities are listed in *Kart-Ways* (Edward Arnold, 1975) in the Design and Craft Education series

Section IV

de Bond, E. (Ed.). *Technology Today*. Routledge & Kegan Paul, 1971

Wiener, N. *The Human Use of Human Beings*. Houghton Mifflin, 1954; Sphere, 1968

Schools Council. *Closer Links Between Teachers and Industry and Commerce* (Working Paper 7). HMSO, 1966

The Institute of Career Officers. *Work Experience in British Secondary Schools*. The Institute of Careers Officers, 1971

Keane, G. R. *Teaching Industry Through Production*. American Industrial Arts Association, 1963

Ward, C. *Work* (Connexions series). Penguin Education, 1971

Index